# LIBRARY OF NEW TESTAMENT STUDIES

## 323

*Formerly The Journal For The Study Of The New Testament Supplement Series*

### Editor
Mark Goodacre

# MATTHEW'S JUDAIZATION OF MARK

Examined in the Context of the Use of Sources
in Graeco-Roman Antiquity

ANNE M. O'LEARY, PBVM

t &t clark

Published by T&T Clark
*A Continuum imprint*
The Tower Building, 11 York Road, London SE1 7NX
80 Maiden Lane, Suite 704, New York, NY 10038

www.tandtclark.com

British Library Cataloguing-in-Publication Data
A catalogue record for this book is available from the British Library


ISBN 0567031047 (hardback)

Typeset by Data Standards Limited, Frome, Somerset, UK
Printed on acid-free paper in Great Britain by Biddles Ltd, Kings's Lynn,
Norfolk

# CONTENTS

## DEDICATION

To *my mother, Joan O'Leary (nee Sexton),*
and *late father, Ted O'Leary, RIP (d. 2002)*
*~ eternal gratitude ~*

# PREFACE

*And he said to them,*
*'Therefore every scribe who has been trained for the kingdom of heaven*
*is like the master of a household who brings out of his treasure*
*what is new and what is old'.* (Mt. 13.52)

This book is a study of Matthew's use of Mark as a source. The genesis of the present study lies in the research that I carried out for the purpose of a doctoral dissertation. The dissertation is entitled, 'John's Use of Matthew as a Source in the Context of the Use of Sources in Graeco-Roman Antiquity'.[1] Its aim is to contribute to the scholarly debate on what is termed the 'John-Synoptic' problem. The thesis presented is that John knew and used Matthew as a source and that the way in which he did so was in accord with the literary conventions of Graeco-Roman antiquity. Thus it confirms the position of the ancient Church, a position that remained practically unchallenged until the first half of the twentieth century.

To this end, Matthew's use of Mark as a source was explored in order to provide a generic model for the examination of the relationship between John and Matthew. The importance of examining the issue of Matthew's use of Mark in the broader context of the literary conventions of their day became clear. Moreover, it also became clear that there was a dearth of in-depth analysis of this topic. Thus what was intended as an introductory part of a chapter for a dissertation now occupies an entire chapter of that work and the whole of this book.

What is wonderfully amazing is the attention Matthew gives to rewriting even the minutest detail of his Markan source, as well as his use of Mark in fashioning the bigger project that became his Gospel. An analysis of each detail or unit taken from Mark in its Matthean context accentuates just how important it was to Matthew to communicate a more judaized portrait of Jesus Christ. His literary portrait became a theological icon for the hearers/readers of his age and all subsequent ages, as it will be for all ages to come. It communicates something unique about the Eternal – specifically, Jesus, the Son of God.

---

1. Anne M. O'Leary, 'John's Use of Matthew as a Source in the Context of the Use of Sources in Graeco-Roman Antiquity' (part-published dissertation; Mary Immaculate College, University of Limerick, 2004).

At the end of the project, I come away with a very deepened appreciation of the literary genius of the author we call Matthew, and the theological riches recorded in the pages of his Gospel. More especially, it has led me to a deeper appreciation of and faith in the person of Jesus Christ who is the chief subject of Matthew's work. I hope that reading these pages will have the same effect on you.

Anne M. O'Leary, PBVM
Mary Immaculate College,
Limerick
*Feast of the Epiphany,* 6 January 2006

ACKNOWLEDGEMENTS

I would like to express my sincere gratitude to the many individuals and groups who helped and supported me in the course of my academic studies, the fruit of which you see reflected in the pages of this book.

I thank my parents, Ted and Joan O'Leary, sisters – Marie, Margaret, Carolyn and Martina – and brothers – Sean, Tadhg and Stephen – and their families. During the challenging years of study and research, I came to know even more deeply the support of a loving family.

I am also deeply indebted to my religious family, the Presentation Sisters. My hope is that this work is in the spirit and tradition of Nano Nagle, our founder, who cherished the Scriptures as the Living Word of God.

I am grateful to the Presentation Sisters of Limerick who provided a community of love and support during the course of my research, and, in particular, Anna Sheehy, PBVM, of my present community.

I thank Tony Egan, OSA, and the Augustinian Community of Limerick who provided a valuable space and place to pursue the research for this book. The welcome and hospitality I received there from the Friars, staff members and friends, were special gifts.

I wish to thank Thomas L. Brodie, OP, Dominican Biblical Centre, Limerick, who supervised my PhD dissertation, part of which you see reflected in the pages of this book. In particular, I thank him for introducing me to the wonderful literary world of Graeco-Roman antiquity.

I owe a great debt of gratitude to Eamonn Conway, Head of the Department of Theology and Religious Studies, Mary Immaculate College, Limerick, who first invited me to Limerick and offered me great assistance during the course of this work. I thank most especially Mary Immaculate College, Limerick, for the scholarship they awarded me that greatly facilitated the undertaking of the study that lead to this book.

This work is the fruit of all my years involved in the study of Scripture. I wish to acknowledge my gratitude to the professors from whom I have learned so much. I thank the professors at St Patrick's College, Maynooth – + Martin Drennan, Maurice Hogan, SCC, and + Michael Neary – who first introduced to me the wonders of the Sacred Scriptures. I take this opportunity to thank the professors of the Loyola School of Theology, Ateneo de Manila University, from whose expertise and varied methods in the use of Scripture I benefited greatly. These include William Abbott, SJ, Carlos Abesamis, SJ, Philip Calderon, SJ, Thomas H. Green, SJ, Nill Guillemette, SJ, and Herbert Schneider, SJ. In particular, I am indebted to Anicia Co, RVM, who supervised my STL dissertation, and to my fellow classmate, Carlito Reyes, PhD elect, for his help and support.

My thanks to Teresa O'Doherty, Head of the Department of Education, Mary Immaculate College, Limerick, and my colleagues in this department, especially Patricia Kieran, Eileen Linehan, RSJ, Fiona McSorley and Eileen O'Sullivan (Director of Teaching Practice), for their support, understanding and good humour while I was undertaking the preparation of this manuscript for the publishers.

I am deeply grateful to Sean Freyne, Director of Mediterranean and Near Eastern Studies, Emeritus Professor of Theology, Trinity College, Dublin, and Wilfred Harrington, OP, Dominican Priory Institute, Tallaght, Dublin, examiners at the *viva*, who were both enthused about the contribution that publishing the section 'Matthew's Judaization of Mark' would make to the current scholarly discussion on the Gospel of Matthew.

In particular, I am grateful to Professor Freyne for introducing me to Continuum/T&T Clark. I want to thank their editors and personnel, in particular Ms Rebecca Vaughan-Williams, for her enthusiasm, guidance and patience in relation to the preparation of this publication.

At various critical stages of this work, I was very blessed with the help and support of a number of friends: Thérèse Arguelles, Venus Guibone, Martin Kenneally, FPM, Aumer Lopez, Breda Moloney, Eleanor Sugrue, PBVM, Tomás Ó Caoimh, CC, Grace McKernan, PBVM, Bede Minehane, FPM, Margaret Murphy, Vincent McCarthy, Maura O'Connor, RSM, Canon Timothy O'Leary, PP, and Frances Rowland. I am sincerely grateful to all of the above, and many others too numerous to mention here.

# ABBREVIATIONS

## BIBLE TEXTS

| | |
|---|---|
| LXX | The ancient Greek translation of the Septuagint |
| MT | Masoretic Text of the Hebrew Scriptures |
| NA$^{27}$ | Nestle-Aland 27th edition of the Greek New Testament |
| NJB | *New Jerusalem Bible* |
| NRSV | *New Revised Standard Version* |

## JOURNALS AND SERIES

| | |
|---|---|
| AB | Anchor Bible |
| ABD | *Anchor Bible Dictionary* |
| ABRL | Anchor Bible Reference Library |
| AJT | *American Journal of Theology* |
| AnBib | Analecta biblica |
| ANTC | Abingdon New Testament Commentaries |
| ARCA | Classical and Medieval Texts, Papers and Monographs |
| ASORLBNEA | American Schools of Oriental Research Library of Biblical and Near Eastern Archaeology |
| BCPE | *Bulletin du Centre Protestant d'Etudes* |
| BETL | Bibliotheca ephemeridium theologicarum lovaniensium |
| Bib | *Biblica* |
| Bib T | *Bible Today* |
| BTB | *Biblical Theology Bulletin* |
| CBQ | *Catholic Biblical Quarterly* |
| CBQMS | *Catholic Biblical Quarterly*, Monograph Series |
| CC | A Continental Commentary |
| CHCLLL | *Cambridge History of Classical Literature II: Latin Literature* |
| ChicStud | *Chicago Studies* |
| CQ | *Classical Quarterly* |
| ETL | *Ephemerides theologicae lovanienses* |
| ExpTim | *Expository Times* |
| GELNTECL | *A Greek – English Lexicon of the New Testament and Other Early Christian Literature* |

| GNS | Good News Studies |
|---|---|
| *GR* | *Greece and Rome* |
| GRS | Greek and Roman Studies |
| *HCBD* | *HarperCollins Bible Dictionary* |
| HCHCB | Hermeneia – a Critical and Historical Commentary on the Bible |
| *Hen* | *Henoch* |
| *HSCP* | *Harvard Studies in Classical Philology* |
| *HTR* | *Harvard Theological Review* |
| IBT | Interpreting Biblical Texts |
| ICC | International Critical Commentary |
| *Int* | *Interpretation* |
| *ISBE* | *International Standard Bible Encyclopedia* |
| *JBC* | *Jerome Biblical Commentary* |
| *JBL* | *Journal of Biblical Literature* |
| JCB | Judaism and Christianity in the Beginning |
| *JDPTL* | *A Journal for Descriptive Poetics and Theory of Literature* |
| *JHS* | *Journal of Hellenic Studies* |
| *JRS* | *Journal of Roman Studies* |
| *JSNT* | *Journal for the Study of the New Testament* |
| JSNTSup | *Journal for the Study of the New Testament*, Supplement Series |
| *JSOT* | *Journal for the Study of the Old Testament* |
| *Lat* | *Latomus* |
| *Mod Phil* | *Modern Philology* |
| *Neot* | *Neotestamentica* |
| NIB | New Interpreters Bible |
| *NJBC* | *New Jerome Biblical Commentary* |
| *Nov* | *Novel* |
| *NovT* | *Novum Testamentum* |
| NovTSup | *Novum Testamentum*, Supplements |
| NTAbh | Neutestamentliche Abhandlungen |
| NTESTI | New Testament Essays in Support of Traditional Interpretation |
| NTM | New Testament Message |
| *NTS* | *New Testament Studies* |
| *OCD* | *Oxford Classical Dictionary* |
| *PTL* | *A Journal for Descriptive Poetics and Theory of Literature* |
| *QJS* | *The Quarterly Journal of Speech* |
| *RB* | *Revue biblique* |
| *RevQ* | *Revue de Qumran* |
| SBL | Society of Biblical Literature |
| SBLAB | Society of Biblical Literature Academia Biblica |
| SBLDS | Society of Biblical Literature Dissertation Series |

| | |
|---|---|
| SBLSBS | Society of Biblical Literature Sources for Biblical Study |
| *SBLSP* | *Society of Biblical Literature Seminar Papers* |
| *Sem* | *Semeia* |
| *SJT* | *Scottish Journal of Theology* |
| SNTSMS | Society for New Testament Studies Monograph Series |
| SPS | Sacra Pagina Series |
| *ST* | *Studia theologica* |
| Sup | Supplementum |
| SupJSJ | Supplements to the Journal for the Study of Judaism |
| *TD* | *Theology Digest* |
| *TDNT* | *Theological Dictionary of the New Testament* |
| *ThH* | *Theologie Historique* |
| TU | Texte und Untersuchungen |
| WBC | Word Biblical Commentary |
| WSA | Works of Saint Augustine: A Translation for the 21st Century |
| WUNT | Wissenschaftliche Untersuchungen zum Neuen Testament |

## MISCELLANEOUS

| | |
|---|---|
| *hapax* | *Hapax legomenon* |
| Gk | Greek |
| Lt. | Latin |
| NT | New Testament |
| OT | Old Testament |
| SM | Sermon on the Mount |

## ANCIENT LITERATURE

*Graeco-Roman, Jewish and Early Christian Writings*

| | | |
|---|---|---|
| *Aen.* | *Aeneid* | Virgil |
| *Ag. Sop.* | *Against the Sophists* | Isocrates |
| *Ages.* | *Agesilaus* | Xenophon |
| *Agr.* | *Agricola* | Tacitus |
| *Alc.* | *Alcibiades* | Plutarch |
| *Alex.* | *Alexander* | Plutarch |
| *Ann.* | *Annals* | Tacitus |
| *Ant.* | *Anthony* | Plutarch |
| *Antid.* | *Antidosis* | Isocrates |
| *Arg.* | *Argonautica* | Apollonius Rhodius |
| *Ars Poet.* | *Ars Poetica* | Horace |

| Att. | *Letters to Atticus* | Cicero |
|---|---|---|
| Aul. Gel. | *Attic Nights* | Aullus Gellius |
| Bacc. | *Bacchae* | Euripides |
| 1–2 Clem. | *1–2 Clement* | Clement |
| Cael. | *Pro Caelio* | Cicero |
| Cato Yng. | *Cato the Younger* | Plutarch |
| Com. Diatess. | *Commentary on Diatessaron* | Ephraem |
| De Cons. Evang. | *De Consensu Evangelistarum* | Augustine |
| De Or. | *De Oratore* | Cicero |
| Did. | *Didache* | Anonymous |
| Eum. | *Eumenes* | Plutarch |
| Epist. | *Epistles* | Seneca |
| Her. | *Heriodes* | Ovid |
| Hipp. | *Hippolytus* | Euripides |
| Hist. Eccl. | *Ecclesiastical History* | Eusebius |
| Hypo. | *Hypotyposeis* | Clement of Alexandria |
| Il. | *Illiad* | Homer |
| Inst. Or. | *Institutio Oratio* | Quintilian |
| Inv. Rhet. | *De Inventione Rhetorica* | Cicero |
| J. Ant. | *Jewish Antiquities* | Josephus |
| J. War | *Jewish War* | Josephus |
| Jub. | *Jubilees* | Pseudonymous |
| Met. | *Metamorphoses* | Ovid |
| Ner. | *Nero* | Suetonius |
| Nic. | *Nicias* | Plutarch |
| Ody. | *Odyssey* | Homer |
| On Imit. | *On Imitation* | Dionysius of Halicarnassus |
| Pan. | *Panegyricus* | Isocrates |
| Per. | *Pericles* | Plutarch |
| Phae. | *Phaedra* | Seneca |
| Phil. | *Philippics* | Cicero |
| Phoc. | *Phocion* | Plutarch |
| Phys. | *Physics* | Aristotle |
| Poet. | *Poetics* | Aristotle |
| Poly. | *Roman History* | Polybius |
| Pom. | *Pompey* | Plutarch |
| Repub. | *Republic* | Plato |
| Rhet. | *Rhetoric* | Aristotle |
| Sol. | *Solon* | Plutarch |
| Virt. | *De Virtutibus* | Philo |

# INTRODUCTION

This book is a study of Matthew's use of Mark as a source. The exercise of examining Matthew's use of Mark has taken the author into the great literary world of the ancients and their methods of composition. The use of musical composition provides a good analogy for the use of literary sources by the authors of both classical and biblical works. Scholars often note this. C.H. Dodd expresses it thus in terms of the Fourth Gospel:

> What he [the author] gives us is no ordinary narrative, where one thing follows another in a simple succession. The links that connect one episode with another are extremely subtle. It is rather like a musical fugue. A theme is announced, and developed up to a point; then a second theme is introduced and interwoven with the first, then perhaps a third, with fresh interweaving, until an intricate pattern is evolved, which yet has the unity of a consummate work of art.[1]

With regard to both music and literature, a knowledge of the direct and indirect influences upon the final work leads to a far greater appreciation and understanding of it. This book is an attempt to help us to 'hear' in Matthew 'the various melodies on the tonescale of his Gospel'[2] that have been sourced from Mark.

The author appreciates the appropriateness of the comparison above, as she is also a music graduate, trained over many years of scholarship to hear themes, motifs and minute details in musical works and to draw upon them for musical composition. This background makes her acutely aware of one major difference between the study of music and classical studies on the one hand and biblical scholarship on the other.

The difference concerns a lack of development in one area of biblical scholarship. The exercise of learning to trace a composer's use of earlier musical models or sources has been part of the methodology used in the

---

1. C.H. Dodd (*About the Gospels*; Cambridge: Cambridge University Press, 1950), p. 40, cited in M.W.G. Stibbe, *John as Storyteller: Narrative Criticism and the Fourth Gospel* (SNTSMS, 73; Cambridge: Cambridge University Press, 1994), p. 14.

2. Adelbert Denaux, 'The Q-Logion Mt 11.27/Lk 10.22 and the Gospel of John,' in Adelbert Denaux (ed.), *John and the Synoptics* (BETL, 101; Leuven: Leuven University Press, 1992), pp. 163–99.

training of music scholars over the past number of centuries, at least in the western world. The exercise of learning to trace an author's use of literary sources also continues to be used in the training of students of ancient classical (and other) literature, as in ancient days. However, with regard to the exercise of learning to trace the evangelists' use of literary sources, it appears to this author that Scripture scholarship is only beginning to take its first steps at something about with which the ancients could run. Dale C. Allison observes this deficiency: 'Our historically conditioned deafness to oblique [and not so oblique] allusions in the Bible can sometimes lead us to doubt their very existence.'[3]

*Statement of the Problem:*[4] The aim of this book is to demonstrate the thesis that Matthew used Mark as a literary source, and that the way in which he did so was in accord with the literary conventions of Graeco-Roman antiquity. The approach we propose here it that of setting the examination of Matthew's use of Mark in the broader context of the use of sources in Graeco-Roman antiquity. Creative imitation (Gk, *mimēsis*; Lt., *imitatio*) was the primary literary convention of the ancient world of the first century CE. It will be demonstrated that Matthew's use of Mark may be viewed fruitfully in terms of this ancient convention.

*The Problem in Context*: From the research on Matthew's use of Mark, three key issues emerged. First, while some commentaries provide details of Matthew's modifications of the verses and pericopae of Mark that he uses, we did not find any in-depth study of Matthew's overall strategy in using Mark as a source. It appears that once the priority of Mark was re-established by and large in the twentieth century and, subsequently, that Matthew had used it as a source, the broader examination of *how* and *why* he did so did not capture the imagination of scholars. Secondly, we found that Matthew's use of Mark has not been examined in depth to date in the context of the use of sources in Graeco-Roman antiquity; and, thirdly, we discovered that Matthew's use of Mark is far more creative and sophisticated than is often presented by scholars who comment on Matthew's modifications of his Markan source.

*Scope and Limitations*: The issue of Matthew's use of Mark is analysed in the context of the literary conventions of Graeco-Roman antiquity. Thus it is an interdisciplinary study involving research into the literary classics and the sacred Scriptures. It is set in the context of ancient, rather than modern, literary criticism. However, Matthew's use of Mark in terms

---

3. Dale C. Allison, *The New Moses: A Matthean Typology* (Edinburgh: T & T Clark, 1993), p. 18.

4. I am indebted to the professors at the Loyola School of Theology, Ateneo de Manila University, Manila, for introducing me to the format used in the introduction above when I was preparing a dissertation for the degree of Licentiate in Sacred Theology (STL).

of what has come to be termed 'Rewritten Bible'[5] or *Midrash* will not be examined.[6]

The literary critical approach adopted here will study the Gospels in their final form without the concern, as with redaction critics, of discerning any hypothetical stages of development. The aim of our approach is to preserve the integrity of the document as a *whole*, as the work of an author, rather than 'shatter the narrative into fragments'.[7]

In the examination of the Gospels, our focus will be upon the way in which the source Gospel contributes to the later Gospel's Christology. We will not focus on how the source Gospel contributes to the later Gospel's ecclesiology, eschatology, soteriology or any other dimension of the theology of the later Gospel.

The scope and limitation of this book allow us to provide positive evidence to make the case for Matthew's use of Mark as a source. We will not examine alternative solutions to the issue of their relationship. The theory of direct dependence most clearly accounts for the data, and, in scientific method, is to be preferred.

*Significance of the Study*: Recent decades have seen the development of several major critical approaches in biblical research – literary criticism, reader-response criticism, structural criticism, to name but a few. The inter-critical approach to Scripture is also a relatively new phenomenon. It shall be used in this book. The approach used here, however, is also inter-critical in a different sense: it involves, first, an analysis of extra-scriptural works of antiquity to discern the conventions of ancient literary criticism, and then, the analysis of Scripture in the light of these conventions. We are aware of no other study of this nature to date in relation to the issue of Matthew's use of Mark.

The analysis of Matthew's use of Mark as a source unravels some literary and theological issues that have heretofore gone unnoticed, or, if noticed, have been misunderstood. Most of all, it greatly enriches our understanding of dimensions of Matthew's Christology.

We may use another musical metaphor, borrowed from Allison, to describe the fruitfulness of this approach. In terms of the function and effect, the exercise of tracing an author's use of literary sources is akin to the function and effect of the 'surround sound-button' on present-day stereoplayers. When used, the listener is able to hear the timbre of the

---

5. See Michael Fishbane, *Biblical Interpretation in Ancient Israel* (Oxford: Clarendon Press, 1988).

6. See Michael D. Goulder, *Midrash and Lection in Matthew* (Speaker's Lectures in Biblical Studies 1969–71; London: SPCK, 1974). The case for Mark as *midrash* is made by Marie Noonan Sabin, *Reopening the Word: Reading Mark as Theology in the Context of Early Judaism* (Oxford: Oxford University Press, 2002).

7. Mary Ann Tolbert, *Sowing the Gospel: Mark's World in Literary-Historical Perspective* (Minneapolis: Fortress Press, 1989), p. 29.

various instruments along with the themes and motifs that make up the texture of the music in much more detail.[8] Thus dimensions of the music may be enjoyed that might otherwise be missed.

Finally, it marks a very significant contribution in terms of offering a new methodological approach which we hope shall be further used, refined and/or modified by other scholars toward advancing the thesis of Matthew's dependence upon Mark, as well as informing us better regarding their differences.

*Methodology*: This book is set out in two parts. Part 1 provides the context in which we examine Matthew's Judaization of Mark. It is entitled, 'Use of Sources in Graeco-Roman Antiquity: Towards a Context and Criteria for Examining Matthew's Use of Mark as a Source'. Part 2 explores how and why Matthew rewrites much of Mark. It is entitled, 'Matthew's Use of Mark as a Source'. Both parts have three chapters each. A conclusion in relation to the thesis and evidence given is provided at the end of each chapter. The book ends with a concluding chapter.

Chapter 1 consists of an overview of the use of sources in antiquity. The purpose of this is three-fold: (1) to provide a context for a more informed discussion of Matthew's use of Mark as a source; (2) to establish criteria for claiming literary dependence of one text upon another; and (3) to establish that the conventions of ancient literary criticism, in particular the convention of imitation (Gk, *mimēsis*; Lt., *imitatio*), are also reflected in the sacred Scriptures.

In Chapter 2 the classical and biblical methodologies of literary, historical and socio-historical criticisms will be used to examine the theory and practice of rewriting in Graeco-Roman antiquity. A select number of texts of various genres from the Graeco-Roman literary world are analysed; and, in each case, the function and effect of the source text in its later literary context is demonstrated.

In Chapter 3 the classical and biblical methodologies of literary, historical and socio-historical criticisms will be used to examine the theory and practice of rewriting in Jewish antiquity. A select number of texts of different genres from the Jewish literary world are analysed – namely, the book of Tobit and Paul's First Letter to the Corinthians (8.1–11.1); and, in each case, the function and effect of the source text in its later literary context is demonstrated.

In Chapter 4 we explore Matthew's use of Mark as a source in general. We present initial examples of how Matthew rewrites Mark. We demonstrate the plausibility of the thesis that Matthew used Mark as a literary source, and that the way in which he did so was in accord with literary conventions of Graeco-Roman antiquity.

In Chapter 5 we explore Matthew's judaization of Mark. Matthew uses

8. Allison, *New Moses*, p. 18.

two main methods. He restructures Mark using key Jewish numerals, and rewrites his Markan source in the light of the Torah. This 'judaization' is the most distinctive hallmark of Matthew's meticulous rewriting of his Markan source.

In Chapter 6 we examine the use of Mark as a source in Matthew 10 and 18 in particular. The rationale for examining Matthew's use of Mark in Matthew 10 and 18 is that much less attention has been given to the issue of *how* and *why* Matthew judaizes Mark in these two linked discourses, relative to the scholarly attention given the strong Jewish tenor of his first discourse (Matthew 5–7).

In Chapters 2–6, for each text examined, we comment *briefly* upon the way in which the literary evidence is directive toward our understanding of its *Sitz im Leben* or context of origin. For this, we draw upon the above critical methods. Moreover, it is hoped that this dimension will be further developed in a future work.

The Conclusion provides a summary of the whole. Here there is, as it were, a 'pulling through of the thread' of the material of the book from beginning to end. This involves a brief résumé of the chapters and their conclusions in turn, after which the key insights that emerge as a result of this study are presented.

*Related Studies*: An extensive range of related studies was consulted for this book. Here, we will cite only the most pertinent studies used in each chapter.[9]

Among the texts used in the examination of non-scriptural sources in antiquity, Damien Nelis's *Vergil's Aeneid and the Argonautica of Apollonius Rhodius* (2001)[10] was influential, and in particular his demonstration of the method of two-tier allusion used in antiquity. For the use of non-scriptural sources in Old Testament Scripture, we are indebted to Dennis R. MacDonald's 'Tobit and the *Odyssey*' (2001)[11] and George W.E. Nickelsburg's 'Tobit, Genesis, and the *Odyssey*: A Complex Web of Intertextuality' (2001).[12] For Paul's use of Torah as a source, we draw upon several key texts: Richard B. Hays, *Echoes of Scripture in the Letters*

---

9. All the relevant studies that were published after 2004 may not be included. However, the more pertinent ones of which we are aware will be included in the relevant footnotes for your consideration.

10. Damien Nelis, *Vergil's Aeneid and the Argonautica of Apollonius Rhodius* (ARCA, 39; Leeds: Francis Carins, 2001).

11. Dennis R. MacDonald, 'Tobit and the *Odyssey*', in Dennis R. MacDonald (ed.), *Mimesis and Intertextuality in Antiquity and Christianity* (Harrisburg, PA: Trinity Press International), pp. 11–40.

12. MacDonald (ed.), *Mimesis*, pp. 41–55.

*of Paul* (1989),[13] C.K. Stockhausen, '2 Corinthians 3 and the Principles of Pauline Exegesis' (1993),[14] and Christopher D. Stanley, *Paul and the Language of Scripture: Citation Technique in the Pauline Epistles and Contemporary Culture* (1992).[15]

Richard A. Burridge's *What Are the Gospels?: A Comparison with Graeco-Roman Biography* (1992)[16] was instructive on the issue of the genre of the Gospels. In establishing the plausibility of the thesis that Matthew had access to a copy of Mark, Richard Bauckham's (ed.) *The Gospel for All Christians: Rethinking the Gospel Audiences* (1998)[17] proved valuable. In relation to the distribution of Mark in Matthew, M. Eugene Boring's The Convergence of Source Analysis, Social History and Literary Structures in the Gospel of Matthew' (1994)[18] provided some key insights upon which we built. For the main matter of literary dependency, we drew from a plethora of studies. In particular, we are indebted to the work of Allison, *The New Moses: A Matthean Typology* (1993),[19] and the three-volume commentary on Matthew by W.D. Davies and Dale C. Allison (1988–2000).[20]

13.  Richard B. Hays, *Echoes of Scripture in the Letters of Paul* (London: Yale University Press, 1989).

14.  C.K. Stockhausen, '2 Corinthians 3 and the Principles of Pauline Exegesis', in Craig A. Evans and James A. Sanders (eds.), *Paul and the Scriptures of Israel* (JSNTSup, 83; Studies in Scripture and Early Judaism, 1: Sheffield: JSOT Press, 1993), pp. 143–64. See C.K. Stockhausen, *Moses' Veil and the Story of the New Covenant: The Exegetical Substructure of 2 Cor. 3.1–4.6* (AnBib, 116; Rome: Pontifical Biblical Institute, 1989).

15.  Christopher D. Stanley, *Paul and the Language of Scripture: Citation Technique in the Pauline Epistles and Contemporary Culture* (New York: Cambridge University Press, 1992).

16.  Richard A. Burridge, *What Are the Gospels?: A Comparison with Graeco-Roman Biography* (Cambridge: Cambridge University Press, 1992).

17.  Richard Bauckham (ed.), *The Gospel for All Christians: Rethinking the Gospel Audiences* (Grand Rapids: William B. Eerdmans, 1998).

18.  M. Eugene Boring, 'The Convergence of Source Analysis, Social History and Literary Structures in the Gospel of Matthew', in E.H. Lovering (ed.), *Society of Biblical Literature Seminar Papers* (Atlanta: Scholars Press, 1994), pp. 587–611.

19.  See n. 3 above.

20.  W.D. Davies and Dale C. Allison, Jr., *A Critical and Exegetical Commentary on the Gospel according to Saint Matthew* (ICC; 3 vols.; Edinburgh: T & T Clark, 1988–2000).

Part 1

USE OF SOURCES IN GRAECO-ROMAN ANTIQUITY: TOWARDS A
CONTEXT AND CRITERIA FOR EXAMINING MATTHEW'S USE OF MARK
AS A SOURCE

# Chapter 1

## USE OF SOURCES IN GRAECO-ROMAN ANTIQUITY

The use of earlier texts as sources was a literary convention practised widely among the authors of the Graeco-Roman world. Judaea was part of the great Graeco-Roman empire before and up to the first century.[1] Therefore, it is not surprising that we also find evidence of this convention in the sacred texts of the Jewish world, including the Gospels of Matthew and Mark.

The recognition and analysis of the literary source(s) used by an author and the way in which he uses them enlarges the meaning of the later text for the hearer/reader.[2] In contemporary terminology this may be described as an exercise in intertextuality.[3] Allison distinguishes between three types of intertextuality: 'borrowing which alludes to no subtext, borrowing which alludes to a series of subtexts, and borrowing which alludes to or cites a specific subtext'.[4] It is the second and third types of borrowing in the practice of the ancients that concern us here.

---

1. Tolbert notes that, 'Judaism too, by the time of the first century CE was thoroughly Hellenized, both in Palestine and especially in the Diaspora. Attempts to divide sharply the Jewish heritage of Christianity from the Greek heritage fail to recognize the degree of Hellenization already part of Jewish culture.' See Tolbert, *Sowing the Gospel*, pp. 37–38. See also Daniel J. Harrington, *The Gospel of Matthew* (SPS, 1; Collegeville: Liturgical Press, 1991), p. 10.

2. Dale C. Allison, Jr., *The Intertextual Jesus: Scriptures in Q* (Harrisburg, PA: Trinity Press International, 2000), p. ix.

3. The term 'intertextuality' originated with the Tel Quel group and became widely know as a result of the work of J. Kristeva. See J. Kristeva, *Desire in Language: A Semiotic Approach to Literature and Art* (ed. L.S. Roudiez; trans. T. Gora, A. Jardine and L. Roudiez; New York: Columbia University Press, 1980). R.O.A.M. Lyne points out a positive advantage of the term 'intertextuality': 'So we have no evidence of Virgil's intentions in the matter of allusion *beyond the evidence of the text* ... this terminology too is objectionable ... but at least it encourages us to state facts about a *text*; more precisely, it allows us to say relatively objective things about something which exists. And if we do this it becomes harder to dodge difficult or unwelcome implications.' See R.O.A.M. Lyne, 'Vergil's *Aeneid*: Subversion by Intertextuality: Catullus 66.39 and Other Examples', *GR* 41 (1994), pp. 187–204 (189). See also Gian Biagio Conte, *The Rhetoric of Imitation: Genre and Poetic Memory in Virgil and Other Latin Poets* (ed. Charles Segal; trans. from Italian; Ithaca, New York: Cornell University Press, 1996), p. 29, n. 11; and Allison, *Intertextual Jesus*, p. ix.

4. Allison, *New Moses*, p. 7.

The focus of this chapter is theoretical. It provides an overview of the use of sources in Graeco-Roman antiquity.[5] The aim is threefold: (1) to give an overview of the context of the use of sources in antiquity; (2) to examine the theory of the use of sources in antiquity, indicating the literary methods and techniques most commonly used by authors to incorporate source texts into their texts;[6] and (3) to outline key criteria by which a reader may discern whether a particular text is the product of literary dependency.[7] These aims will be fulfilled under the following headings:

1.  The Context: Widespread Practice of Literary Borrowing
2.  The Theory and Practice of Rewriting
3.  Criteria for Establishing Literary Dependence

Determining and examining the methods and techniques used by authors focuses our attention on their work of literary appropriation (section 2. below). The testing of the criteria for establishing the case for literary dependency focuses our attention on the role of readers in recognizing the same (section 3. below). Thus our approach is *both author centred and reader centred*.[8]

---

5.   Antiquity here refers to the period from the eighth century BCE, the period when Homer was writing, to the end of the first century CE, when the canonical Gospels were completed.

6.   In classical terminology the product of imitation is called the *mimēma*. See David West and Tony Woodman (eds.), *Creative Imitation and Latin Literature* (Cambridge: Cambridge University Press, 1979), p. 4. Different writers use different terminology to distinguish the source text and the end text. Ellen van Wolde uses 'genotext' for the older text and 'phenotext' for the later text. She cites Claes, *De mot zit in de mythe: Antieke intertextualiteit in het werk van Hugo Claus* (Leuven, 1981) as the source of her terminology. See Ellen van Wolde, 'Trendy Intertextuality?', in Spike Darisma (ed.), *Intertextuality in Biblical Writings: Essays in Honour of Bas van Iersel* (Kampen: Uitgeversmaatschappij J.H. Kok–Kampen, 1989), pp. 43–49 (45). A. Maria van Erp Taalman Kip uses the term '*praetext*' for the source text. See A. Maria van Erp Taalman Kip, 'Intertextuality and Theocritus 13', in Irene J.F. de Jonge and J.P. Sullivan (eds.), *Modern Critical Theory and Classical Literature* (New York: Leiden, 1994), pp. 151–69 (156). Carey A. Moore uses the term 'Urtext' for the source text. See Carey A. Moore, *Tobit: A New Translation with Introduction and Commentary* (AB, 40A; London: Doubleday, 1996), p. 17. Allison terms the model text 'hypotext' and the later text a 'hypertext' or 'subtext.' See Allison, *Intertextual Jesus*, pp. ix, 2. See MacDonald (ed.), *Mimesis and Intertextuality*, p. 2. We will use the terms 'source text' and 'later text', 'earlier author' and 'later author', as does Stanley, *Paul*, as it keeps the sense of historical chronology to the fore.

7.   In this age of 'trendy intertextuality' we must guard against phantom parallels. Hence the need for examining the texts in their historical context and with appropriate criteria. See van Wolde, 'Trendy Intertextuality?', pp. 43–44.

8.   Allison makes an excellent case when he argues for the validity of seeking 'authorial intention' when analysing an ancient text. See Allison, *New Moses*, pp. 6–8.

## 1. *The Context: Widespread Practice of Literary Borrowing*

The most common method of literary composition in the Graeco-Roman world from the fourth century BCE[9] onwards was the rewriting of earlier texts by means of creative imitation (Gk, *mimēsis*; Lt., *imitatio*).[10] Texts composed by earlier authors provided the inspiration and source material for later authors' works. In fact, the art of systematic rewriting prevailed in the literary world until approximately the 1800s.[11] The advent of the printing of the *Enclycopēdia* in France, among other things, led to a shift in emphasis in the western literary world. Volumes such as these, it was thought, would preserve what was known about the past and so, subsequently, writing came to be more an exercise of innovation rather than preservation.[12]

It is generally true that ancient authors were more interested in preserving the oral and literary treasures of preceding generations than modern authors are.[13] This does not mean, however, that they preserved texts as they were, unaltered. While some composed texts by incorporating elements of earlier texts in pedantic fashion, most often ancient authors used their sources in such creative ways that had quite a dynamic effect on the matter. Composition was seen as a means of reviving or retelling the more essential aspects of ancient material.[14]

In antiquity, subject matter was regarded as common property. It was taken from the common stock of themes, traditions, events and myths that already existed. Ancient authors concerned themselves not so much with what to write but how to write it. Isocrates (436–338 BCE) declares that, 'for the deeds of the past are, indeed, an inheritance common to us

---

9. For a good brief description of the process we call 'Hellenism', see Tolbert, *Sowing the Gospel*, p. 37.

10. Nelis, *Vergil's Aeneid*, p. 12. For an extended bibliography of authors who use Hellenistic *imitatio*, see Nelis, *Vergil's Aeneid* , p. 13, n. 56. See also George Lee, 'Imitation in the Poetry of Virgil', in Ian McAuslan and Peter Walcot (eds.), *Virgil* (GRS, 1; New York: Oxford University Press, 1990), pp. 1–14 (1); J.J. Gahan, 'Imitation and Aemulation in Seneca's Phaedra', *Lat* 46 (1987), pp. 380–87 (380); R.J. Tarrant, 'Senecan Drama and Its Antecedents', *HSCP* 82 (1978), pp. 213–63 (214).

11. G.C. Fiske, *Lucilius and Horace: A Study in the Classical Theory of Imitation* (New York Westport, CT: Greenwood Press, rev. edn, 1971), p. 15. Van Wolde notes that, 'man himself, with his own ideas and position, becomes the centre of attention. That is why the 19th century, the Romantic period, is capable of a definite break with the ideal of *imitatio*. *Inventio* had become the ideal, replacing the age-old *imitatio*.' See van Wolde, 'Trendy Intertextuality?', p. 44.

12. W.J. Ong, *Rhetoric, Romance and Technology* (Ithaca, NY: Cornell University Press, 1971), pp. 276–79.

13. Van Erp Taalman Kip, 'Intertextuality', p. 168.

14. D.A. Russell, 'De Imitatione', in David West and Tony Woodman (eds.), *Creative Imitation and Latin Literature* (Cambridge: Cambridge University Press, 1979), pp. 1–16 (3).

all' (*Pan.* 9).[15] Moreover, he praises, 'not those who speak on subjects on which no one else has spoken before', but those who know how to treat the old subjects as no one else had (*Pan.* 10).[16] To the ancient mind, then, originality was about reinterpreting, re-expressing and sometimes supplementing traditional matter so that it became more meaningful in the author's own age.[17] Rewriting was also then an exercise in contemporization.

For Quintilian (c. 40–96 CE), the practice of rewriting was fundamental to the teaching of rhetoric in Graeco-Roman schools (*Inst. Or.* 10.1.3).[18] Such schools were dotted all over Asia Minor, Syria and Judea, and in Greek areas like the Decapolis. Schools played a central part in the process of Hellenization.[19] We know that, 'the educational system for teaching Greek grammar remained amazingly stable over many centuries throughout the Roman Empire'.[20] The success of the system can be deduced from the fact that, from the Maccabean period onwards, conservative Jews sought to safeguard their own school system.[21]

Isocrates provides the earliest surviving reference to rhetorical imitation in schools. He exhorts the teacher to be a worthy example for the students to imitate: 'for the rest he [the teacher] must in himself set such an example (παράδειγμα) of oratory that the students who have taken form under his instruction and are able to pattern (μιμήσασθαι) after him will, from the outset, show in their speaking a degree of grace and charm which is not found in others' (*Ag. Sop.* 18).[22]

---

15.　See Harold Ogden White, *Plagiarism and Imitation during the English Renaissance: A Study in Critical Distinctions* (Cambridge: Harvard University Press, 1935), p. 7.

16.　See Ogden White, *Plagiarism*, p. 6. All citations given for the classical works are taken from the editions of the Loeb Classical Series.

17.　Allison states that, 'the expansion of meaning through allusion, is a common feature of traditional western rhetoric. The generalization includes ancient Jewish and Christian literature, whose authors were ... adept ... at adding force and augmenting sense through implicit interaction with authoritative predecessors. Examples are, for practical purposes, endless. The Hebrew Bible, which is itself increasingly recognized to be a collection of interacting texts, is constantly quoted and alluded to in the Dead Sea Scrolls, in the Apocrypha and the Pseudepigrapha, in the NT, and in rabbinic sources. The Tanak was trailed by Jewish and Christian writers who, as members of a text-based religion, incessantly occupied themselves with it.' See Allison, *Intertextual Jesus*, p. 2.

18.　See Richard McKeon, 'Literary Criticism and the Concept of Imitation in Antiquity', *Mod Phil* 34 (1936), pp. 1–35 (27); and Donald Lemen Clark, 'Imitation: Theory and Practice in Roman Rhetoric', *QJS* 37 (1951), pp. 11–22 (11).

19.　Burridge, *What Are the Gospels?*, p. 252.

20.　Tolbert, *Sowing the Gospel*, p. 36. Tolbert also provides a useful bibliography of the studies of education in antiquity, up to 1984. See Tolbert, *Sowing the Gospel* , p. 36, n. 3

21.　E.B. Castle, *Ancient Education and Today* (Harmondsworth: Penguin, 1961), p. 184.

22.　See Isocrates, *Antid.*, 175, 301–3; and Cicero, *De Or.* 2.21.89–90. See also McKeon, 'Literary Criticism', p. 26; Clark, 'Imitation', p. 12; Thomas Louis Brodie, 'Greco-Roman

The student of rhetoric in antiquity was also encouraged to read and memorize the work of the great writers[23] and to do so as often as possible.[24] While the end of rhetoric was oral delivery in different public fora, the means was the writing and rewriting of speeches beforehand.[25] George Kennedy points out, 'this rhetorical *mimēsis* or imitation, in which one studied a writer and tried to reproduce his style became such a major interest to teachers of rhetoric that in later Hellenistic times it tended to overshadow everything else'.[26]

It is not surprising then that the principles and techniques underlying rhetorical imitation become fundamental to all the major literary genres of the ancients – such as epic, tragedy, *bioi* and historiography.[27] Familiarity with these various genres was 'considered as the minimum formal rhetorical equipment of any literate person from the Hellenistic period on'.[28]

## 2. *The Theory and Practice of Rewriting*

The Greek mind had long been familiar with the notion of imitation. Plato (c. 428–c. 384 BCE) regarded the natural world as an imitation (διὰ μιμήσεως) of the eternal and unchanging forms of ultimate being (*Repub.* 3.392d-94c; 4.500e).[29] Accordingly he classified poetry into three groups:

---

Imitation of Texts as a Partial Guide to Luke's Use of Sources', in Charles H. Talbert (ed.), *Luke-Acts: New Perspectives from the Society of Biblical Literature Seminar* (New York: Crossroad, 1984), pp. 17–46 (18, n. 8, and 20, n. 27).

23.   Clark, 'Imitation', p. 19.

24.   Horace recommends the incessant reading of the Greeks' models: 'handle Greek models by night, handle them by day' (*Ars Poet.* 268–69). Dionysius of Halicarnassus emphasized that constant reading imparts affinity of style (*On Imit.*, Frag. 6 Us.); Quintilian regards careful repeated reading to be an important prelude to imitation (*Inst. Or.,* 10.1.19–20). See Brodie, 'Greco-Roman Imitation', pp. 20 and 40, nn. 29–31.

25.   George Kennedy notes that, 'the rhetorical theory of the schools found its immediate application in almost every form of oral and written communication: in official documents and public letters, in private correspondence, in the law courts and assemblies, in speeches at festivals and commemorations, and in literary composition in both prose and verse'. See George Kennedy, *New Testament Interpretation through Rhetorical Criticism* (Chapel Hill: University of North Carolina Press, 1984), p. 10.

26.   George Kennedy, *The Art of Persuasion in Greece* (Princeton, NJ: Princeton University Press, 1963), p. 332.

27.   Fiske, *Lucilius and Horace*, p. 25.

28.   Francis Cairns, *Generic Composition in Greek and Roman Poetry* (Edinburgh: Edinburgh University Press, 1972), pp. 6–7.

29.   For a discussion of *mimēsis* and Plato, see McKeon, 'Literary Criticism', pp. 3–16, 20.

'simple narrative in the person of the author; narrative conveyed by "imitation" (μίμησις); and that which mixes both sorts'.[30] Aristotle (384–322 BCE) taught that art imitates nature (*Phys.* 2.2.194a22; 2.8.199a15-17; *Poet.* 4.1448b4-23; 9.1451b9).[31] Because the ancient Greeks considered writing to be an exercise about imitating men in action by the use of 'word pictures',[32] they came to apply the term *mimēsis* to the literary activity of the imitation of earlier texts by later authors.

The earliest writings that formulate the principles underlying the practice of imitation in any great detail occur in works dated from the first century BCE.[33] Only a relatively small volume of these theoretical accounts are extant. However, those we do have, such as Cicero's (106–43 BCE) *De Oratore* and Quintilian's *Institutio Oratoria*,[34] are instructive. Also instructive is the evidence provided by authors who either cite their models – for example, Livy (c. 59 BC–17 CE)[35] – or outline something of their theory as well as naming their models, such as Plutarch (c. 40–120 CE).[36] Some authors cite the sources used by other authors – for example, Terence (b. c. 190 BCE) names three of the Greek plays that Plautus (d. 184 BCE) used as sources.[37] By comparing the known later texts with the known source texts one can discern much about the literary conventions of the time (as we shall see below).

Far more common are the numerous texts that, without explicit references, reveal their source(s) to the person schooled in the conventions regarding the use of sources in Graeco-Roman antiquity. Virgil's (70–19

---

30.    Burridge, *What Are the Gospels?*, p. 27.

31.    For a discussion of *mimēsis* and Aristotle, see McKeon, 'Literary Criticism', pp. 16–26.

32.    Charles Sears Baldwin, *Ancient Rhetoric and Poetic: Interpreted from Representative Works* (New York: Macmillan Company, 1924), p. 141.

33.    George Kennedy notes that, 'the earliest work to discuss literary imitation of orators is the small, partially fragmentary, treatise *On Imitation* by Dionysius of Halicarnassus written at the end of the first century. The concept is fundamental to all of Dionysius' writings on rhetoric.' See George Kennedy, *Classical Rhetoric and Its Christian and Secular Tradition from Ancient to Modern Times* (Chapel Hill: University of North Carolina Press, 1980), p. 118.

34.    Quintilian provides a detailed list of useful authors, and the accompanying general reflections (*Inst. Or.* 10.1–2). See West and Woodman, *Creative Imitation*, pp. 5–6.

35.    P.G. Walsh, *Livy: Historical Aims and Methods* (Cambridge: Cambridge University Press, 1976), pp. 116–17.

36.    Michael Roberts notes that, 'Plutarch (c. 50–120 CE) records that Demosthenes was in the habit of paraphrasing his own as well as other people's speeches (1)'. See Michael Roberts, *Biblical Epic and Rhetorical Paraphrase in Late Antiquity* (ARCA, 16; Liverpool: Francis Carins, 1985), p. 7, n. 77.

37.    Ogden White, *Plagiarism*, p. 12, n. 2.

BCE) rewriting of Homer's *Illiad* and *Odyssey* in the *Aeneid* is undoubtedly the most famous example.[38]

An analysis of the literature of the last centuries BCE and the first century CE reveals that the process of imitation can be examined in terms of three stages generally: (1) Selection: a stage of selecting and gathering one or several source texts by an author; (2) Gestation: a gestating period when the author take time to absorb the source text(s) and to choose the appropriate genre to suit his literary and ideological (or theological, in the case of Jewish sacred texts) purposes;[39] and (3) Transformation: the stage of applying one or more literary methods and techniques to integrate the source text(s) into its new literary context.[40]

The methods of 'interpretation' (Gk, ἑρμηνεία;[41] Lt., *interpretatio*)[42] and paraphrase (Lt., *paraphrasis*) were frequently employed in the practice of rewriting in antiquity.

The term ἑρμηνεία was used in antiquity in several senses. It was used to refer to the method of replacing poetic vocabulary with its simple prose equivalent and to describe the work of translating texts.[43] Roman authors looked upon Latin adaptations from Greek as new works, whether the adaptation was of style or content, or both.[44] The Romans held such works in very high esteem, often higher than the original invention.[45]

---

38. Fiske, *Lucilius and Horace*, pp. 28–35. For details about other examples such as Hermogenes (c. 200 BCE), *On Ideas of Style*, and Horace (65–8 BCE), *Ars Poetica*, see Fiske, *Lucilius and Horace*, pp. 28–35.

39. Lucilian (d., c.102/101 BCE) bemoaned the decline of the quality of literary borrowing in his day, which he primarily attributed to the taking of short cuts by authors in imitating the ancients. See Ogden White, *Plagiarism*, p. 3.

40. See Seneca, *Epist.* 84.3, 7. The images of honey-making and food digestion used by Seneca (c. 4–65 CE), and Macrobius (fourth/fifth century CE), are instructive here. First, there is the selecting and gathering – of pollen or food; second, there is the time needed to work on it – in the case of honey, to distribute it among the combs, and in the case of food, to digest it; finally, something totally new is produced – pollen is transformed into honey, food, into energy. While these stages marked a general pattern among writers in antiquity, they are not mutually exclusive of one another. See also Brodie, 'Greco-Roman Imitation', p. 22; Fiske, *Lucilius and Horace*, p. 44; and Ellen Finkelpearl, 'Pagan Traditions of Intertextuality in the Roman World', in Dennis R. MacDonald (ed.), *Mimesis and Intertextuality in Antiquity and Christianity* (Harrisburg, PA: Trinity Press International, 2001), pp. 78–90 (83).

41. The word ἑρμηνεία (Lt., *interpretatio*) is associated etymologically with Hermes. In Graeco-Roman mythology, Hermes was a mythical spokesperson whom, it was thought, interpreted the lofty messages of heaven and brought them down to earth. He was noted for his simple and clear communication. See Thomas L. Brodie, 'Luke-Acts as a Systematic Rewriting and Updating of the Elijah-Elisha Narrative in 1 and 2 Kings' (unpublished doctoral dissertation; Rome: St. Thomas Aquinas University, 1984), p. 6.

42. See Plato, *Ion* 534e.

43. Roberts, *Biblical Epic*, p. 16.

44. Ogden White, *Plagiarism*, p. 12.

45. Fiske, *Lucilius and Horace*, p. 49.

The method of paraphrasing involved several literary techniques, for example, the techniques of variation (Gk, πρόποι; Lt., *variatio*)[46] and emulation (Gk, ζῆλος; Lt., *aemulatio*).[47] Quintilian writes of it thus: 'For I would not have our paraphrase to be a mere interpretation, but an effort to vie with and rival our originals in the expression of the same thoughts ... for we should not despair of the possibility of finding something better said than it has been said before' (*Inst. Or.* 10.5.48).[48] The successful writer in antiquity, however, avoided plagiarism.[49]

The terms 'interpretation' (*interpretatio*) and 'paraphrase' (*paraphrasis*) were sometimes used interchangeably in antiquity.[50] This indicates a certain overlap in these methods of rewriting as they evolved. It also indicates that the labelling for the various methods and techniques involved in the practice of literary borrowing came later. R.O.A.M. Lyne points out that this is indeed the case: 'Poets operate techniques and procedures that are categorized and labelled a long time after the event. This is obviously in the nature of things: the artist creates, the scholar shuffles behind in his footsteps labelling.'[51]

It is not always easy to distinguish between methods of inventive imitation and paraphrase. In general, however, a paraphrase followed the broad outline of its source whereas inventive imitation treated it with far more creativity and in far greater detail.[52]

More inventive than the methods of 'interpretation' and 'paraphrase' is the method of creative imitation. The techniques used in the practice of creative imitation varied in range, some being relatively simple, and others quite complex.[53] It is not always easy to categorize them, as some

46. Roberts, *Biblical Epic*, pp. 11, 20

47. MacDonald, *Mimesis*, p. 1. Brodie, 'Greco-Roman Imitation', p. 21. A.J. Woodman notes that, 'Livy wrote in his preface: "New historians always think either that they have some more exact knowledge to impart to the subject matter or that their literary skill will improve on the inferior standards of their predecessors".' See A.J. Woodman, *Rhetoric in Classical Historiography* (London: Croom Helm, 1988), pp. 93, 131.

48. See Clark, 'Imitation', p. 20; Roberts, *Biblical Epic*, p. 20.

49. Fiske, *Lucilius and Horace*, p. 27.

50. See Brodie, 'Luke-Acts', pp. 8–9.

51. Lyne, 'Vergil's *Aeneid*', p. 198. Cicero's Antonius in *De Oratore* maintains that the reason the rhetorical handbooks do not give rules for history is that the rules were obvious (*De Or.* 2.62). See Woodman, *Rhetoric*, p. 259. Jeff Wills notes this phenomenon also. He writes: 'Anyone trying at present to describe a variety of types of repetition must inevitably christen many of them with new names, or at least adapt unpopular or redundant ancient ones. The second difficulty is the ancient confusion of names and the ambiguity of distinctions which makes even most traditional terms unsuitable.' See Jeff Wills, *Repetition in Latin Poetry: Figures of Allusion* (Oxford: Clarendon Press, 1996), p. 9.

52. See Brodie, 'Luke-Acts', p. 12.

53. Sometimes two or more techniques are being used together, and it may be advantageous to analyse them in combination. Most often, however, we shall identify the

simple techniques are used masterfully and some of the more complex techniques appear deceptively simple.

Among the common examples of the more simple techniques[54] are elaboration, invention (*inventio*),[55] addition or omission,[56] positivization or negativization,[57] amplification (*amplificatio*),[58] contemporization[59] and universalization.[60] We may also add to this list the techniques of 'variation' and 'emulation' mentioned above. Examples of the more common complex techniques used in antiquity include conflation or

---

most specific technique used in a given unit of material. This point has already been made by David R. Bauer. See David R. Bauer, *The Structure of Matthew's Gospel: A Study in Literary Design* (JSNTSup, 31; 3rd repr.; Sheffield: Sheffield Academic Press, 1996), p. 19.

54. We will use the Latin names. However, not all of the techniques were labelled in antiquity, as noted above.

55. For example, when Euripides described Hippolytus' fatal chariot accident, he spent one line on Hippolytus' head: 'And his dear head [was] pounded on the rocks' (*Hipp.* 4.1238). This is rewritten five centuries later by Seneca into a five-line stanza of vivid detail:

The ground was reddened with a trail of blood;
His head was dashed from rock to rock; his hair
Torn off by thorns, his handsome face despoiled
By flinty stones; wound after wound destroyed
For ever that ill-fated comeliness (*Phae.* 4.1092-96).

See Brodie, 'Greco-Roman Imitation', pp. 23, n. 68, and 24, n. 69.

56. Seneca writes: 'We should increase what we have inherited ... and he who shall be born a thousand ages hence will not be barred from his opportunity of adding something further' (*Epist.* 64.7; cf. Quintilian, *Inst. Or.* 12.1). See Ogden White, *Plagiarism*, p. 8; and D.A. Russell and M. Winterbottom (eds.), *Ancient Literary Criticism: The Principal Texts in New Translations* (Oxford: Clarendon Press, 1972), p. 406.

57. Brodie provides an example of *positivization* and *internalization* from Virgil's use of Homer in the *Aeneid*. In the *Iliad*, the eternally angry Achilles who promises to pursue his quest for revenge to the end ('As long as breath remains in my bosom [/] And my good knees have their strength', *Il.* 9.609), is replaced, in the *Aeneid*, with the promise of eternal love by Aeneas to Dido, a love which has been internalized ('While I remember who I am [/] And while the breath still governs this frame', *Aen.* 4.336). See Brodie, 'Greco-Roman Imitation', pp. 25, 42. Positivization, in excess, formed the basis of the encomiastic literature.

58. For an interesting example of *amplification* from Callimachus, *Hymn* (1.72), which, appears later to have been expanded into four lines and amplified by means of the use of triple variation (5.72–74), see Wills, *Repetition*, p. 182.

59. Baldwin notes that, 'imitation is creative when it adapts the art of the past to the interpretation of the present'. See Baldwin, *Ancient Rhetoric*, p. 215. The literary movement know as Atticism is an exception. See Kennedy, *Classical Rhetoric*, p. 118. See also Fiske, *Lucilius and Horace*, p. 50.

60. Virgil *universalizes* Roman *pietas* as an ideal. For example, in his account of the games, he rewrites his sources in order to demonstrate that virtue supersedes race (*Aen.* 5.442-71//*Arg.* 2.90–97//*Ody.* 18.96-98//*Il.* 23.689-91). See Chapter 2, section 1. b below.

contamination (*contaminatio*),[61] correction (*correctio*),[62] compression or synthesis,[63] internalization,[64] and distribution (*distributio*).[65]

The above list of techniques is not exhaustive. One may also detect other simple or more complex techniques from the analysis of ancient texts (as we shall see below). Moreover, authors sometimes used more than one technique at a time to bring about the desired literary, ideological or theological effect.

### 3. *Criteria for Establishing Literary Dependence*

The key question arises: What criteria can we use to establish a case of deliberate literary borrowing?[66] Detecting literary genetics is usually a complex task. The ancients tell us little about how we ought to proceed in this regard. In the ancient Graeco-Roman and Jewish world literary borrowing was such a cultural convention that such criteria were unnecessary.[67]

The criteria we use today for identifying source texts are not new, but 'their formulation into an explicit methodology might be viewed as a new departure'.[68] As a general criterion, Gian Biagio Conte cautions that, in

---

61. Quintilian notes admiringly that Cicero, through the constant practice of imitation, combined 'the force (*vim*) of Demosthenes, the copious flow (*copiam*) of Plato, and the charm (*iucunditatem*) of Isocrates' (*Inst. Or.* 10.1.108). See Brodie, 'Greco-Roman Imitation', p. 21; and Richard Heinze, *Virgil's Epic Technique* (trans. Hazel Harvey, David Harvey and Fred Robertson; London: Bristol Classical Press, 1993), p. 204.

62. T.J. Luce cites an example from Livy's account of the Spanish campaign. Livy *corrects* the information provide by Antias' annals by appealing to Cato's account of the campaign (34.15.9). See T.J. Luce, *Livy: The Composition of History* (Princeton, NJ: Princeton University Press, 1977), p. 164. For other examples of the use of the technique of correction, see Wills, *Repetition*, pp. 68–71, 174–75.

63. Luce provides a rather amusing example of *compression* or *synthesis* from Livy: Livy *compresses* the separate accounts of a banquet and a private meeting in another room, found in his model, Polybius, into one scene where he has some of the diners asked to get up and leave in order to facilitate the meeting (*dimissi aliis*) (Livy, 36.29.3-11//Poly., 20.11; cf. Livy, 33.21.1-5//Poly.,18.41). See Luce, *Livy*, pp. 207, 212–14. See also Brodie, 'Greco-Roman Imitation', p. 24.

64. See note 57 above. See also Brodie, 'Greco-Roman Imitation', p. 25.

65. Luce cites an example from Livy: Livy *distributes* the account of the peace treaty with Antiochus, found in his model, Polybius (Livy, 38.38.1–39.2//Poly., 21.41-43). Luce observes in regard to this that Livy 'gives the terms, with one or two minor omissions, accurately and in order, except that the names of those to be surrendered to Rome is delayed some thirty-two lines, coming next to last in the series'. See Luce, *Livy*, p. 210.

66. Lyne, 'Vergil's *Aeneid*', p. 189. See Allison, *Intertextual Jesus*, p. 9; Finkelpearl, 'Pagan Traditions', pp. 78–79.

67. Allison, *Intertextual Jesus*, p. 13.

68. Stanley, *Paul*, p. 32.

so far as possible, we read a literary text or reference in terms of the cultural models that it presupposes.[69] We do not automatically have access to such cultural modes. John Hollander explains that, 'when such access is lost in a community of reading, what may have been an allusion may fade in prominence; and yet a scholarly recovery of the context would restore the allusion, by revealing intent as well as by showing means'.[70]

In relatively recent times reliable criteria for establishing literary dependency have been honed from analyses of ancient texts in relation to their cultural modes. It is part of the scholarly recovery mentioned above. Both classical scholars and biblical scholars who also engage with classical texts have proffered valuable directives in this regard – Hays (1989),[71] Stanley (1992),[72] Allison (1993, 2000),[73] R.F. Thomas (1999),[74] Timothy W. Berkley (2000),[75] Brodie (2001)[76] and MacDonald (2001).[77] It is upon the work of these scholars that this study draws.

---

69. Gian Biagio Conte, *Genres and Readers: Lucretius, Love Elegy, Pliny's Encyclopedia* (trans. Glenn W. Most; London: The Johns Hopkins University Press, 1994), p. 133. Nelis gives an example: 'Too long judged as a failed attempt to write a Homeric epic or as a weak and inferior precursor of the *Aeneid*, readable only because of the love story in the third book, Apollonius has constantly been the victim of ill-judged comparison with Homer and Vergil. More recently, in the context of a renewed interest in and better understanding of Hellenistic poetry, several studies have led to a more just appreciation of the *Argonautica* as a brilliantly experimental attempt to renew the epic genre and as a sophisticated work perfectly in keeping with the criteria for poetic excellence commonly associated with Hellenistic poetry in general and Callimachus in particular.' See Nelis, *Vergil's Aeneid*, pp. 7–8.

70. John Hollander, *Figure of Echo: The Mode of Allusion in Milton and After* (Berkley: University of California Press, 1981), pp. 65–66.

71. Hays, *Echoes of Scripture*, pp. 30–31.

72. Stanley, *Paul*, pp. 31–61.

73. Allison, *New Moses*, 19–23; *idem, Intertextual Jesus*, pp. 10–14.

74. R.F. Thomas, 'Virgil's *Georgics* and the Art of Reference', in Philip Hardie (ed.), *Virgil: Critical Assessments of Classical Authors* (4 vols.; London: Routledge, 1999), II, p. 60.

75. Timothy W. Berkley, *From a Broken Covenant to a Circumcision of the Heart: Pauline Intertextual Exegesis in Romans 2.17-29* (Atlanta: SBL, 2000), pp. 47–66.

76. Thomas L. Brodie, *Genesis as Dialogue: A Literary, Historical, and Theological Commentary* (Oxford: Oxford University Press, 2001), pp. 427–31; *idem*, 'Towards Tracing the Gospels' Literary Indebtedness to the Epistles', in MacDonald (ed.), *Mimesis*, pp. 104–16.

77. MacDonald (ed.), *Mimesis*, pp. 2–3.

## a. *External Criteria*

*Primary Criteria*

### 1. *Date*

It must be established that the source text predates the text for which dependency upon it is claimed.[78]

### 2. *Accessibility*

The source text must be known to have been quite widely available and/or specifically available to the author at the time of his writing the later text.[79]

*Secondary Criteria*

### 3. *Status of Text*

The likelihood of one text being dependent on another is increased if the source text was held in high regard or was popular in the tradition at the time when the author was writing the later text.[80]

### 4. *Analogues*

The existence of other examples of literary borrowing of the same source text by other (earlier or contemporary) authors strengthens the case for dependency.[81]

## b. *Internal Criteria*

*Primary Criteria*

### 1. *Parallels*

(a) *Common vocabulary*: Common vocabulary is usually the first positive indicator of a possible case of literary dependency. Common groups of words or vocabulary-clusters sometimes indicate a literary connection. In fact, a 'hook-word' or phrase may be enough to make the link between the source text and the later text.[82] If the words have the same grammatical

---

78. Brodie, *Genesis*, p. 427; Allison, *New Moses*, p. 21.
79. Brodie, *Genesis*, p. 427; MacDonald (ed.), *Mimesis*, p. 2; Hays, *Echoes of Scripture*, pp. 29–30.
80. Allison, *Intertextual Jesus*, p. 11; *idem*, *New Moses*, p. 22.
81. MacDonald (ed.), *Mimesis*, p. 2; Allison, *New Moses*, p. 22.
82. For the terminology of 'hook-word', we are indebted to Stockhausen. See Stockhausen, '2 Corinthians 3', p. 155. See also Allison, *New Moses*, p. 20; William Freedman, 'The Literary Motif: A Definition and Evaluation', *Nov* 4 (1971), pp. 123–31 (123); Charles H. Lohr, 'Oral Techniques in the Gospel of Matthew', *CBQ* 23 (1961), pp. 403–35 (422–23).

form, or even if they have a different grammatical form but occur in similar order, the case for dependency is strengthened.[83]

(b) *Common themes, events, circumstances and/or structure*: The presence of common themes, events, circumstances and/or structures serve as positive indicators for literary dependence.[84] Where they occur in common order, along with common vocabulary, the possibility of dependence is greatly increased.[85]

The higher the frequency of the occurrences outlined in (a) and (b) above, the stronger the case for dependency.[86]

### 2. *Distinctive Details*

The incorporation of distinctive details by authors into their texts was a literary convention in antiquity: 'Ancient authors frequently include unusual detail to alert readers to the presence of their models; one might call them intertextual [or *literary*] *flags*' (italics added)[87].

If the alleged source text(s) and the later text share a correspondence of vocabulary that is shared by no other or few other text(s), it strengthens the case for literary dependency between the texts in question and lessens the possibility that such similarities are commonplace *topoi*. The occurrence of such distinctive traits reflects 'a degree of complexity which oral tradition cannot handle'.[88] The satisfying of this criterion often clinches the case for dependency of one text upon another.

*Secondary Criteria*[89]

### 3. *Systematic Use of Source*

The probability of dependence is increased if all or most of the source text is reflected in some way in the later text, that is, where the later text is a systematic rewriting of an earlier work.[90] This criterion will not be treated

---

83.   Berkley, *Broken Covenant*, pp. 61–62.

84.   Allison, *New Moses*, p. 20.

85.   Berkley, *Broken Covenant*, pp. 63–64.

86.   Berkley, *Broken Covenant*, p. 61.

87.   MacDonald (ed.), *Mimesis*, p. 2. See Berkley, *Broken Covenant*, p. 61; Allison, *New Moses*, p. 23. Stanley considers what he terms 'abnormal expressions' as secondary indications of dependency. See also Stanley, *Paul*, p. 59.

88.   Brodie, *Genesis*, p. 427.

89.   The case for dependency is also strengthened if it can be demonstrated that the source text or other texts by the same earlier author are ones in which the later author shows interest or if the style of incorporating a source text by an author is demonstrated elsewhere by him. The satisfying of these criteria for all of the authors to be analysed in this book lies beyond our scope here. See Thomas, 'Virgil's *Georgics*', p. 60; Hays, *Echoes of Scripture*, p. 30; Berkley, *Broken Covenant*, p. 63; Allison, *New Moses*, pp. 21–22; Stanley, *Paul*, p. 59.

90.   Brodie, *Genesis*, p. 429.

separately, but will be noted where appropriate when analysing an author's use of his source(s) below.

Dependency is also affirmed if the presence of the source text (or elements of it) can be found to explicate or enhance the meaning of its literary context in terms of the later text's theme(s), plot(s), ideology or theology.[91] Evidence of this will be given with each text analysed below.

No single criterion can establish dependency satisfactorily.[92] Nor are all criteria of equal weight or significance. Both the quality (that is, density, volume, distinctiveness of the evidence) and quantity (satisfying the greatest number of criteria together) are important. Some criteria are primary and must be satisfied if a claim of literary dependence is to be made. Other criteria are secondary. If they are satisfied, the evidence provided by them may be considered as confirmatory of the evidence established in relation to primary criteria. Secondary criteria may not, however, be taken alone to establish the case of literary dependency. Nor should they be used as a negative test to exclude cases of dependency that commend themselves on other grounds.

Not all the above criteria will be satisfied equally in every test case.[93] The present study requires that, as a minimum, the primary external and internal criteria be satisfied before a case for dependency is deemed to be successfully established.[94] Moreover, while the application of criteria will be as systematic as possible, we will apply Hays' wise caution: 'To run explicitly through this series of criteria for each of the texts that I treat would be wearisome. I trust the reader's competence to employ these criteria and to apply appropriate discounts to the interpretative proposals that I offer throughout.'[95]

The application of criteria such as the above draws attention to the fact that every composition is to some degree an exercise in comtemporization. In other words, the way in which the author uses his source(s) is not only directive with regard to his literary and ideological or theological purposes, it is directive toward a better interpretation of the socio-

91.   Thomas, 'Virgil's *Georgics*', p. 60. Allison notes that, 'ancient writers did not typically borrow in order to show off or to add surface ornamentation ... most ancient authors were ... accustomed to borrowing from well-known classics in order to add meaning'. See Allison, *Intertextual Jesus*, p. 19. See also MacDonald (ed.), *Mimesis*, p. 3; Hays, *Echoes of Scripture*, p. 31.

92.   Allison, *New Moses*, p. 22.

93.   Allison, *Intertextual Jesus*, p. 11. See Brodie, *Genesis*, pp. 428–29; MacDonald (ed.), *Mimesis*, p. 2.

94.   We will not discuss negative indicators here. It can be assumed in each text examined above that were the presence of negative testimony sufficiently strong we would not offer the cases for analysis. Hence on Stanley's scale of A to E of probability ratings for claiming dependence, only A to C apply here. See Stanley, *Paul*, p. 58.

95.   Hays, *Echoes of Scripture*, p. 32.

historical context or *Sitz im Leben* in which or to which he is writing. Therefore, after the internal evidence of each text is examined, we will comment *briefly* on this where appropriate. In this way we are effecting the methodology given by Mary Ann Tolbert who states that, 'certainly the results of literary analysis may well supply useful information for historical reconstructions of the milieu of the Gospel [or any text], but the determination of that information must logically follow, not precede, the completion of thorough literary evaluation'.[96]

It is very important to be clear that differences between texts do not rule out the possibility of dependency. 'Longinus' (1st century CE) notes humorously that, 'total accuracy is apt to be small minded; in great works, as in large fortunes, something ought to be disregarded'.[97] An author may select only some element(s) from a particular source text. However, in every case where dependency is claimed, 'the source text remains a visible sign of the norm against which the imitating text emphasises its difference'.[98] Thus the issue is not whether there are differences, because of course there will be differences between the source text and the later text; the issue is whether 'the differences are intelligible'.[99]

While some element of subjectivity is unavoidable, by applying further criteria for adjudicating interpretations we shall attempt to make the exercise as objective as possible.[100]


## 4. Conclusion

The Graeco-Roman world of antiquity was a context in which the practice of rewriting was widely pervasive and very highly regarded. Earlier literary sources were taken to be common property, and it behoved an author to fashion something new out of the old. We learn of the methods and techniques of literary imitation from the extant works of authors such as Quintilian and Cicero.

Ancient writers strove from youth to old age to acquire literary

---

96.    Tolbert notes that this observation had already been made in 1901 by William Wrede, *Das Messiasgeheimnis in den Evangelien* (Göttingen: Vandenhoeck & Ruprecht, 1901), pp. 2–3), but has largely gone unheeded by historical critics. See Tolbert, *Sowing the Gospel*, p. 4.

97.    'Longinus', *On the Sublime* 33.2. See Lee, 'Imitation', p. 12.

98.    Finkelpearl, 'Pagan Traditions', p. 86.

99.    Brodie, *Genesis*, p. 431.

100.    Russell, analysing the process of detecting Quintilian's use of sources, notes wisely that, 'it needs critical intelligence ... to comprehend thoroughly not only the words of the models but their purposes and methods'. See Russell, 'De Imitatione', p. 6.

versatility by the constant practice of rewriting.[101] The process of rewriting involved one or more methods and techniques. The most common method of rewriting was that of creative imitation. The techniques involved in this method varied, ranging from quite simple to quite complex. Some of these techniques were not labelled until modern times.

External criteria (date, accessibility, status of text, analogues) and internal criteria (parallels, distinctive details, systematic use of source) may be applied to detect evidence of literary dependency in ancient texts. For our purposes, these have been honed from the work of both classical and biblical scholars involved in analysing the use of sources in antiquity and will be applied to selected texts below.

---

101. Roberts notes that, 'Sopater undertook to paraphrase a text of Homer (*Iliad* 17.629-42, or parts of it) in 72 different ways and of Demosthenes (*De Corona* 60) in 74.' See Roberts, *Biblical Epic*, pp. 12, 18. Of Lucian's (b. c. 120 CE), *How to Write History* (34), Clark writes: 'In his *How to Write History*, Lucian of Samosata is typical of antiquity when he takes it for granted that the power of expression is acquired by long practice and studious imitation of the classics.' See Clark, 'Imitation', p. 12.

# Chapter 2

## REWRITING: EVIDENCE FROM GRAECO-ROMAN TEXTS

The texts of the great authors are the greatest proof of the practice of rewriting in antiquity. It is to them that we now turn our attention. In this chapter, a variety of texts that wholly or in part reflect the use of a source or sources will be analysed. These texts are selected from the Graeco-Roman classical tradition. They reflect a variety of genres – epic, tragedy, historiography and *bioi* – and are analysed using the criteria that have been established for claiming literary dependence above. In each example, the function and effect of the source text(s) within its later literary context are outlined.[1] The aim is to demonstrate the methods and techniques used by Graeco-Roman authors to incorporate earlier sources into their works. These texts will be examined under the following headings:

1. Virgil's Use of Homer's *Iliad* and *Odyssey* and Apollonius' *Argounautica* as Sources
2. Seneca's Use of Euripides' *Hippolytus* and *Bacchae*, Virgil's *Aeneid* and Ovid's *Heriodes* and *Metamorphoses* as Sources
3. Historiography and *Bioi*: Use of Sources by Livy and Plutarch

## 1. *Virgil's Use of Homer's* Iliad *and* Odyssey*, and Apollonius'* Argonautica *as Sources*

Virgil uses Homer's *Iliad* and *Odyssey*, as well as Apollonius Rhodius' (3rd century BCE) *Argonautica*, as literary sources for his *Aeneid*. The aim in this section is to demonstrate this by outlining both the literary techniques by which Virgil incorporates these sources into his text, and the function and effect of the earlier Homeric and Apollonian material in its later Virgilian context.

The rationale for beginning our examination of Graeco-Roman literature with Virgil's *Aeneid* is twofold: first, the *Aeneid* has proved to be the most famous example of the use of sources in classical antiquity; and, secondly, it was studied as such – a reworking of Homer – across the

---

1. Van Erp Taalman Kip, 'Intertextuality', p. 156.

empire at the time of Jesus and up to the time of the composition of the Gospels.[2]

Virgil's epic, the *Aeneid*, narrates the story of the founding of Rome. Virgil's selection of his source material and the manner in which he transforms it is determined by his ideological concerns – poetical, ethical and political.[3] Poetically, he creates an epic for the Roman people, one that rivals the poems of the Greek literary giant, Homer, and later Hellenistic literary master, Apollonius.[4] Ethically, he explores the making of a Roman hero, Aeneas, who struggles to embody the Roman virtue of *pietas* and the ethical ideals of the Stoics. Politically, he universalizes the significance of Roman history.[5]

For the Romans of antiquity, the epic genre was the highest form of literature and Homer's epics were the highest examples of that form.[6] Virgil most likely chose the genre of a mythological epic with its blend of cosmic and historical elements, because of the elevated status of its form. Moreover, his rewriting of the narratives of Homer's epics would immediately elevate his own message among his hearers/readers.[7]

### a. *External Criteria Applied*
*Primary Criteria*

### 1. *Date*

Homer's epics date from the eighth century BCE[8] and Apollonius' epic to the second century BCE.[9] Both sources, therefore, precede Virgil's *Aeneid*

---

2. Colin Graham Hardie, 'Virgil', *OCD* (2nd edn), pp. 1123–28 (1126).

3. See Georg N. Knauer, 'Vergil's *Aeneid* and Homer', in Philip Hardie (ed.), *Virgil: Critical Assessments of Classical Authors* (4 vols.; London: Routledge, 1999), III, p. 98.

4. See Nelis, *Vergil's Aeneid*, p. 8.

5. Viktor Pöschl summarizes it thus: 'The *Aeneid* is a poem of humanity, not a political manifesto. There are three levels of reality: (1) Cosmos, the sphere of divine order, the world of ideas and law; (2) Myth, the heroic world of poetic persons and destiny; (3) History, the world of historical and political phenomena. These are inlaid, one with another, and at the same time they are stratified. Myth, as the poetic intersymbol, partakes of both upper and lower strata. In one direction it incorporates Roman history, and in the other, the eternally valid laws of the universe.' See Viktor Pöschl, *The Art of Vergil: Image and Symbol in the Aeneid* (trans. Gerda Seligson; Michigan: University of Michigan Press, 2nd edn, 1966), pp. 23–24.

6. R. Deryck Williams, 'The *Aeneid*', in E.J. Kenny and W.V. Clausen (eds), *The Cambridge History of Classical Literature II: Latin Literature* (Cambridge: Cambridge University Press, 1982), pp. 333–69 (333).

7. Nelis, *Vergil's Aeneid*, p. 400.

8. C.M. Bowra notes that, 'literary evidence gives at least a *terminus ad quem* in the seventh century …' See C.M. Bowra, 'Homer', *OCD* (2nd edn), p. 524.

9. E.A. Barber and C.A. Trypanis, 'Apollonius Rhodius', *OCD* (2nd edn), p. 84.

and in terms of chronology are not problematic for establishing the case of Virgil's literary dependency upon them.

## 2. *Accessibility*

The works of Homer had become standardized by the late second century BCE, primarily due to the work of Alexandrian scholars.[10] They were the most readily available books in antiquity and were used as school texts for writing exercises in imitation.[11] The survival of manuscripts of the *Argonautica* into the Middle Ages is a strong indication of their wide availability also in antiquity.[12]

### Secondary Criteria

## 3. *Status of Text*

The Homeric epics retained their elite status as models for teachers and students well into the period of Roman imperialism.[13] In fact, their status can be illustrated by the sheer bulk of surviving Homeric texts.[14] The occurrence of various graffiti illustrating the recitation of Homer's works would seem to indicate that their influence extended beyond the educated and elite.[15] The status of Apollonius' *Argonautica* is such that it was

---

10. Stanley, *Paul*, pp. 270, 354.

11. Dennis Ronald MacDonald notes that, 'among their first reading assignment was as selection of verse from *The Odyssey*. Among papyri that survive from the early empire are scraps of lines from *The Iliad* and *The Odyssey* copied as a writing exercise ...'. See Dennis Ronald MacDonald, *Christianizing Homer: The Odyssey, Plato and the Acts of Andrew* (Oxford: Oxford University Press, 1994), p. 17. MacDonald, in another work, notes that, 'the Iliad was the most readily available book in Greek antiquity and retained its elite position well into the Roman Imperial Period. A school text paraphrases the death of Hector, proof that teachers targeted it for mimesis.' See MacDonald (ed.), *Mimesis*, p. 4. See also Tolbert, *Sowing the Gospel*, p. 36, n. 4. Nicholas Horsfall notes that, 'Quintilian lays down that school reading should begin with Homer and Virgil, at the outset imperfectly understood ...' See Nicholas Horsfall (ed.), *A Companion to the Study of Virgil* (Leiden: Brill, 1995), p. 250.

12. Barber and Trypanis, 'Apollonius Rhodius', p. 84.

13. Horsfall notes that, 'Virgil was read, copied and recopied, committed to memory times without number ... and the whole process of comprehension and contamination went on uninterrupted for centuries'. See Horsfall (ed.), *Companion*, pp. 298–99.

14. MacDonald, *Christianizing Homer*, p. 17. Tolbert notes that, 'it is a tribute to the importance of this culture that, next to copies and fragments of the New Testament, the greatest number of manuscripts of any work that have survived from the ancient world are copies of Homer's *Iliad*'. She attributes this datum to B. Metzger, *The Text of the New Testament: Its Transmission, Corruption, and Restoration* (New York: Oxford University Press, 1964), p. 34. See Tolbert, *Sowing the Gospel*, p. 37.

15. Horsfall (ed.), *Companion*, pp. 251–52. Rosalind Thomas notes that, 'much reading and writing was done by slaves, especially in Rome, ensuring that it was by itself of low status'. See Rosalind Thomas, 'Literacy', *OCD* (3rd edn), pp. 868–69 (869).

considered to be the only epic before Virgil 'that in subject and material could aspire to a comparison with Homer'.[16]

### 4. *Analogues*

There is ample evidence of the use of Homer's epics as sources by authors in antiquity, for example, Livius Andronicus' (3rd century BCE) employed the work of Hellenistic commentators on Homer for his translation of the *Odyssey*, and the pseudo-Plutharchan, *On the Life and Poetry of Homer*.[17] Apollonius' *Argonautica* was imitated by poets such as Gnaeus Naevius (b. 3rd century BCE) and Lucius Accius (170–c. 86 BCE).[18]

### b. *Internal Criteria Applied*

The extent and complexity of the creative rewriting involved in the *Aeneid* has been demonstrated in two monumental works: Georg N. Knauer's *Die Aeneis und Homer* (1964)[19] and, more recently, Nelis's *Virgil's Aeneid and the Argonautica of Apollonius Rhodius* (2001). Knauer's work demonstrates the systematic nature of Virgil's use of Homer's texts: 'Vergil has in fact incorporated the whole *Iliad* and the whole *Odyssey* into the *Aeneid*, incomparably transforming the Homeric Epics.'[20] Knauer traces parallels between the large-scale narrative patterns of Virgil and Homer, along with many parallels of vocabulary. An overview of the extent and complexity of Virgil's use of Homer can be gleaned from the summarizing charts in Knauer's book.[21]

Inspired by the work of Knauer, Nelis demonstrates how the *Argonautica* of Apollonius provided an invaluable model for Virgil's sophisticated reworking of Homer.[22] His research shows how 'Vergil's epic is built out of a consistent, structured pattern of imitation based on awareness of Apollonius' imitation of the *Iliad* and the *Odyssey*, and that

---

16. Horsfall (ed.), *Companion*, p. 251.

17. Philip Russell Hardie, 'Epic', *OCD* (3rd edn), p. 530.

18. Damien P. Nelis, 'Hellenistic Poetry at Rome', *OCD* (3rd edn), p. 679; Richard L. Hunter, 'Apollonius Rhodius', *OCD* (3rd edn), pp. 124–26 (126).

19. Georg N. Knauer, *Die Aeneis und Homer: Studien zur poetischen Technik Vergils mit Listen der Homerzitate in der Aeneis* (Hypomnemanta, 7; Göttingen: Vandenhoeck & Ruprecht, 1964).

20. Knauer, 'Vergil's *Aeneid*', p. 96. See Brooks Otis, 'The Originality of the Aeneid', in D.R. Dudley (ed.), *Virgil* (London: Routledge & Kegan Paul, 1969), pp. 27–66 (28).

21. See Knauer, *Die Aeneis und Homer*, appendix 3.

22. Francis Cairns had earlier recognized that 'Virgil looks through Apollonius to the latter's source' but does not demonstrate it in detail as Nelis does. See Francis Cairns, *Virgil's Augustan Epic* (Cambridge: Cambridge University Press, 1989), p. 195.

the direct influence of the *Argonautica* is present from the *Aeneid's* first line to it's closing scene.'[23]

Two-tier or multi-tier allusion is a literary device whereby a text demonstrates not only evidence of the author's immediate model but also of that model's model(s).[24] Francis Cairns' research demonstrates that, 'this device whereby a writer shows his awareness of his model's model by introducing something from that ultimate model not present in the more immediate model into his own imitation of his nearer predecessor, is standard Roman practice'.[25] It is a type of contamination and it accounts for the way in which the *Aeneid* reflects these three epics simultaneously, on different levels, and to different degrees throughout.

As well as demonstrating literary artistry, the effect of two-tier allusion is that the reader familiar with the ultimate model is *sent back* to it, mentally or literally, and the message of the later text is thereby amplified for him/her.[26]

We will examine the games in honour of the death anniversary of Anchises in Book 5 of the *Aeneid*. They provide a good example of a narrative that demonstrates something of the simple, as well as the more complex, techniques involved in rewriting.[27] We will compare the games of *Aeneid* 5 in general, and the boxing match in particular, with those of Virgil's sources, the *Iliad* (Book 23), *Odyssey* (Books 8 and 18) and the *Argonautica* (Book 2).

### 1. Parallels

The overall pattern of events at the Virgilian games bears a general similarity to the pattern of events at the funeral games for Patroclus in the *Iliad* (23.659-95) and the Phaecian games in the *Odyssey* (8.100-254).[28] A

---

23.  Nelis, *Vergil's Aeneid*, p. 7. Cairns notes that, 'the background of the *Aeneid* is just as complex as that of Persius 5.161ff., since in addition to the Homeric epics, it contains (notably) Apollonius' *Argonautica*. Apollonius himself has subtly harmonized many Homeric features with the changed taste of Hellenistic and later readers. This allowed Virgil paradoxically to "improve" on Apollonius by "looking through" him to Homer, thereby giving his reminiscences of Apollonian events and characters a homeric ethos.' See Cairns, *Augustan Epic*, p.195.

24.  This method is variously expressed, as Nelis notes: 'In order to define the classic case in which a poet imitates both a model and that model's model, the terms "double allusion", "window reference" and "two tier allusion" have been coined, and the imitator has also been said to "look through" one model to the other.' See Nelis, *Vergil's Aeneid*, p. 5.

25.  Cairns, *Augustan Epic*, p. 195. See Nelis, *Vergil's Aeneid*, pp. 2–9.

26.  Thomas, 'Virgil's *Georgics*', II, p. 59.

27.  D.A. Kidd, 'Imitation in the Tenth *Ecologue*', in Hardie (ed.), I, pp. 404–17 (405).

28.  Cairns, *Augustan Epic*, p. 230.

number of the games are common to both the Virgil and Homer (see Table 2.1 below).[29]

Table 2.1: *Order of the Games*[30]

| *Il.* 23.659-95 Funeral Games of Patroclus | *Ody.* 8.100-254 Phaecian Games | *Aen.* 5.104-386 Anniversary Games |
|---|---|---|
| 1. Chariot race | 1. Running (nautical | 1. Naval race |
| 2. Boxing | games) | 2. Running |
| 3. Wrestling | 2. Wrestling | 3. Boxing |
| 4. Running | 3. Jumping | 4. Archery |
| 5. Duel in armour | 4. Discus | [*Acestes' shot] |
| 6. Weight-throwing | 5. Boxing | |
| 7. Archery | [*Odysseus' discus | |
| [*Javelin] | throw] | |

[*events outside the official games]

The games of *Aeneid* 5 are closer to those of *Odyssey* 8 with regard to the number of competitive events (4, in the *Aeneid*; 5, in the *Odyssey*). Both include an incident of a solo 'competitor' performing after the formal games to close the competition ('shooting', in the *Aeneid*; 'throwing', in the *Odyssey*). Further, Virgil's placing of the games (Book 5) before Aeneas' descent into the underworld (Book 6), mirrors the order found in the *Odyssey* where Homer places the games (Book 8) before Odysseus' descent into the underworld (Book 11).

We also find parallels between the opening of Virgil's boxing match and that of the boxing match of the *Iliad* (*Iliad* 23). It is one of the games in honour of Patroclus. Virgil, however, *reorders* the Iliadaic sequence (see Table 2.2 below):[31]

---

29.  Knauer's insight is that, 'the structural correspondence provides a clue to the Homeric prototype ...' See Knauer, 'Vergil's *Aeneid*', p. 97.

30.  Brodie concretizes the significance of the presence of similar ordering thus: 'If two people, independently of each other, arrange the numbers 1 to 5 at random, the chance that they will arrange them in the same order is less than one in a hundred. If the numbers are 1 to 10 the chance is less than one in a million.' See Brodie, *Genesis*, p. 429.

31.  Nelis, *Vergil's Aeneid*, p. 13.

Table 2.2: *Opening Scene of the Boxing Match*

| *Il.* 23.653-75 | *Aen.* 5.363–86 |
| --- | --- |
| 1. Achilles presents the prizes to be won | 1. Aeneas invites the boxers to come forward |
| 2. Achilles invites the (best) boxers to come forward | 2. Achilles presents the prizes to be won |
| 3. Epeius steps forward to claim victory | 3. Dares steps forward to claim victory |

These correspondences provide further initial evidence of Virgil's use of Homer.[32] Precise verbal parallels also betray the influence of Homer upon Virgil. Virgil repeats three proper names from Homer's games: (1) Virgil's 'Salius' (*Aen.* 5.298, 321, 335, 347, 352, 356) corresponds to Homer's Ἅλιος in *Odyssey* 8 (vv. 119, 370); (2) Virgil's 'Euryalus' (*Aen.* 5.295) is homonymous with both the winning wrestler of *Odyssey* 8, Εὐρύαλος ('Euryalus', v. 127) and the defeated boxer of *Iliad* 23, Εὐρύαλος ('Euryalus', vv. 677–99); and (3) Virgil's 'Nautes', a name which occurs in the *Aeneid* after the games (v. 704), is a homonym of Ναυτεύς of *Odyssey* 8 which occurs at the beginning of Phaecian games (v. 112).[33]

### 2. Distinctive Details

Single similar occurrences, verbal or otherwise, are significant tell-tale indications of literary dependence. Entullus, the winner of the boxing match in the *Aeneid*, and Epeius, the victor of the game in *Iliad* 23, are mentioned only once in their respective epics (*hapax*).[34] In terms of numerical correspondence, both the *Aeneid* 5 and *Odyssey* 8 list 16 competitors by name.[35]

### 3. Simple Rewriting

As well as incorporating the vocabulary and events of his sources in parallel order, there is evidence of Virgil's use of other simple literary techniques to incorporate his source texts into his *Aeneid* to suit his purposes.

*Positivization by Addition and Omission*: Apollonius, in his reworking of the Homeric boxing matches, had made his match lengthier than both of

32. Cairns, *Augustan Epic*, p. 231. See Heinze, *Virgil's Epic*, p. 203.
33. Cairns, *Augustan Epic*, p. 230.
34. Cairns, *Augustan Epic*, p. 225.
35. Cairns, *Augustan Epic*, pp. 231–32.

Homer's. Virgil appears to have noticed this, as his boxing match even surpasses Apollonius' one in terms of length (*Aen.*, 122 verses; *Arg.*, 31 verses).[36] Virgil omits a number of the more brutal Homeric games of the *Iliad* 23 and *Odyssey* 8 (wrestling, the duel in armour and weight throwing from the *Iliad*; wrestling, jumping and discus from *Odyssey* 8; see Table 2.1 above).

In the Iliadic boxing match the only stimulus given to a would-be competitor is the boastful challenge given by Epeius to *anyone* to fight him (*Il.* 23.667-75). In the Odyssean boxing match two stimuli are given to a *specific subject*, namely, Odysseus, to entice him to box: first, Laodamus, the son of Alkinos, charmingly invites him to compete (*Ody.* 8.145-51); then Euryalus distastefully challenges him to do so (*Ody.* 8.159-64). Virgil has Dares, like the Iliadic Epeius of *Iliad* 23, place the challenge. However, he does so to a *specific subject*, Entullus (cp. Irus of *Ody.* 18.25-31). Also, he *adds* a second subject, Acestes, to the parallel scene, as in *Odyssey* 8. Acestes, unlike Euryalus, is a non-competitor who encourages Entullus at length to take up Dares' challenge (*Aen.* 5.387-93). Acestes' language is positive, imitating that of Laodamus who encourages Odysseus ('Entellus, once bravest of heroes', *Entelle, heroum quondam fortissime, Aen.* 5.389; cp. 'for there is no greater glory for a man', οὐ μὲν γὰρ μεῖζον κελός ἀνέρος, *Ody.* 8.147).

Thus Virgil draws upon both his Homeric and Apollonian models for the purposes of the positivization of his games.

### 4. *Complex Rewriting: Positivization by Conflation*

The complex techniques of rewriting are obviously more difficult to trace than the more simple ones. Moreover, they tend to extend over longer sections of the text.[37] Here, we shall examine Virgil's reference to 'rattling cheeks' (*crepitant malae*, 5.436) in the violent opening exchange of the boxing match. It provides an example of how Virgil *conflates* his sources by the use of two-tier allusion. By presenting the Virgilian, Apollonian and Homeric texts as layers, one upon another, it becomes easier to trace the pattern of Virgil's rewriting (see Table 2.3 below).

---

36. Nelis, *Vergil's Aeneid*, p. 16. See Cairns, *Augustan Epic*, p. 240.
37. Kidd, 'Imitation', I, p. 408.

Table 2.3: *Opening of the Boxing Matches of the* Iliad, Argonautica *and* Aeneid
(Literary Technique = Two-Tier Allusion)

| BOXERS | VIOLENT OPENING EXCHANGE | NOISE MADE BY BOXERS' TEETH |
|---|---|---|
| *ILIAD* 23<br>Epeius v.<br>Euryalus | σὺν δέ σφι βαρεῖαι χεῖρες ἔμιχθεν<br>and their hands clashed together in heavy blows (23.687) | δεινὸς δὲ χρόμαδος γενύων γένετ'<br>Terrible then was the grinding of their teeth (23.688) |
| *ARGON-AUTICA* 2<br>Amycus v.<br>Polydeuces | προπάροιθε βαρείας χεῖρας ἐπ' ἀλλήλ ... ἀυτιωντες<br>they raised their heavy hands and matched their might in deadly strife (2.68) | ὡς τοῖσι παραήιά τ' ἀυφοτέρωθεν, καὶ γένυες κτύπεον, βρυξὴ δ'ὑπετέλλετ' ὀδόντων, ἄσπετος<br>and the blows resound one after another; so cheeks and jaws crashed on both sides, and a huge clattering of teeth arose (2.82-84) |
| *AENEID* 5<br>Dares v.<br>Entellus | *multa viri nequiquam inter se vulnera iactant, multa cavo lateri ingeminant*<br>Many hard blows they launch at each other to no avail, but many they reign on hollow flank (5.433-34) | *et pectora vastos dant sonitus, erratque auris et tempora circum crebra manus, duro crepitant sub vulnere malae*<br>while their chests ring loudly; hands flash about ears and brows and cheeks rattle under the hard strokes (5.436) |

In the boxing match of the *Iliad* (23.687), Homer refers to the noise made by the grinding of teeth by a boxer who is gearing up before a fight. Apollonius picks up this reference (*Arg.* 2.82-84). However, he also adds a reference to another source of the noise, namely, that which results from the grinding of teeth *after* the boxer's jaw has been punched by his opponent. In the *Aeneid*, the noise of the grinding of teeth comes from the punched jaw (*duro crepitant sub vulnere malae, Aen.* 5.436). Traditionally, Virgil had been seen by some commentators to pick up Homer's reference, but to misunderstand it.[38] By adding the Apollonian tier into the

---

38.   Nelis, *Vergil's Aeneid*, p. 17; Hunter, 'Apollonius Rhodius', p. 126.

equation, it becomes clear that the *Argonautica* was the immediate model for Virgil, and the *Iliad* the ultimate source of the reference.[39]

In the next example from the games, we wish to illustrate how extraordinarily systematic Virgil was in his use of these epic sources. Here, we will present a more extended example of Virgil's use of the technique of two-tier allusion, that is, Virgil's *looking through* Apollonius to Homer, and sometimes only to one or other.[40] We will do so by examining the six stages of the game under the headings:

A: Preliminaries to the Fight
B: Initial Confrontation
C: Age, Skill and Physical Power
D: Response of the One Challenged
E: Speech
F: Ending

In the Virgilian match, the character Dares, in his role as boastful challenger, corresponds to the Iliadic Epeius, the Odyssean Irus and the Apollonian Amycus; and the character Entullus, the one challenged, is modelled on the Iliadic Euryalus, the Odyssean Odysseus and the Apollonian Polydeuces.

*A: Preliminaries to the Fight*: A positive initial indication that the *Argonautica* reflects the Iliadic boxing match is to be found in the close verbal and thematic parallels between their respective accounts of the preliminaries to the fight ('And Tydues' son, famed for his spear, attended to Euryalus, encouraging him with words', *Il.* 23.681 // 'and to him came Castor and mighty Talaus, son of Bias, and they quickly bound the gauntlets about his hands, often bidding him be of good courage', *Arg.* 2.62-64; cf. *Arg.* 2.20-21 // *Il.* 23.677).

*B: Initial Confrontation*: Apollonius' use of the *Iliad* as a source is immediately confirmed in the initial confrontation of the boxers (cf. *Arg.* 2.32-58 // *Il.* 23.684). It is at this point of the match that Virgil picks up the

39. Nelis, *Vergil's Aeneid*, pp. 11–12, 17.
40. Nelis, *Vergil's Aeneid*, pp. 14–16. Cairns notes that, 'At *Iliad* 23.807–9 Achilles seems to be offering as prizes in the spear duel a sword to the victor (807f.), and arms (presumably Sarpedon's, cf. 798-800), to be "held in common" by both victor and loser (809). The spear duel appears, as modern commentators have noted, somewhat implausible in this and other respects. It may be suggested that Virgil (or a previous commentator), encouraged by τεύχεα ἑσσαμένω (arming themselves) in line 803, took the offending line τεύχεα δ' ἀμφότεροι ξυνήϊα ταῦτα φερέσθων (809) to mean not "let them take these (i.e. Sarpedon's) arms as a jointly owned prize" but "let them don the same (i.e. equal) arms <for the fight>" i.e. interpreting ταῦτα as ταὐτά = τὰ αὐτά. On this hypothesis *Iliad* 23.809 would indeed be the source of the equal arms motif of *Aeneid* 5.400-25.' See Cairns, *Augustan Epic*, p. 241.

story. In fact, at this point, there is a higher density of correspondence between the respective accounts of the initial confrontation between the boxers of Virgil (*Aen.* 5.401-21) and his immediate model, Apollonius (*Arg.* 2.32-59), than with Virgil and his ultimate model, Homer (*Il.* 23.683-84).

Virgil *transfers* the gesture of the laying down of gloves of the Apollonian servant character, Lycoreus, to the one challenged, Entellus. His description of the gloves as dangerous ('oxhides all stiff with unsewn lead and iron'; *terga boum plumbo insuto ferroque rigebant, Aen.* 5.404-405) imitates that of Apollonius' description ('gauntlets made of raw hide, dry, exceedingly tough ... dry oxhides'; δοιοὺς, ἑκάτερθεν ἱμάντας ὠμούς, ἀζαλέους, περὶ δ'οἵγ' ἔσαν ἐσκληῶτες ... ῥινούς τε Βοῶν ... ἀζαλέας, *Arg.* 2.52, 58). Apollonius' description already picks up an element of the vocabulary of his Iliadic source ('well-cut thongs of the hide of an ox of the field'; ἱμαντες ἐυτμήτους βοὸς ἀγραύλοιο, *Il.* 23.684).

Further, Virgil *reverses* the order of the symbolic cloak shedding: Apollonius' Amycus does it before the laying down of the gloves; Virgil's Entullus does it afterwards (cf. *Aen.* 5.421 // *Arg.* 2.32).

*C: Age, Skill, and Physical Power*: In the matter of age, skill and physical power, Virgil's text reflects the *Odyssey* (18.17-74). Homer's Odysseus is disguised as an old beggar whose powerful physique is revealed. Virgil's Entullus is in fact old but still has a powerful physique. Both Odysseus and Entullus are reluctant competitors (*Aen.* 5.395).

*D: Response of the One Challenged*: Irus, the challenger in *Odyssey* 18, becomes terrified of his opponent, Odysseus, who first appears to be the weaker one (*Ody.* 18.75). In *Argonautica* 2, Apollonius takes up the idea of including an element of emotion from the *Odyssey*, but he transfers it from the challenger, Amycus, to the one challenged, Polydeuces. Further, he reverses the quality of the emotion: instead of being terrified, he has Polydeuces remain undaunted by his opponent (*Arg.* 2.61-64).

Virgil *undoes this reversal* by having his challenger, Dares, become terrified by his opponent, Entellus, as was Homer's Irus. Further, he has the one challenged, Entullus, appear initially as the weaker one. This is a good example of a literary *correction* or 'opposition-in-imitation' (*oppositio in imitando*), where 'the poet provides unmistakable indications of his source, then proceeds to offer detail which contradicts or alters that source'.[41]

---

41. Thomas, 'Virgil's *Georgics*', II, p. 68. For other examples of literary correction in the games, see Cairns, *Augustan Epic*, pp. 234, 242-43. It was quite acceptable for authors to correct their sources in antiquity. For comments on same, see Woodman, *Rhetoric*, pp. 90, 93, 130. Heinze notes a serious qualification in this regard: 'However, one thing is obligatory,

*E: Speech*: Virgil's Entullus, in his speech before the match, explains that his gloves are those with which Eryx fought Hercules on that very spot, and which he, Entullus, had used in his youth (*Aen* 5.410-20).

Odysseus' speech recalls his expertise in his youth with a view to intimidating his opponent (*Ody.* 8.179-84). Virgil takes the idea of a speech from the *Odyssey* and *conflates* it with the reference to Hercules from the *Argonautica* (1.1163-362). The inclusion of a reference to such a deity here by Virgil helps to amplify the notion of the power behind the one being challenged, and, by implication, the fear that his opponent should have. Entullus, by showing himself connected to the gods, makes himself an even more intimidating opponent than Odysseus (*Aen.* 5.412).

All the more striking then is the fact that Entullus indicates at the end of his speech that he will fight with normal gloves, rather than his own very dangerous ones. This gesture marks a *reversal* when compared with the use of dangerous gloves by the boxers of *Iliad* 23 and *Argonautica* 2 respectively. It is another mark of Virgil's positivization of the games.

In his lengthy speech, Entullus gives his reasons for his acceptance of the challenge – his love of praise and glory rather than greed, his courage in his old age rather than reticence. For him, the end is not the demolition of the opponent. Rather, he presents a superior reason for fighting, namely, the Roman virtue of *pietas* (*Aen.* 5.394-435).

*F: Ending*: Sometimes several techniques are employed together, providing double or multiple references to an author's previous model(s).[42] For example, at the end of Virgil's boxing match, the phrase 'they spar, hand with hand' (*immiscentque manus minibus, Aen.* 5.429), which describes the opening round of punches, recalls the phrase from the beginning of the fight at the Iliadic funeral games of Patroclus – 'their hands clashed together' (χεῖρες ἔμιξθεν, *Il.* 23.687). A closer examination, however, shows the vocabulary of Virgil's phrase to be closer to a phrase given at a later stage of the Apollonian boxing match – 'the brutal play of fists' (χεροῖν ἐναντία χεῖρας, *Arg.* 2.78). Virgil's positioning of the phrase, therefore, follows Homer but his vocabulary is closer to that of Apollonius.

The ending also, however, marks a departure by Virgil from his models. He has age win over youthfulness, strength over skill, modesty over arrogance, and an alien over a national. This does not occur in either of

---

that the poet should know the traditional version and should not contradict it out of sheer ignorance. Therefore, when he deviates from it, he should make at least a covert reference to the true version in order to reassure learned readers.' See Heinze, *Virgil's Epic*, pp. 200–201. Baldwin makes another pertinent observation: 'The notion that imitation must be subversive of originality betrays a crude conception of both.' See Baldwin, *Ancient Rhetoric*, p. 213.

   42. See Nelis, *Vergil's Aeneid*, p. 2.

the Homeric boxing games[43] (cp. *Aen.* 5.443-48, 468-71 // *Arg.* 2.90-98 // *Ody.* 18.96-98 // *Il.* 23.689-91).[44]

Deliberate points of departure mark the most advanced form or rewriting.[45] Departures from tradition were not made lightly in antiquity.[46] This departure serves to amplify hugely Virgil's ethical and political values. He has one of his fellowmen lose to a foreigner because morally he is below the standard of the Trojan ideal. For Virgil, virtue supercedes race. In this way he universalizes the ideal of Roman *pietas*.

The above analysis of Virgil's games (*Aeneid* 5), and in particular the boxing match, shows something of the extent to which Virgil could make use of sources from 'totally different epochs'.[47]

At the time of Virgil's writing, the virtue of *pietas* was the most esteemed of all virtues among the Romans.[48] The exercise of virtue leads to a situation of concord.[49] This appears to be his agenda in transforming 'a simple narrative of adventure into a complex narrative of motivation'.[50]

It is useful to restate briefly the techniques used by Virgil in the rewriting of the games of the *Iliad*, *Odyssey* and *Argonautica*. The more simple techniques noted above include parallel order of events, parallel vocabulary, the transferring of gestures and the reversal, addition/ omission of words or events.

The more complex techniques that were dealt with in greater detail above include the following:

*Emulation*: Apollonius had made his boxing match longer than Homer's. Virgil's is longer than all of his models.

*Positivization*: Virgil positivizes his boxing match thus: he omits the bloodier games of Homer's epics; he adds a character whose language is positive – Acestes; and has Entullus choose to play with normal rather than dangerous gloves, and provide a virtuous response upon his victory.

---

43. Cairns, *Augustan Epic*, p. 240.

44. Nelis, *Vergil's Aeneid*, p. 18. Cairns notes that, 'the notice of Servius on *Aeneid* 5.389 states that, (*sic*) according to Hygnius, (*sic*) Entellus was a Trojan'. See Cairns, *Augustan Epic*, p. 227. See also Heinze, *Virgil's Epic*, p. 200.

45. Kidd, 'Imitation', I, p. 6.

46. Heinze, *Virgil's Epic*, p. 200.

47. E.J. Kenney, 'Books and Readers in the Roman World', in Kenny and Clausen (eds), *The Cambridge History of Classical Literature II*, p. 344.

48. William Chase Greene, 'Pietas', *OCD* (2nd edn), p. 833.

49. Concord is a motif that was associated with games in general in antiquity. See Cairns, *Augustan Epic*, pp. 228, 236, 237, 247.

50. Otis, 'Originality', p. 41. Heinze notes that, 'Virgil takes a scene ... develops it, so to speak, backwards or forwards, by giving it either a motivation or consequences that differ from those which it had in it's source'. See Heinze, *Virgil's Epic*, p. 206.

*Conflation*: Virgil's phrase – 'they spar, hand with hand' (*Aen.* 5.429) – at the opening of his boxing match reflects the influence of the Iliadic boxing match in terms of position and the Appollonian boxing match in terms of vocabulary.

*Two-Tier Allusion*: Virgil's reference to the noise made by 'rattling cheeks' after a violent punch (*Aen.* 5.436) had traditionally been seen to be a misunderstanding of Homer's reference to the noise made by a boxer gearing up before a match (*Il.* 23.688). When we include the Apollonian epic into the analysis, and look from Virgil's *Aeneid* through it to Homer's *Illiad*, we see that Virgil's immediate model is Apollonius' boxing match (*Arg.* 2.82-84) (already a rewriting of the boxing match of Homer's *Iliad*), and his ultimate model is Homer's *Iliad*.

*Correction*: In Homer's *Odyssey*, Irus, the challenger in the boxing match, becomes terrified (*Ody.* 18.75). Apollonius transfers the element of emotion from the challenger, Amycus, to the one challenged, Polydeuses. However, he reverses the response: unlike Amycus, Polydeuses remains undaunted (*Arg.* 2.61-4). Virgil undoes the reversal, and has the challenger in his boxing match, Dares, become terrified of his opponent, Entullus, just as Irus was in the *Odyssey* (*Aen.* 5.406-8).

*Amplification*: Entullus' speech at the boxing match in the *Aeneid* is modelled on that of Odysseus in the *Odyssey* (*Aen.* 5.409-20; *Ody.* 8.179-84). However, Virgil embeds in it an element from the *Argonautica*, namely, that of the boxer being connected to the gods. Thus he amplifies the power of Entullus, making him intimidating to his opponent.

*Systematic Rewriting*: The games of the *Aeneid* in general, and the boxing match in particular, are clearly a systematic rewriting by Virgil of those of the *Iliad*, *Odyssey* and *Argonautica*.

## 2. Seneca's Use of Euripides' Hippolytus and Bacchae, Virgil's Aeneid and Ovid's Heriodes and Metamorphoses as Sources

Seneca (c. 4–65 CE) sourced much of his materials for his *Phaedra* from the works of his Greek predecessors.[51] Euripides' (c. 485–406 BCE) *Hippolytus* is his primary literary source.[52] According to C.S. Segal's analysis, 'the

---

51. Brodie, 'Greco-Roman Imitation', p. 23. See Michael Coffey and Roland Mayer, (eds), *Seneca Phaedra* (Cambridge: Cambridge University Press, 1990), p. 1; Elaine Fantham, 'Virgil's Dido and Seneca's Tragic Heroines', *GR* 22–23 (1975–76), pp. 1–10 (1); and Tarrant, 'Senecan Drama', p. 262.

52. Coffey and Mayer, *Seneca Phaedra*, p. 6.

ghost of Euripides haunts every line'.[53] As well as this primary source, however, Seneca draws upon at least four other sources – Euripides' *Bacchae*, Virgil's *Aeneid* and Ovid's (43 BCE–18 CE) *Heriodes* and *Metamorphoses*.

The rationale in choosing to examine Seneca's *Phaedra* is threefold: first, it demonstrates that literary dependence and the practice of rewriting transcended literary genres in antiquity; secondly, it shows that authors often used several sources of quite different genres for their compositions (Seneca uses the genres of tragedy, epic poetry and letters for his *Phaedra*); thirdly, Seneca is roughly contemporaneous with Jesus, Paul and the origin of the Gospel genre.

Seneca's *Phaedra* is a tragedy that tells the story of the illicit passion of a stepmother, Phaedra, for her stepson, Hippolytus. In terms of matter, it mirrors Euripides' tragedy, *Hippolytus*. Euripides' other play, the *Bacchae*, is a story in which the activities of a tyrant, Dionysius of Syracuse (c. 430–367 BCE) are first presented and then vindicated. Virgil's *Aeneid*, as we saw above, is an epic narrative about the founding of Rome and the idealization of the virtue of *pietas*. Ovid's *Heriodes* is a set of paired love letters, with the lady responding to the (absent) gentleman's letter.[54] His *Metamorphoses* is an epic poem that gives an account of the movement from Chaos to Order (Cosmos), culminating in the apotheosis of Julius Caesar.[55]

### a. *External Criteria Applied*
*Primary Criteria*

### 1. *Date*

Euripides' works date from the fifth century BCE. Virgil's *Aeneid* dates from the first century BCE. Ovid's works date from before or at the turn of the era. The works of all three authors precede Seneca's *Phaedra* in terms of chronology. Therefore, their dating is not problematic for establishing the case of Seneca's literary dependency on them.

### 2. *Accessibility*

Seneca was educated as a youth in Rome by the best available teachers. He studied grammar, rhetoric and philosophy.[56] Later, he gained an elevated status, first, as tutor to young Nero, and then as advisor and minister to Nero after his accession in 54 CE. Seneca later withdrew from

---

53. C.S. Segal, *Language and Desire in Seneca's Phaedra* (Princeton, NJ: Princeton University Press, 1986), p. 202.

54. Edward John Kenney, 'Ovid', *OCD* (2nd edn), pp. 763–65 (764).

55. Kenney, 'Ovid', pp. 763–65 (764).

56. A. Ker and Leighton Durham Reynolds, 'Seneca', *OCD* (2nd edn), p. 976.

public life and devoted himself to reading and philosophical inquiry. When one considers that first-century Rome saw 'an explosion of commercial book production',[57] it is quite implausible to assume that Seneca could not have had access to copies of the texts of the literary giants of the distant past, such as Euripides, and the immediate past, such as Virgil and Ovid. By Seneca's day, Virgil's works were already standard school textbooks.[58]

*Secondary Criteria*

### 3. *Status of Text*

About 200 CE, a selection of ten of Euripides' plays was collated for use in schools. His *Bacchae* was included in this collection. Both this play and his *Hippolytus* won prizes at competitions such as those held at Dionysia.[59] Clearly, these works were held in high regard among authors up to and including Seneca. Some eighty titles of Euripides' plays remain extant today.

The high status of Virgil's *Aeneid* has already been noted. As for Ovid, it is recorded that 'by AD 8 he was the leading poet of Rome'.[60] It would be quite incredible to imagine that his mature *Heriodes*, and technically brilliant *Metamorphoses*, would not have caught Seneca's attention.[61]

### 4. *Analogues*

While we have no known account of the use of Euripides' *Hippolytus* and *Bacchae* as sources, other than by Seneca, we know that the influence of Euripides' literary techniques was far-reaching. This is especially the case in relation to Middle Comedy, for example, Aristophanes' (c. 445–385 BCE) *Cocalus*.[62]

Virgil's *Aeneid* was widely used as a source. As noted above, contemporary critics used it. Most famous among them is Macrobius (n.d.), who used it in his *Saturnalia* (an academic symposium of seven volumes) to set out the parallels between Virgil's *Aeneid* and Homer's epics, along with other Virgilian sources, for the purpose of demonstrating

---

57.   Loveday Alexander, 'Ancient Book Production and the Circulation of the Gospels', in Bauckham, (ed.), *The Gospel for All Christians*, pp. 71–105 (88).

58.   See ch. 2., section 1. a. above.

59.   Donald William Lucas, 'Euripides', *OCD* (2nd edn), pp. 418–21 (418–19). See Alan Wardman, *Plutarch's Lives* (London: Paul Elek, 1974), p. 175.

60.   Kenny, 'Ovid', p. 763; Michael Dewar, '*Siquid Habent Ueri Uatum Praesagia*: Ovid in the 1st–5th Centuries A. D.', in Barbara Weiden Boyd (ed.), *Brill's Companion to Ovid* (Leiden: Brill, 2002), pp. 383–412 (385–87, 393).

61.   Kenney, 'Ovid', pp. 764–65.

62.   Lucas, 'Euripides', p. 421.

Virgil's literary genius (*Saturnalia* 3–6).[63] Many post-Augustan Latin writers, namely, Persius (34–62 CE), Lucan (39–65 CE) and Statius (c. 45–96 CE), used Ovid's poetry, most especially his *Metamorphoses*, as a source.[64]

### b. *Internal Criteria Applied*

One of the models for Seneca's character, Phaedra, is Virgil's Dido (*Aeneid* 4). They share parallels of theme and plot structure. Both Phaedra's and Dido's passionate love is one-sided, undeclared, over-whelming, and immoral – Phaedra's incest with a stepson, Hippolytus; Dido's infidelity to her husband, Sychaeus. Both women share their dilemma with a confidante – Phaedra to her nurse, and Dido to Anna. Both infatuated women confront their respective loves, only to be rejected ultimately.

### 1. *Parallels*

In terms of parallel vocabulary and imagery, there are several examples in Seneca's *Phaedra* that demonstrate his dependence upon the aforementioned works of both Euripides and Virgil. One such example is Seneca's use of the simile of a rock resisting the sea. In the *Hippolytus,* Euripides has the nurse urge Phaedra to be more brazen in pursuing her stepson, Hippolytus, but Phaedra resists the nurse's entreaty as a rock resists the sea (*Hipp.* 304-305). Seneca portrays his Phaedra as victim in her own eyes, but much less so in the eyes of the narrator. Segal notes this subtlety: 'In Seneca the (step)mother, instead of being an agent of wrongdoing, is, ostensibly at least, the victim of wrongdoing (891-93) . . .'.[65]

The idea of resistance is also found in Virgil's *Aeneid*.[66] Virgil describes how, in the underworld, Aeneas was as unmoved as an oak at the approach of Dido ('But by no tearful pleas is he moved, nor in any yielding (*tractabilis*) mood does he pay heed to any words . . . even as when northern Alpine winds . . . emulously strive to uproot a (*sic*) oak strong', *Aen.* 4.438-40; cp. 7.586-90). Seneca, in the creation of the nurse's description of Hippolytus, *fuses* Euripides' simile of rock-resisting sea with Virgil's oak-resisting wind simile and embellishes both: [Nurse] 'Like a hard crag, intractable (*intractabilis*) on every side, that resists the seas and flings the attacking waves far back, so he [Hippolytus] rebuffs my

---

63.   Roland Gregory Austin, 'Macrobius', *OCD* (2nd edn), p. 635.

64.   Dewar, '*Siquid Habent*', pp. 383–412.

65.   Segal, *Language and Desire*, p. 171.

66.   Seneca and Virgil also share a common metaphor of passion, that is, passion as a fire fuelled by the wound of love (cp. *Phae.* 101-104//*Aen.* 4.1-5, 66-69); and both authors provide catalogues of the symptoms of love (cp. *Phae.* 105-108, 362//*Aen.* 4.74-79, 86-89). See Fantham, 'Virgil's Dido', pp. 4–5.

words' (*Phae.* 580-83).[67] By means of this double-reference, Seneca *amplifies* the portrait of Hippolytus as stubborn.

Seneca's use of literary sources is also obvious elsewhere. For example, in the *Aeneid*, Anna addresses her frustration to her mistress, Dido (*Aen.* 4.31-53). Seneca uses this, but has the parallel character, the nurse, address her frustration to the Chorus rather than to her mistress, Phaedra (*Phae.* 267-73). The nurse appears to have despaired of her mistress ever listening to her advice to take action. The style of the nurse's grand descriptive address, complete with epithets, reflects the influence of Virgil's epic. However, in the epic genre, a speech as grand as this would normally be found on the lips of a primary character, rather than a secondary one, such as a lowly nurse.[68]

An examination of the issue of marriage in Seneca's *Phaedra* shows up something rather interesting. Seneca's Phaedra hopes that she might cloak her offensive intentions by marrying Hippolytus: 'If I carry out what I have begun, perhaps I shall conceal the crime behind the torch of marriage' (*Phae.* 596-7). Here, Seneca's theme and vocabulary recall the fourth letter of Ovid's *Heriodes*. Ovid writes: 'Theseus pierced her [Phaedra's] side ... yes, and she was not even wed to him and taken to his home with the nuptial torch ... our fault can be covered under the name of kinship' (*taedaque accepta iugali ... /cognato poterit nominee culpae tegi* (*Her.* 4.121, 137). However, the word 'iugalis' is also used three times in the context of Virgil's Dido material (*vinclo sociare iugali*, 4.16; *vincla iugalia*, 4.59; *lectumque iugalem*, 4.496), where the idea of marriage as concealment for the offence occurs (*Aen.* 4.172).

Clearly, Seneca mirrors both Virgil and Ovid in terms of thought and vocabulary. What is less clear, however, is whether we have here an example of *conflation* by means of two-tier allusion. Is Ovid in fact rewriting Virgil at this point, and was Seneca aware of it? Or did Seneca draw separately upon both Virgil and Ovid?[69] The former appears not at all unlikely when one considers that, 'Virgil is everywhere in Ovid'.[70] Whichever is the case, however, on the issue of marriage, Seneca's 'textuality involves a kind of double vision',[71] as both earlier authors' works are reflected in the later text.

## 2. *Distinctive Details*

It has been noted that the term *tractabilis* (Lt., *tractare* = 'to handle', 'to maul'), albeit a rare word in ancient texts, is part of Virgil's vocabulary.

---

67. Fantham, 'Virgil's Dido', p. 4.
68. Fantham, 'Virgil's Dido', p. 2.
69. Fantham, 'Virgil's Dido', pp. 7–8.
70. Horsfall (ed.), *Companion*, pp. 257, 258–67.
71. Segal, *Language and Desire*, p. 202.

Virgil applies its negative form to an African tribe – 'the bordering country is Lybian, a race unconquerable in war' (*genus intractabile bello, Aen.* 1.339) and applies its positive form to describing the sky – 'and the skies intractable' (*dum non tractibile caelum, Aen.* 4.53). Seneca favours the negative form, '*intractabilis*', which occurs nowhere *in the whole of his ten tragedies* except the three occurrences in the *Phaedra* (*intractabilem*, 229; *intractabilem*, 271; *intractabilis*, 580). This is strong evidence of a literary link between Seneca's *Phaedra* and Virgil's *Aeneid*.

### 3. *Complex Rewriting: Emulation by Conflation and Negativization*
The ending of Senaca's *Phaedra* provides a fascinating example of complex rewriting from antiquity. For the ending, Seneca draws not only on Euripides' *Hippolytus* and Virgil's *Aeneid* but also upon two other sources, namely, Euripides' *Bacchae* and Ovid's *Metamorphoses*.

In both Euripides' *Hippolytus* and Seneca's *Phaedra*, Hippolytus dies as a result of the curse of his father, Theseus; in both, the curse causes Hippolytus to be dragged by horses that a sea-creature causes to bolt; and in both, the news of his death is brought by the messenger, as is usual in tragic drama.[72]

For the ending, however, Seneca and Euripides differ: Euripides has Hippolytus reconciled, albeit briefly, with his father. Seneca has Hippolytus refuse utterly to be reconciled with his father. He has him suffer death by dismemberment (*Phae.* 1093-94), and has his father, Theseus, gather up the parts of his dead son's body. Both Virgil and Ovid also describe a death by dismemberment (*Aen.* 7.765-67; 10.534-43; *Met.* 15.524-29).[73] However, the high density of verbal parallels in parallel order between Ovid's *Metamorphoses* and Seneca's *Phaedra* leaves little doubt that it is Ovid's work, rather than Euripides' *Hippolytus*, which was his primary model here (see Table 2.4 below).

---

72. Gahan, 'Imitation', p. 381.
73. Gahan, 'Imitation', p. 381, n. 7.

Table 2.4: *Death by Dismemberment in Ovid and Seneca*[74]

| Ovid's *Metamorphoses* | Seneca's *Phaedra* |
|---|---|
| 15.506 *profugo* (of the chariot of Hippolytus) | 1000 *profugus* (of Hippolytus himself) |
| | 1026 *immugit* (of the sea) |
| 15.510 *dare mugitus* | 1036 *taurus* ... 1081 *corniger* (of the sea creature |
| 15.511 *corniger* ... *taurus* | |
| | 1043 *naresque* (of the sea creature) |
| 15.513 *naribus* | 1096 *vulnere* (of the injuries of Hippolytus) |
| 15.525 *stipe* | 1099 *stipite* (of the stake by which the body of Hippolytus is partly held fast) |
| 15.526 *membra* | |
| 15.529 *vulnus* | 1097 *membra* (of the body of Hippolytus) |

We find another element of literary intrigue in Seneca's description of the dismemberment of Hippolytus. It is more lurid than Ovid's. J.J. Gahan argues that this is because Seneca *conflates* Ovid's letter, *Metamorphoses*, with another of Euripides' plays, namely, the *Bacchae*, for the end of his tragedy (*Phae.* 1093-1114). In the *Bacchae*, Pentheus is killed by his mother, Agave, and his body is dismembered like that of Hippolytus. Parts of Pentheus' portioned body lie under hard rocks (στύφλοις πέτραις, *Hipp.* 1137-38). Seneca rewrites this element in his *Phaedra*: he has Hippolytus' face ravaged by a hard stone (*durus lapis*, *Phae.* 1095).[75]

In Euripides' *Bacchae*, Cadmus twice orders his men to put the dead weight of the dismembered pieces of his grandson, Pentheus, on the stage (ἔπεσθε ... ἔπεσθε, *Bacc.* 1216-17). The double command of Cadmus is noticed by Seneca. He has the father, Theseus, issue a double command to bring the pieces of his own son's body, Hippolytus, to him: 'Here carry the remains of that dear body; that mass of limbs heaped randomly together, give me them (***Huc, huc*** *reliquias uehite cari corporis pondusque et artus temere congestos date, Phae.* 1246-8). Seneca, like Euripides, refers to the weight of the dead body (*pondusque*, *Phae.* 1248 // βράος, *Bacc.* 1216) and the scattering of its parts (*dispersa foede membra*, *Phae.* 1246 // διασπαρακτόν, *Bacc.* 1220). However, where Euripides has Pentheus' mother, Agave, ask if the parts of Pentheus' body are set in order (ἐν ἄρθροις, *Bacc.* 1299), Seneca in his rewriting presents the Chorus as having to tell Hippolytus' father, Theseus, to put the parts of his son's body in order (*laceri corporis in ordinem*, 1257).[76] Thus he *amplifies* both the

---

74. This table is based on the data provided by Gahan, 'Imitation', p. 386, n. 23.
75. Gahan, 'Imitation', pp. 382–83.
76. Gahan, 'Imitation', pp. 383–84.

poignancy and the sense of tragedy. Seneca *emulates* his source, Euripides' *Bacchae*, by making his play's ending even more tragic.

Seneca's models – Euripides, Virgil and Ovid – pour like literary streams into the whole of his *Phaedra*. Out of the works of these models, he creates something new, yet familiar, for the hearer/reader acquainted with his sources.[77]

That he negativizes the parts he selects from his sources indicates that his strategy is in part a literary one – the emulation (*aemulatio*) of earlier great works of the Greek and Roman literary masters. Its severity, however, runs wholly counter to the contemporary ideal of concord and the Roman virtue of *pietas* discussed above. It bears the hallmark of Seneca's later life. With a deadly Nero in power, this adept politician retired from the public domain. Shortly after, he took his own life.[78]

It is useful to restate briefly the techniques used by Seneca in the reworking of his sources. The more simple techniques evident in the above sample include parallel themes, parallel vocabulary in parallel order, and distinctive details.

The sample of complex rewriting analysed above demonstrated Seneca's method of combining sources and techniques to achieve the following literary strategy:

*Emulation by Conflation and Negativization:* In rewriting the matter of death by dismemberment, Seneca uses the vocabulary of Ovid's *Metamorphoses* in the same parallel order. Further, he also conflates some of Ovid's vocabulary with lurid details taken from Euripides' *Bacchae*. The effect is that his tragedy is more tragic than either of these sources.


## 3. *Historiography and* Bioi*: Use of Sources by Livy and Plutarch*

We now turn to two more of the great authors of antiquity: first, Titus Livius or Livy, author of the *History of Rome* (*Ab urbe condita libri*), and second, Plutarch, the author of the grand collection of parallel *Lives*. Authors of both history and *bioi* in antiquity made free use of earlier literary sources.[79]

---

77. Gahan, 'Imitation', p. 384. Further, Gahan notes that, 'an educated Roman audience of roughly the first half of the first century AD was probably about the last generation so thoroughly schooled in Greek that we can assume of them a real knowledge of Euripides.' See, p. 387. Gahan adds an interesting detail: he cites H.I. Marrou (*A History of Education in Antiquity*; trans. G. Lamb; London, 1956, 259ff.), who cautions that, 'we should not overestimate the speed of the decline'. See also Gahan, 'Imitation', p. 387, n. 24

78. Durham Reynolds Leighton, Miriam T. Griffin, and Elaine Fantham, 'Annaeus Seneca (2), Lucius', *OCD* (3rd edn), pp. 96–98 (96).

79. Burridge, *What Are the Gospels?*, p. 174.

Livy, in his production of the *History of Rome* (142 vols.), drew upon many sources. Unlike many authors in antiquity, he himself cites several of them.[80] Sometimes he even quotes source(s) against one another.[81] We will give two brief examples of Livy's use of the works of Polybius of Megapolis (c. 200–118 BCE) and Claudius Quadrigarius (*apud* Aulus Gellius, c. 130–80 CE, *Attic Nights*) as sources. Polybius was the author of the 40-volume *Histories* (only five of which are wholly extant).[82] Claudius was one of the late-Roman annalists.[83]

Plutarch produced 22 pairs of parallel *Lives*. In each set, he pairs the life of a Greek and Roman together. His account of the Greek *Lives*, in particular, reflects the influence of many models.[84] We will present examples of Plutarch's use of the works of both Thucycides (b. c. 460/455 BCE) and Cicero as sources.

Thucycides was author of an eight-volume (incomplete) *History of the Peloponnesian War*, the war between Athens and Sparta (431–404 BCE).[85] Cicero was a prolific author. He composed orations, rhetorical and philosophical works, and letters. We will examine Plutarch's use of Cicero's second *Philippic*, one of Cicero's 14 extant *Philippicae* orations.[86]

The rationale for choosing to analyse the works of these authors is threefold: first, as with the previous section, it serves to demonstrate that literary dependency and the practice of rewriting transcended literary genres in antiquity; secondly, it serves as preparatory background for the

---

80.　For a list of such sources, see Walsh, *Livy*, pp. 115–17. See also Alexander Hugh McDonnald, 'Tubero', *OCD* (2nd edn), p. 1098.

81.　For examples, see John Briscoe, *A Commentary on Livy: Books 31–33* (Oxford: Clarendon Press, 1973), p. 8. Briscoe notes that, 'it can, however, be argued that in the cases where the alterations are particularly far reaching the contamination of Polybius occurred in the annalists, and was not produced by L. combining Polybian and annalistic accounts. There can be no doubt that L. read Polybius for himself. The stylistic changes and verbal parallels can only be explained on that hypothesis. If that is not enough, the case is proved by the fact that L. can quote Claudius and Antias as variants to the Polybian version.' See Briscoe, *Commentary*, p. 8.

82.　Frank William Walbank, 'Polybius', *OCD* (2nd edn), pp. 853–54 (853).

83.　Walsh notes that annalists such as Quadrigarius had himself drawn from the existing Roman sources. Such sources included the *annals maximi* which comprised 80 books compiling the history of Rome, the *libri lintei* or magistrates lists, *senatus consulta* or records of the senate and some private archives. See Walsh, *Livy*, p. 114. See also Ernst Breiseach, *Historiography: Ancient, Medieval and Modern* (London: University of Chicago Press, 2nd edn, 1994), pp. 41, 53.

84.　Plutarch's literary models include, Euripides, Thucydides, Xenophon (c. 428/427–c. 354 BCE), Plato, Theophrastus (c. 370–288/285 BCE), Aristophanes (c. 257–180 BCE). See Wardman, *Plutarch's Lives*, pp. 154–61.

85.　Henry Theodore Wade-Gery, 'Thucydides', *OCD* (2nd edn), pp. 1067–69 (1067).

86.　In all, 58 of Cicero's orations are extant. See John Percy Vyvian Dacre Balsdon, 'Cicero', *OCD* (2nd edn), pp. 234–36 (236).

discussion on the genre of two Gospels, namely, Matthew and Mark, below (ch. 4); thirdly, in terms of chronology, these authors closely frame the time of Jesus and the composition of the Gospels.

By the first century BCE, Roman historiography had developed as an independent genre-type. As with all other literary genres of antiquity, it was based on the techniques of rhetoric.[87] Cicero's *De Oratore* contains a very valuable two-part discussion on historiography – a critique of preceding Roman historians (2.51-61), and an outline of how he thought history should be written (2.62-64).[88] Cicero's ideal was two fold: first, history ought to be written by an orator trained in the method and principles of rhetoric and, secondly, the hard core of history ought to be true.[89]

The aim of the historian in antiquity was to create not just dull annals, but an artistic composition that would be 'an ethically satisfying patriotic synthesis'.[90] The techniques of invention (*inventio*)[91] and elaboration were often used to this end. The material invented and/or elaborated upon, if not entirely true, was expected to be plausible (*probabilis*).[92] In antiquity, truth and invention were seen as complementary.

Concomitant with the development of Roman historiography (*historia*) in the first century BCE came the development of the genre of Roman *bioi*: 'By the first century AD there was a clear generic grouping of Βίος literature, which was widespread from Rome to Alexandria, across the social classes from the high-brow to the popular texts.'[93] As with all literary genres it was highly influenced by the development of Graeco-Roman historiography, the principles of rhetoric and the biographical

87. T.P. Wiseman, *Roman Studies: Literary and Historical* (Liverpool: Francis Cairns, 1987), p. 258.

88. Woodman, *Rhetoric*, p. 74.

89. S.P. Oakley, *A Commentary on Livy: Books 6–10: Volume I: Introduction and Book VI* (Oxford: Clarendon Press, 1997), p. 8. See Wiseman, *Roman Studies*, pp. 245, 249; Woodman, *Rhetoric*, p. 75.

90. Wiseman, *Roman Studies*, p. 247. See Breisach, *Historiography*, p. 58.

91. 'Invention' (*inventio*) was the first of the five techniques used by rhetoricians in creating speeches (*narratio*). Oakley notes that, 'the practice of the wholesale fabrication of the occasion for a speech was widespread ...' See Oakley, *Livy*, p. 10. Christopher Pelling notes an important point made by M.I. Finley (*Ancient History: Evidence and Models*. London, 1985), namely, that, 'the ability of the ancients to invent and their capacity to believe are persistently underestimated.' See Christopher Pelling, *Literary Texts and the Greek Historian* (London: Routledge, 2000), p. 44.

92. See Josephus, *Ant.* 20.156-57. R.M. Ogilvie writes: 'Indeed, Aristotle went so far as to say that "one could praise someone for doing something, even if there were no evidence, if he were the kind of person who might have done it" (*Rhet.* 1367).' See R.M. Ogilvie, 'Livy', in Kenny and Clausen (eds), *The Cambridge History of Classical Literature II*, pp. 458–66 (462).

93. Burridge, *What Are the Gospels?*, p. 153. See Craig S. Keener, *The Gospel of John: A Commentary* (2 vols.; Peabody, MA: Hendrickson, 2003), I, p. 11.

tradition of Greece.[94] Some form of biography can be attested as early as the fifth century BCE in Greece. However, the term *bios*, 'life' or *bioi*, 'lives', only began to be used in the Hellenistic period.[95] Plutarch used the term to distinguish his own work from the works of historiography (οὔτε γὰρ ἱστορίας γράφομεν ἀλλὰ Βίους, *Alex.* 1.2; cf. *Per.* 2.4).[96]

Xenophon (c. 428/427–c. 354 BCE) had introduced a bi-part division into his biographical work, *Agesilaus:*[97] first, a chronological account of the events (πράξεις) of a subject's life; and then, a systematic treatment of his character (ἦθος).[98] Later, Cicero, when writing about historiography, distinguished between two elements – content and style (*res et verba*), and added that the former ought to include a biographical account of the chief subject (*De Or.* 2.63-64).[99] Thus it becomes clear that right up to the first century CE, *bioi* and historiography were not rigidly defined but were often 'generic mixtures' of related genres (*genera proxima*).[100]

In each of his peripatetic parallel *Lives*, Plutarch focuses wholly on one main subject throughout. His task is the revelation of the character of his subject (cf. *Alex.* 1.1-3).[101] This is what determines his selection of source material: 'For it is not Histories that I am writing, but Lives; and in the most illustrious deeds there is not always a manifestation of virtue or vice, nay, a slight thing like a phrase or jest often makes a greater revelation of character than battles where thousands fall' (*Alex.* 1.1-2; cf. *Cato Yng.* 37.5; *Phoc.* 5.4).

---

94. Woodman, *Rhetoric*, p. 4.

95. Patricia Cox notes that, 'the earliest surviving reference to it is in Damascius' *Life of Isidorus* dating from the end of the fifth century AD'. See Patricia Cox, *Biography in Late Antiquity: A Quest for the Holy Man* (Berkley: University of California Press, 1983), p. 6, n. 11. See also Burridge, *What Are the Gospels?*, pp. 70–74.

96. Burridge, *What Are the Gospels?*, p. 62.

97. Agesilaus (444–360 BCE) was the lame king who inherited the Spartan throne after Sparta had defeated Athens in the Peloponnesian War. Because of his lust for conquest, however, he violated the laws of Lycurgus against imperialistic ventures by fighting too much with the same enemy. By the time Agesilaus died, Sparta had gone into decline. In the *Agesilaus*, Xenophon borrows from his earlier work *Hellenica* 3–4. See Donald Ernest Wilson Wormell, 'Agesilaus', *OCD* (2nd edn), p. 27; Derek John Mosley, 'Xenephon', *OCD* (2nd edn), pp. 1141–44; Burridge, *What Are the Gospels?*, pp. 129–30.

98. Cox, *Biography*, p. 8; Burridge, *What Are the Gospels?*, p. 130.

99. See Oakley, *Livy*, pp. 8–9.

100. Burridge, *What Are the Gospels?*, pp. 47, 63–69, 80. See also Frank William Walbank, 'Chamaeleon', *OCD* (2nd edn), p. 226; C.B.R. Pelling, 'biography, Greek', *OCD* (3rd edn), pp. 241–42 (241). On the relationship between biography and enconium, see Woodman, *Rhetoric*, pp. 10–15.

101. Woodman, *Rhetoric*, p. 6; Cox, *Biography*, p. xiii. See Cox, *Biography*, p. 12, n. 32. See also Burridge, *What Are the Gospels?*, pp. 134–35, 143; Pelling, *Literary Texts*, p. 45; and Breisach, *Historiography*, p. 71.

a. *External Criteria Applied*

*Primary Criteria*

### 1. *Date*

As is clear from the dates cited above, in terms of chronology, the afore-named sources of both Livy and Plutarch are not problematic for establishing the case of literary dependency.

### 2. *Accessibility*

Where people travelled, texts were transported. This was particularly the case between ancient Greece and Rome.[102] Polybius' account of the history of the rise of Rome would have attracted great interest among the Romans, and so would an Italian author, such as Livy, bent on carrying out a similar literary exercise;[103] likewise, Thucycides' *History of the Peloponnesian War* would have been sought out by Plutarch for an accurate source for his Greek *Lives*. The Roman materials such as Claudius' (10 BCE–54 CE) annals and Cicero's *Philippicae* orations would have been quite accessible to authors such as Livy and Plutarch in the first-century book-generating city of Rome. Plutarch's regard for Cicero as a model is reflected in his account of his life, *Cicero*.

*Secondary Criteria*

### 3. *Status of Text*

The status of Polybius is indicated by the fact that his literary style was modelled and remodelled by historians up to the first century CE.[104] His *History*, which was Livy's main source for his *History of Rome*, was regarded by Livy himself as history *par excellence* (cf. Livy, 30.45.5; 33.10.10).

Dionysius of Halicarnassus' (active in Rome, c. 30 BCE) critical essay entitled *Thucydides* is evidence that Thucydides' *History* (one of Plutarch's main sources for his Greek *Lives*) was held in high regard as, in it, Dionysius expresses his indebtedness to him.[105]

The status of Cicero's *Second Philippic* may best be inferred from the

---

102. Harry Y. Gamble, *Books and Readers in the Early Church: A History of Early Christian Texts* (New Haven: Yale University Press, 1995), pp. 176–89. See Horsfall (ed.), *Companion*, pp. 293–300.

103. The *Life* of Polybius reads like a travelogue: born in Greece, he became envoy to Egypt but was later deported to Rome. He travelled west as far as Spain and south as far as Africa. This data gives an idea of the great degree of movement of people by land and sea in the second century BCE. See Walbank, 'Polybius', *OCD* (2nd edn), pp. 853–54 (853).

104. Luce, *Livy*, p. 141, n. 3; Cecil Maurice Bora, 'Historiography, Roman', *OCD* (2nd edn), pp. 523–26 (523).

105. Donald Andrew Frank Moore Russell, 'Dionysius', *OCD* (2nd edn), p. 351.

status of its author. At the time of writing, Cicero had the prestige (*auctoritas*) of being a senior consular. He lobbied the Senate with his *Philippicae* orations (44–43 BCE) in order to try and secure the same deadly fate for Anthony as Caesar received in 44 BCE (*Att.* 15.11.2).[106]

### 4. *Analogues*

The *Histories* of Posidonius (c. 135–c. 50/51 BCE), the Roman historiographer, provides a relatively close analogue to Livy's use of Polybius' *Histories* as a source.[107] The most famous analogue to the use of Thucydides is the aforementioned *Thucydides* by Dionysius. In it, he both cites and analyses in detail the style and method of Thucydides.[108] With regard to Cicero, his rhetorical and philosophical works, more so than his orations, were used as literary sources by later authors, such as Sallust (c. 86–35 BCE).[109]

### b. *Internal Ariteria Applied*
### 1. *Livy*

Livy is considered to be the first Roman historian to fulfil Cicero's ideals as a historiographer (*De Or.* 2.54.1.6-7), that is, one who 'conceived his task as one of source selection and adaptation, not breakdown and restoration'.[110] It was he who introduced the fully developed periodic structure into the writing of history.[111] He blocks his 45-volume *History of Rome* chronologically in three stages. Each stage consists of a pentad of books that is based on a particular topic: Books 1–15, for Early Roman history; 16–30, for the Punic Wars; and 31–45, for the Conquest of the East.[112] Each book covers a year, following the custom of the annalists.[113] Each unit episode therein has a beginning, usually sourced from annalists, a middle, usually sourced from a historian, and an end, again sourced from the annalists.[114] The episodes are connected skilfully by various links

---

106. Balsdon, 'Cicero', p. 235.

107. Bora, 'Historiography, Roman', p. 523; Piero Treves, 'Posidonius', *OCD* (2nd edn), pp. 867–68 (868).

108. Moore Russell, 'Dionysius', p. 351; Wade-Gery, 'Thucycides', pp. 1069–70.

109. See Woodman, *Rhetoric*, p. 117; George Makay Paul, 'Sallust', *OCD* (2nd edn), pp. 946–47 (946).

110. Luce, *Livy*, p. 150. See also, Briscoe, *Livy*, p. 16.

111. Briscoe, *Livy*, p. 16.

112. Luce, *Livy*, p. 185.

113. Ogilvie, 'Livy', p. 462.

114. Briscoe, *Livy,* p. 10. Walsh observes that, 'Livy often divides his narrative into episodes constructed according to Aristotelian precepts governing tragedy; they have a beginning, middle and end'. See Walsh, *Livy*, p. 179.

or transitions (for example, accounts of journeys),[115] or by a change of literary technique.[116]

*Parallels*: Livy's method of using sources is often to choose one main source and to supplement it with others.[117] Over two-thirds of his material on eastern affairs is sourced from Polybius, most likely because of his 'pro-Roman Tendenz'.[118] This is clear from the very close correspondence they share in terms of vocabulary, order and numerical citations[119] (see Table 2.5 below).

Table 2.5: *Parallels between Livy and Polybius*[120]

| Livy | Polybius |
| --- | --- |
| 31.14.11–18.8 | 16.25-26, 28-34 |
| 32.32.9–37.5 | 18.1-12 |
| 32.40.8-11 | 18.16–17.5 |
| 33.2.1 | 18.17.6 |
| 33.5.4–13.15 | 18.18-27, 33-4, 36-39 |
| 33.20.2-3 | 18.41a.1 |
| 33.21.1-5 | 18.41 |
| 33.27.5-28 | 18.43, 40.1-4 |
| 33.30-35 | 18.44-48 |
| 33.39-40 | 18.49-51 |

*Simple Rewriting*: Livy usually prefers to omit material from his source rather than to paraphrase it. However, he does sometimes select a significant scene for lengthy *elaboration* while greatly *abbreviating* the beginning and ending (cp. Livy, 45.12.3-8 // Poly., 29.27).[121] Often he uses a link phrase like 'about that time it chanced that ...' *(per eos forte dies)* and moves directly to the central description; or, he uses the pluperfect

---

115. Walsh, *Livy*, p. 180.

116. Luce provides a good example of where Livy changes his technique several times. Within one short section on the material on the East, when he is rewriting Polybius 44–48, Livy rewrites by means of: (1) close adaptation (Livy, 30 // Poly., 44; Livy, 34 // Poly., 47); (2) simple rewriting (Livy, 31 // Poly., 45); (3) elaboration (Livy, 32–33 // Poly., 46); and (4) exact parallel (Livy, 35 // Poly., 48). See Luce, *Livy*, pp. 219–20.

117. Ogilvie, 'Livy', p. 461. See Walsh, *Livy*, p. 124.

118. Keener, *John*, I, p. 14, and n. 110.

119. Regarding Books 30–45 of Polybius' *Roman History*, Walsh notes that, 'since the emphasis in these 15 books is on Eastern expansion, almost three quarters of the narration is attributable to the information of Polybius'. See Walsh, *Livy*, p. 135.

120. Based on the list provided by Briscoe. See Briscoe, *Livy*, p. 1.

121. Luce, *Livy*, p. 206.

tense to move quickly over events preceding the main event of the narrative (Livy 6.17.7; 22.33.1; 33.3.6; 42.17).[122]

In terms of simple rewriting, his style of rewriting is also marked by love for detail, and by *clarification* (σαφήνεια) of matters already presumed to be known. The following comic incident illustrates his love for graphic detail, but with a twist. According to his model, Claudius, the Gaul was naked when he fought the duel with Manlius Torquatus (*apud* Aul. Gel., 9.13). Livy has the Gaul clothed, giving descriptive details of his bright garments and shining armoury.[123] This is just one of the ways in which he rewrites his sources in order to make them better suited to the Roman political and social sensibilities of his day (cf. Livy, 7.10.7).

*Complex Rewriting: Contemporization by Positivization*: The best examples of complex rewriting by Livy are perhaps found in his use of his Roman sources. Let us return to the account of the slaying of the Gaul by Manlius Torquatus.

This account is one of the very few occasions when Livy rewrites an entire episode and not just a detail from his source. Because his version marks a complete departure from that of the account recorded by Claudius (*apud* Aul. Gel.), scholars traditionally proposed Livy's literary independence of Claudius. While there are some close verbal parallels between both texts, a most significant clue to Livy's use of Claudius' account is evident in the event of the slaying of the Gaul. Claudius has Manlius chop off the Gaul's head. Livy, again contemporizing to suit the Roman sensibilities of his day, states that, 'the Gaul's body was not violated in any way, save for the removal of the neck chain, which – all bloodied – Manlius put around his own neck' (7.9.11).[124] The detail of the bloodied chain betrays the source here: if there is no slaying and Manlius is explicitly forbidden to strike above the belly, how else does one account for the bloodied chain?

Sent back to his source, the hearer/reader can be surer of Livy's agenda. His rewriting elevates restraint as the practical ideal to be imitated in difficult situations, and highlights it as one of the virtues that enabled Rome to master Italy first, and then the rest of the empire.[125]

---

122. Cited in Walsh, *Livy*, p. 179.
123. Walsh, *Livy*, pp. 180–90.
124. Luce, *Livy*, pp. 225–26.
125. James Boykin Rives, 'Livy (Tacitus Livius (*RE* 9))', *OCD* (3rd edn), pp. 877–79 (879).

## 2. *Plutarch*

Formal comparisons (σύγκρισις) are found in 19 of the 22 pairs of Plutarch's parallel *Lives*.[126] All of these paired *bioi* conclude with a short epilogue in which Plutarch usually outlines the key strengths of the paired subjects.

*Parallels*: The first 30 chapters of the life of *Anthony* show 'a resounding similarity'[127] to the second *Philippic* by Cicero. This *Life* reflects many striking thematic parallels to Cicero's speech – positively, the subject's inherent nobility, brilliance as a soldier and general, and popularity among the people; and negatively, the subject's desire for luxury, and some personal foibles. Towards creating a more vivid account of the character or essence of his subject, Plutarch sometimes *supplements* the details of his source: for example, Anthony's vomiting on his tribuna (cp. *Ant.* 9.6 // *Phil.* 2.63), or his surprising return to his wife, Fulvia, by night, even when duty called (cp. *Ant.* 10.8-9 // *Phil.* 2.77-78).[128]

Sometimes too, Plutarch *reverses* the plot found in his source. He rewrites Cicero's hostile portrait of Anthony and creates a more positive one of him, as one able to bring about a situation of greater concord. This positivization of Anthony is reflected throughout his account. For example, in Cicero's second *Philippic*, Anthony, who attempts to crown Caesar, and Trebonius, who tries to subvert Caesar, are clearly enemies. Plutarch *reverses* this: he has these two characters amicably share a tent. Moreover, Plutarch's Anthony, while aware of the plot to overthrow his friend Caesar, does not tell him (cp. *Ant.* 13 // *Phil.* 2.34; cf. *Ant.* 2.4-8 // *Phil.* 2.44-48).[129] C.B.R. Pelling concludes that, 'such adaptations of the second *Philippic* are eloquent, for they suggest that Plutarch did know the work at first hand: the rewriting is so clearly tailored to the interests and themes of the present *Life*'.[130]

*Simple Rewriting*: For an example of simple rewriting in Plutarch we turn to his life of *Nicias*. This work reflects a revisiting of the Greek tradition, in particular, Thucydides' *History*. At the outset, Plutarch declares that he cannot rival (*aemulatio*) Thucydides, who is 'so emotional, vivid, varied,

---

126. Wardman, *Lives*, p. 3. See D.A. Russell, 'On Reading Plutarch's *Lives*', *GR* 13 (1966), pp. 139–54 (150).
127. C.B.R. Pelling, 'Plutarch's Method of Work in the Roman Lives', *JHS* 99 (1979), pp. 74–96 (89). See *idem*, 'Truth and Fiction in Plutarch's *Lives*', in D.A. Russell (ed.), *Antonine Literature* (Oxford: Clarendon Press, 1990), pp. 19–52 (29).
128. C.B.R. Pelling, 'Plutarch's Adaptation of His Source Material', *JHS* 100 (1980), pp. 127–40 (130–31).
129. Pelling, 'Plutarch's Adaptation', p. 130, n. 14. See *idem*, 'Truth and Fiction', p. 38.
130. Pelling, 'Plutarch's Method', p. 90.

brilliant' (*Nic.* 1.1, 4).[131] Rather, Plutarch's aim is to 'try and collect material that is not well known but scattered among the other authors, or found in ancient dedications or decrees. Nor is this an accumulation of useless erudition: I am conveying material that is helpful for grasping the man's nature and character' (*Nic.* 1.5).[132]

Well over half of Plutarch's account of the Sicilian war in *Nicias* comes from Thucydides' *History* (6–7). His rewriting, however, *negativizes* the very positive portrayal of Nicias found in Thucydides' account. For example, Plutarch *adds* a complaint about Nicias' distractedness, always gazing homeward for his ship (*Nic.* 14.1-2), and has 'everyone' criticizing him for his plan of action (*Nic.* 16.9; 17.2).

In *Nicias*, the crowd eventually have pity on the protagonist in his final hours. They come to a deep moral insight (*internalization*): 'Nor was it only the sight of the man that was so moving. They were dispirited too when they thought … how this pious man, who had performed so many religious duties with such great splendour, was faring no better than the lowliest and humblest of his army' (*Nic.* 26.4-6).[133] Compared to Thucydides' account, Plutarch's more negative account of the main subject is, in fact, toward a positive end, namely, to present compassion and humility before the gods as the appropriate response to the issue of unjust retribution.[134]

*Complex Rewriting: Positivization by Variation and Re-ordering*: The story of the ostracism of Hyberbolus (*Nicias* 10–11), found in Plutarch's *Nicias* and another of his *Lives*, *Alcibiades* (13–15), provides us with a different kind of example of complex rewriting, namely, variation (*variatio*), whereby the same author composes several varying accounts of the same event.

In *Nicias*, the ostracism occurs after the trick on the Peloponnesian ambassadors and the Mantinea campaign (418 BCE); in *Alcibiades*, it occurs the other way around.[135] Further, Plutarch provides a third version of the same event in his account of the life of *Aristides* (7). There, he stresses that ostracism befalls only men of distinction, and cites Nicias and Alcibiades as examples of the same (cf. *Alc.* 13.9; *Nic.* 11.6-8). The triple accounting of the same event is an example of Plutarch's literary dexterity and inventiveness. All three of the aforementioned *Lives* were written

131. Pelling, 'Truth and Fiction', p. 25. See A.E. Wardman, 'Plutarch's Methods in the *Lives*', *CQ* (1971), pp. 254–61 (258).

132. Wardman, *Lives*, p. 155. See F.E. Brenk, *In Mist Apparelled: Religious Themes in Plutarch's Moralia and Lives, Mnemosyne* (Sup, 48; Leiden: Brill, 1977), p. 184.

133. Pelling, *Literary Texts*, p. 48.

134. Pelling states it thus: 'Intelligent reconstruction is Plutarch's strength; focalizing through concerned spectators is his hallmark.' See Pelling, *Literary Texts*, p. 49.

135. Pelling, *Literary Texts*, p. 49.

during the same period of time.[136] He rewrites the same source material to suit the different, but very specific, literary and ideological purposes of each one.

An analysis of these three accounts shows up several other factual contradictions. Plutarch admits the occurrence of contradictory details: 'I am not unaware of Theophrastus' version that it was Phaeax, not Nicias, who contended against Alcibiades ...' (*Nic.* 11.10).[137]

Similarly, in the Roman *Lives*, Plutarch sometimes *re-orders* his source material to serve his literary and ideological purposes. In *Caesar*, for example, he places all Caesar's foreign travels together topologically – the trip to Nicomedes (1.7), an adventure alone (1.8–2.7) and the trip to Rhodes (3). A comparison with the account of Suetonius' (b. c. 69 CE) *The Lives of the Caesars* shows that this ordering, created by two antedatings, while not quite accurate, creates a much more elegant account and a more positive portrait of the subject, Caesar.[138]

Plutarch also *re-orders* the account of Caesar's success as a rhetorician, placing it after his return from Rhodes, rather than before (so Suetonius).[139] As Rhodes was a famous centre of study, we may infer from his *re-ordering* of this account that Caesar's rhetorical success was as a result of his being taught by the masters in Rhodes. Plutarch positivizes his sources concerning Caesar by means of his 'imaginative "creative reconstruction" of the truth as he saw it, in order to illustrate the way "it must have been" '.[140]

The historiographer and the biographer of antiquity provided accounts of the same reality but from two different perspectives: 'The historian narrated the lives of persons in the context of events, and the biographer analysed the personalities who brought forth the events.'[141] Their aims were closely linked. Both sought generally to provide models (*exempla maiorum*) and ideals in order to enhance the social, moral and political fibre of their *patria*.[142]

While it is difficult to draw conclusions on the basis of such brief

---

136.  Pelling, *Literary Texts*, pp. 49–51. For the dating of Plutarch's *Lives*, see C.P. Jones, 'Towards a Chronology of Plutarch's Works', *JRS* 54 (1966), pp. 61–74.

137.  Pelling, *Literary Texts*, pp. 49–51.

138.  Pelling, 'Plutarch's Adaptation', pp. 129–30. Woodman notes that Plutarch 'speaks disparagingly of tragedy' (cf. *Sol.* 29.6-7). See Wardman, *Plutarch's Lives*, pp. 169, 176.

139.  For the Roman *Lives*, Plutarch's sources were far less plentiful. His rewriting of them, however, resulted in biographical works that had hitherto been unmatched. A comparison of his account of *Caesar* with Suetonius' account of the same subject reveals Plutarch's use of the method of chronological displacement.

140.  Burridge, *What Are the Gospels?*, p. 174. See Pelling, 'Plutarch's Adaptation', p. 128.

141.  Breisach, *Historiography*, p. 71.

142.  Cox notes Cicero's comment that the purpose of history is the 'calling to our minds illustrious and courageous men and their deeds, not for any gain but the honor that lies in praising their nobility by itself (*De finibus* 1.10.36)'. See Cox, *Biography*, p. 13, n. 32.

studies, the aspect of positivization common to both authors analysed is noteworthy. The positivization by Livy fits well as a critical response to the advanced moral and political decline that surrounded him, and over which Augustus' leadership appeared weak.[143] Moreover, that this is the case is affirmed by evidence found in some of his other books (e.g., Livy 1.10; 3.2.5; 6.5; 7.4-5).[144] It concurs with Ernst Breisach's assessment of Livy's agenda: 'Clearly for Livy, the rise of the state to greatness was based on its people possessing a number of proper character traits (*virtutes*) and not, as for Polybius, on a proper constitutional arrangement.'[145]

Research indicates that most of Plutarch's writing was done after 96 CE. C.P. Jones notes that, 'the inference is inescapable that, like Tacitus, Plutarch felt constrained to silence during the reign of Domitian, towards whose memory he later displayed cordial dislike'.[146] His positivization of Caesar was, from his perspective, a critical response to a nation in need of rebuilding. That this is his agenda is affirmed from his other works, especially the Roman *Lives*.[147]

It is useful to restate briefly the techniques used by both Livy and Plutarch in reworking their sources as outlined above. The more simple techniques evident in the samples of their respective works analysed include: for Livy, parallels in terms of vocabulary and order, examples of omission, abbreviation, elaboration and the addition of details; for Plutarch, addition by invention, negativization and internalization.

The sample of complex rewriting analysed above demonstrates something of the methods and techniques used by Livy and Plutarch to achieve their respective literary and ideological purposes. They are as follows:

*Contemporization by Positivization*: In Livy's *History of Rome*, the Gaul's body is not violated, as in his model's (Claudius') account, in accordance with the sensibilities of his day.

*Positivization by Re-ordering*: Plutarch, in his three variant accounts of the ostracism of Hyperbolis in three different *Lives*, re-orders the material in order to positivize the chief subject in each – Nicias, Alcibiades and Aristides.

143.  Woodman, *Rhetoric*, p. 138; Boykin Rives, 'Livy', p. 879.
144.  Ogilvie, 'Livy', p. 463.
145.  Breisach, *Historiography*, p. 64.
146.  Jones, 'Towards a Chronology', p. 73.
147.  Russell, 'Plutarch's *Lives*', p. 141; Wardman, *Plutarch's Lives*, pp. 39, 42.

## 4. Conclusion

The aim of this chapter has been to demonstrate the methods and techniques used by Graeco-Roman authors to incorporate earlier sources into their works.

To this end we examined evidence from texts of various genres – epic, tragedy, historiography and *bioi*. We selected the works of four Graeco-Roman authors, namely, Virgil's *Aeneid*, Seneca's *Phaedra*, Livy's *History of Rome* and Plutarch's Greek and Roman *Lives*. In each case, we first applied and satisfied the primary external criteria outlined above. Then we applied the internal criteria for demonstrating literary dependence based on the evidence of the text.

In the texts selected, we find that some techniques are used by all of the above authors' to achieve their literary and ideological purposes. These include: parallel vocabulary, themes and events, in parallel order, and distinctive details in the form of shared particular words.

Each of the above authors also used some of the following techniques, namely – abbreviation, addition, amplification, clarification, conflation, correction, elaboration, emulation, internalization, negativization, omission, positivization, re-ordering, two-tier allusion and variation. We also found evidence of the systematic rewriting of primary sources, for example, Virgil's rewriting of Homer's epics in the *Aeneid* and Livy's rewriting of part of Polybius for his *History of Rome*.

In each case, an increased awareness of *how* and *why* an author uses his earlier source(s) increased our understanding of his literary agenda. For example, Virgil's positivization of his Homeric sources appears to be for the purpose of universalizing the ideal of Roman *pietas*, while Seneca's negativization of his sources in his version of the *Phaedra* appears to bear witness to the tragedy that befell a once esteemed citizen of the empire such as himself.

The above provides the contemporary hearer/reader of texts from the Graeco-Roman world with an insight into the wonderful skill, creativity and, sometimes, complex use of sources by ancient authors.

## Chapter 3

### REWRITING: EVIDENCE FROM JEWISH TEXTS

We now turn to examine the practice of rewriting in Jewish antiquity. In this chapter, we examine the sacred works of two Jewish authors, namely, the author of the book of Tobit and Paul. The aim is to demonstrate that the methods and techniques used by Graeco-Roman authors to incorporate earlier sources into their works are also found reflected in Jewish sacred works. Their texts reflect different genres – romance and epistle – and are analysed using the criteria that have been established for claiming literary dependence above. In each example, the function and effect of the source text(s) within its later literary context is outlined.

These texts will be examined under the following headings:[1]

1.  Tobit's Use of Genesis, Deuteronomy and Homer's *Odyssey* as Sources
2.  Paul's Use of Torah as a Source in 1 Cor. 8.1–11.1

### 1. *Tobit's Use of Genesis, Deuteronomy and Homer's* Odyssey *as Sources*

The author of Tobit used Genesis, Deuteronomy and Homer's *Odyssey* as literary sources. The aim in this section is to demonstrate that the way he did so was in accord with Graeco-Roman literary conventions.

The core of the story of the book of Tobit grapples with 'two problems and one divine solution'.[2]

The first problem is Tobit's: Tobit, a righteous man, is made poor because the corrupt king of Israel, Jeroboam, misappropriates his money. Tobit also becomes blind. He sends his son Tobiah on a journey to recover his money. Raphael, who, unknown to Tobiah, is an angel of God, accompanies him. Raphael aids him in retrieving his father's wealth

---

1. All Scripture citations in the body of the text will be from the LXX or *NRSV* unless otherwise stated. The citations in the tables may be modified to reflect the Greek more accurately, where appropriate.

2. Dennis R. MacDonald, 'Tobit and the *Odyssey*', in MacDonald (ed.), *Mimesis*, pp. 11–40 (16). See J.R.C. Cousland, 'Tobit: A Comedy in Error?' *CBQ* 65 (2003), pp. 535–53 (548–50).

and, in the process, marrying his kinswoman, Sarah. He also helps him to find a successful remedy for his father's blindness.

The second problem is Sarah's: she has been plagued by a demon that has killed her first *seven* husbands on their respective wedding nights.[3] Tobiah, upon Raphael's advice, was able to break this demonic power and marry Sarah, his kinswoman.

For both problems, the author's account demonstrates that God, through his angel-in-disguise, provided the solutions.[4]

The book of Tobit is best classified as a Jewish romance[5] that was originally written in Aramaic.[6] It is a Jewish literary tapestry onto which non-Jewish source(s) like threads are woven in function of the author's Jewish theology.[7] Frank Zimmerman states this point quite eloquently: 'In the loom of the Tobit tale, the woof comes from the folklore of mankind, and the warp and the pattern, the vitality and the colour from the religious experience of the Jewish people.'[8]

Carey A. Moore indicates the variety of literary forms which are contained within it: monologue (Tob. 1.3–2.14; 3.10) and dialogue (2.13-14; 5.9-22; 6.6-17); prayers (3.2-6, 11-15) and hymns of thanksgiving (8.5-9, 15-17; 11.14b-15a; 13.1-18); biblical quotations (2.6 // cf. Amos 8.10) and wisdom sayings (Tob. 4.2-21; 12.6-10); demonology (3.8; 6.13-17; 8.1-3) and angelophany (3.16-18; 12.11-22); and, finally, a deathbed testimony (14.3-11).[9]

It has long been noticed that deuterocanonical and pseudepigraphal

---

3. For the theological significance of the number *seven*, see ch. 5, section 1. c. below.

4. Etymologically, the name Raphael means 'angel of healing' ('Ραφαήλ).

5. Moore, *Tobit*, p. 21. Alexander A. Di Lella concurs with this analysis. See Alexander A. Di Lella, 'The Deuteronomic Background of the Farewell Discourse in Tob 14.3-11', *CBQ* 41 (1979), pp. 380–89 (387). *Joseph and Aseneth* is a Jewish example of a lower-class romance novel. For further details, see Moore, *Tobit*, p. 17. Will Soll holds that, 'the designation "Jewish Sacred Book" is as far as we are able to go at present in describing the genre of the final form of Tobit'. See Will Soll, 'Misfortune and Exile in Tobit: The Juncture of a Fairy Tale Source and Deuteronomic Theology', *CBQ* 51 (1989), pp. 209–31 (220, n. 38).

6. See Joseph A. Fitzmyer, *The Dead Sea Scrolls and Christian Origins* (Grand Rapids: William B. Eerdmans, 2000), p. 149 and also pp. 39, 145. Moore considers the original language to be Hebrew. See also Moore, *Tobit*, p. 57. Fitzmyer also points out that, 'the Qumran Aramaic and Hebrew texts, however, do agree in general with the long recension of S and the Vetus Latina …' See Fitzmyer, *Dead Sea Scrolls*, p. 140. Moore also notes that, 'more recent translations, including the Jerusalem Bible, the New English Bible, the New American Bible, the New Revised Standard Version, and the Revised English Bible, have used G[II] …' See Moore, *Tobit*, p. 56.

7. The very word 'text' comes from the Latin verb, *texere*, which means 'to weave.' See Moore, *Tobit*, pp. 12–20, 26. See also Soll, 'Misfortune and Exile', pp. 219–20, 231; Di Lella, 'Deuteronomic Background', p. 387.

8. Frank Zimmerman, *The Book of Tobit: An English Translation with Introduction and Commentary* (New York: Harper, 1957), p.12, cited in Moore, *Tobit*, p. 20.

9. Moore, *Tobit*, pp. 26–27.

writings imitate classical biblical literature, both in terms of form and content. These creative imitations range from single words or verses to complete literary genres.[10] Among such literature, the book of Tobit offers much to a discussion on the appropriation of literary sources.[11] It not only appropriates classical biblical sources, but it also appropriates non-Israelite sources to form the literary patchwork that it is.[12]

### a. *External Criteria Applied*
*Primary Criteria*

#### 1. *Date*
It is difficult to date the book of Tobit. Sometime during the time of the second Temple (300–200 BCE) seems to be appropriate.[13] The dating of the book, although problematic in itself, is not problematic for the claiming of literary dependence upon the texts under study here – Genesis, Deuteromomy and Homer's *Odyssey* – as these texts are dated well before the second century.

#### 2. *Accessibility*
Copies of the Torah were widely accessible by the second century BCE, not only in Israel but also in the far-flung Jewish diaspora settlements. Copies of Homer's *Odyssey* circulated throughout the Graeco-Roman world, including Mesopotamia, where it originated, and near where the narrative of Tobit is set. As noted above, Homer's epics were used as models for teachers and students, well into the Roman imperial age.[14]

*Secondary Criteria*

#### 3. *Status of Text*
Genesis and Deuteronomy were held in the highest regard by the Jews because of being part of the canon of sacred Jewish Scripture. Homer's epics were unrivalled in terms of status among the secular literary works of antiquity.

---

10. Steven Weitzman, 'Allusion, Artifice, and Exile in the Hymn of Tobit', *JBL* 115 (1996), pp. 49–61 (49). Weitzman notes that, 'to be sure, the evocation of "classical" biblical texts such as the Pentateuch was one of the most common compositional techniques among Jewish authors in the early postbiblical period'. See *idem*, 'Allusion', p. 61.

11. George W.E. Nickelsburg, 'Tobit, Genesis, and the *Odyssey*: A Complex Web of Intertextuality', in MacDonald (ed.), *Mimesis*, pp. 41–55 (41).

12. George W.E. Nickelsburg, 'The Search for Tobit's Mixed Ancestry: A Historical and Hermeneutical Odyssey', *RevQ* 17 (1996), pp. 339–49 (339–40).

13. See Fitzmyer, *Dead Sea Scrolls*, p. 145.

14. See ch. 2, section 1. a. above.

## 4. *Analogues*

Several examples of the literary appropriation of Genesis and Deuteronomy are extant: *Genesis Apocryphon* is dependent upon Genesis;[15] Paul's Letters and the Gospel of Matthew exhibit direct dependence upon Deuteronomy, as we shall see below.[16] With regard to Homer's *Odyssey*, Apollonius and Virgil, among others, used it as a source and model for their respective epics, the *Argonautica* and *Aeneid*, as was demonstrated above.[17]

### b. *Internal Criteria Applied*

Scholars repeatedly link the book of Tobit to the books of Genesis (chs 24, 29, 37, 39–50),[18] Deuteronomy[19] and Job.[20] To a lesser degree it has been associated with Judges,[21] 2 Kings,[22] Second- and Third-Isaiah,[23] Daniel 3 and 6,[24] and *1 (Ethiopic) Enoch*.[25] Outside the Jewish tradition, parallels to the Ahiqar,[26] the tales of the Grateful Dead and the Monster in the Bridal Chamber, Homer's *Odyssey*, and other folk tales have been alleged.[27] As noted above, in looking at Tobit, our focus will be on the author's use of Genesis, Deuteronomy and Homer's *Odyssey*, which are his primary sources.

---

15. See J.A. Fitzmyer, *The Genesis Apocryphon of Qumran Cave 1: A Commentary* (Rome: Biblical Institute, 2nd edn, 1971).

16. See ch. 3, section 2. b., and ch. 5, section 2. below.

17. See ch. 2, section 1. b. above.

18. Moore, *Tobit*, p. 8; MacDonald, 'Tobit and the *Odyssey*', p. 15; Cousland, 'Tobit', pp. 549–51.

19. Moore, *Tobit*, p. 8; Cousland, 'Tobit', p. 550.

20. Moore, *Tobit*, p. 8; MacDonald, 'Tobit and the *Odyssey*', p. 14.

21. Alexander Di Lella, 'The Book of Tobit and the Book of Judges: An Intertextual Analysis', *Hen* 22 (2000), pp. 197–205.

22. Nickelsburg, 'Tobit, Genesis, and the *Odyssey*', p. 41.

23. Moore, *Tobit*, pp. 8, 21; Nickelsburg, 'Mixed Ancestry', p. 340.

24. Nickelsburg, 'Mixed Ancestry', p. 341.

25. George W.E. Nickelsburg, 'Tobit and Enoch: Distant Cousins with a Recognizable Resemblance', in David J. Lull (ed.), *Society of Biblical Literature Seminar Papers* (Atlanta: Scholars Press, 1988), pp. 54–68. See Moore, *Tobit*, p. 46.

26. Fitzmyer comments on this legend thus: 'Moreover, the ancient story of Ahiqar, to which an allusion is made in the Book of Tobit came to light only in 1907 when the Aramaic form of that story was discovered among the papyri of Elephantie.' See Fitzmyer, *Dead Sea Scrolls*, p. 134.

27. Nickelsburg, 'Tobit, Genesis, and the *Odyssey*', p. 41; *idem*, 'Mixed Ancestry', pp. 340–41; MacDonald, 'Tobit and the *Odyssey*', p. 14; Moore, *Tobit*, pp. 8–14. Further, Fitzmyer, in his analysis of the Dead Sea Scrolls, concludes that, '[similarly] there is nothing in these Qumran texts that helps in the literary interpretation of the book, nothing about the Grateful Dead, the Monster in the Bridal Chamber, the tractate of Khons, or the Tale of the Two Brothers. The only thing clear is the allusion to the story of Ahiqar in the Aramaic version ...' See Fitzmyer, *Dead Sea Scrolls*, p. 141. See also Di Lella, 'Book of Tobit', pp. 197–205.

## 1. *Parallels*

The similarity between the type of characters in Tobit and Homer's *Odyssey* (1–4; 15–16) is very striking. It provides strong initial evidence that some sort of borrowing has occurred. Equally striking are the parallels between the characters in Tobit and the Isaac story in Genesis 27–29[28] (see Table 3.1 below).

Table 3.1: *Type Characters in* Tobit, Genesis, *and the* Odyssey[29]

| Type | Tobit | Genesis 27–29 | *Odyssey* |
|---|---|---|---|
| *Father* | Tobit | Isaac | Odysseus |
| *Mother* | Anna | Rebekah | Penelope |
| *Son* | Tobiah | Jacob | Telemachus |
| *Deity* | God | God | Zeus |
| *Angel-in-* | Raphael | Angels appear | Athena |
| *Disguise* | (alias Azariah) | in vision | (alias Mentes) |
| *Male Relative* | Raguel | Laban | Menelaus |
| *Male Relative's Wife* | Edna | —— | Helen |
| *Male Relative's Daughter* | Sarah | Rachel | Hermione |
| *Animal* | Dog | —— | Dogs |

In terms of events, some sections of the narrative of Tobit parallel the material of Genesis but not the *Odyssey*; other sections parallel the material of the *Odyssey*, but not Genesis; yet other sections again parallel the material of both Genesis and the *Odyssey*. Moreover, where the book of Tobit parallels with the *Odyssey*, the significant events in both follow in almost exactly the same order. This is also the case where the book of Tobit parallels with the story of Jacob in Genesis 29.

## 2. *Distinctive Details*

One distinctive detail shared between the book of Tobit and Genesis is the time-reference. In the former, Tobiah's father-in-law, Raguel, requests him to stay 'fourteen days' after the wedding (= 7 days × 2, Tob. 10.7; cf. 8.20). This clearly seems to have been sourced from the Genesis narrative, where Jacob offers to stay with his father-in-law, Laban, for '*seven* years'

---

28.  Nickelsburg, 'Tobit, Genesis and the *Odyssey*', pp. 54–55.
29.  Based on the table provided by MacDonald. See MacDonald, 'Tobit and the *Odyssey*', pp. 33–34.

first (Gen. 29.18, 20), and then for 'another *seven* years' (= 7 years × 2, in total; Gen. 29.27, 30).[30]

However, the idea of using money as bait by an older relative to detain the new groom from returning to his home as used in the book of Tobit is found in *Odyssey* 4, but not in Genesis 29.

Another distinctive detail shared between the book of Tobit and the *Odyssey* has to do with the shift in physical location in their respective narratives. In both, the shift from a faraway place to the home place occurs at precisely the same point in the narrative. The shift occurs in both texts after the request by the older relatives for the sons to stay longer. In the book of Tobit, the narrative moves from Ecbatana back home to Nineveh. In the *Odyssey*, the narrative moves from Sparta back home to Ithaca.[31]

Other distinctive details point us further toward the thesis of the dependence of the book of Tobit on both Genesis and the *Odyssey*. With regard to the welcome-home scenario of these books, hugs and tears may indeed be considered *topoi* of such scenes. However, consider that the expression 'light of my eyes' (τὸ φῶς τῶν ὀφθαλμῶν) that Tobit uses in relation to his son, Tobiah, is found nowhere else *in the whole of the Old Testament* (Tob. 11.14), but it is found in the *Odyssey*. Penelope uses the same metaphor in the same context in relation to her son, Telemachus. She cries: 'You have come, Telemachus, sweet light' (γλυκερὸν φάος, *Ody.* 16.38).[32]

With such solid initial evidence affirming Tobit's dependence on the *Odyssey*, other details can be taken more seriously. For example, it is not usual for a 'Jewish' angel to lie, as does Raguel in Tobit (cf. Gen. 28.12; 32.1; Job 4.18). Nor are dogs among the usual Jewish household animals (Tob. 6.2; 11.4).[33] Such details further point toward a literary relationship between Tobit and the *Odyssey*, because in the *Odyssey* the divine messenger-in-disguise does lie and 'dogs were Telemachus' special signature' (*Ody.* 2.11; 16.4-10; 17.62).[34]

Narrative incongruities may indicate where an author has fused material. They often act as positive pointers to the author's source. Let

---

30. For a comment on the theological significance of the number seven, see Ch. 5, section 1. c. below.

31. MacDonald, 'Tobit and the *Odyssey*', p. 36.

32. MacDonald, 'Tobit and the *Odyssey*', pp. 29–30.

33. MacDonald, 'Tobit and the *Odyssey*', p. 35. Fitzmyer notes some textual variations, for example, 'the Aramaic text b breaks off in 6.2 just where one would look for mention of a dog that goes along on the journey with Tobiah and the angel. The dog is mentioned not only in the Greek short recension (Tob 5.17) and the Vulgate (11.9), but also in the long recension of S and the Vetus Latina (6.2), but is missing in the medieval Aramaic and Hebrew forms.' See Fitzmyer, *Dead Sea Scrolls*, p. 141.

34. MacDonald, 'Tobit and the *Odyssey*', p. 35.

us take, as an example, the well-known enigma of the issue of Raguel's question in Tob. 7.7: Raguel, the distant relative, asks Tobiah of the well-being of his father, Tobit, in spite of the fact that (as is revealed immediately in the narrative), he already knows of Tobit's ill health. For a 'welcome-from-afar' scene in a narrative, a question about the welfare of a relative is totally appropriate on the lips of another relative. However, in the book of Tobit, Raguel's asking of a question, to which he knows the answer, can be explained, if we cast an eye to the Homeric model at this point: Menelaus, the distant relative, is already well aware of the sufferings of his relative, Odysseus, prior to the arrival of Odysseus' son, Telemachus (*Ody.* 4.155-86). Thus a thread taken from the *Odyssey* remains visible in the literary fabric of Tobit.[35]

### 3. *Complex Rewriting: Torahization by Distribution*
When we turn to the issue of a suitable bride for Tobiah, we find close parallels with Genesis. While Tobit's account shares some parallels with the account of Jacob's quest for a bride (Genesis 29), it shares even more with the account of Isaac's similar quest (Genesis 24). In terms of methodology, the author of Tobit *distributes* (*distributio*) the elements of the Isaac story in Genesis 24 throughout his narrative.

Close to death (Gen. 24.1 // Tob. 3.6; 4.2), both fathers send a trusted loved one on an all-important mission – Eliezer, to secure a wife for Isaac; Tobiah, to get the money from Gabael (Gen. 24.3-4, 37-38 // Tob. 4.1-2, 20). Add to this, the *distribution* of elements of Genesis 24 in Tobit, the trail of which has been outlined by Moore:

1. Both fathers felt strongly about their only child marrying within the family (Tob. 1.9; 4.12-13; 6.10-12, 15; 7.10, 12; 8.7 // Gen. 24.3, 4, 7, 38-40)
2. A trusted person played a major role in securing each bride (Tob. 5.3-16; 6.10 // Gen. 24.2-66)
3. In both accounts an angel played a role (Tob. 3.16-17; 6.4-5; 12.14 // Gen. 24.7)
4. Neither negotiator for a bride's hand would eat until the marriage was agreed upon (Tob. 7.11 // Gen. 24.33)
5. Each family of the bride offered her freely and blessed her (Tob. 7.11-12, 15 // Gen. 24.51, 60)
6. The love of each groom for his bride was almost instantaneous (Tob. 6.8 // Gen. 24.66-67)
7. Each bride left her homeland to live with her in-laws (Tob. 7.3; 10.7-12 // Gen. 24.58-59)[36]

---

35. MacDonald, 'Tobit and the *Odyssey*', p. 37.
36. The numbering is added. See Moore, *Tobit*, pp. 8–9.

By means of the *distribution* of elements of Genesis 24 within Tobit, the author of Tobit torahizes his narrative for his Jewish hearers/readers in exile.

The cumulative evidence given above indicates a substantial literary relationship between the book of Tobit and both Genesis and the *Odyssey*. The dependence of the book of Tobit upon the *Odyssey* affirms the reality of literary *conflation* of Jewish and classical Greek writings by the second century.[37] In terms of the interpretability, that is, the function and effect of these source texts in their new context, MacDonald writes succinctly: 'By borrowing both from Genesis and from Homer, the author generated his dominating characterizations and plot in order to promote the importance of God's providence and Jewish endogamy.'[38]

However, MacDonald does not elaborate further on this point, as we will now do. An analysis of how the author of Tobit used another source, the book of Deuteronomy, provides the key.

### 4. *Complex Rewriting: Torahization by Framing*

From our study above, we observe that the parallel material between the book of Tobit and Homer's *Odyssey* spans Tob. 2.11–12.16; and the parallel material between the book of Tobit and the two stories from Genesis spans Tob. 2.7–11.15 (except for Tob. 14.11; cp. Gen. 12.2; 48.16). What becomes apparent is that these two sources do not account for the opening and closing material of the book, that is, Tob. 1.1–2.10, and Tobit 12–14.

Tobit opens with a solemn designation of the text as a 'book', and a genealogy. This has been shown to be modelled upon the style of the prophetic and wisdom books: 'This book tells the story of Tobit son of Tobiel son of Hananiel son of Aduel son of Gabael son of Raphael ... of the tribe of Naphtali, who in the days of King Shalamaneser of the Assyrians was taken into captivity from Thisbe' (Tob. 1.1-2; cf. Eccl. 1.1-3; Isa. 1.1; Jer. 1.1-3; Hos. 1.1; Ezek. 1.1-3). The portrayal of the chief character, Tobit, from the outset of the book, as an innocent man who suffers in spite of his righteousness and mercy, echoes that of Job (Tob.

---

37. Scholars have noted some very striking similarities between the book of Tobit and the apocryphal book of *Jubilees*. Moore cites the following parallels: Tob. 10.4-6//*Jubilees* 27; and especially Tob. 5.17-21//*Jub.* 27.13-18. See Moore, *Tobit*, p. 46. Nickelsburg finds in the book of *Jubilees* closer parallels to the section about the grief of Tobiah's mother, Anna, upon his departure and the warm welcome Tobiah receives upon his return (Tob. 5.18-21// *Jub.* 27.13-18; Tob. 11//*Jub.* 31.3-9). See Nickelsburg, 'Tobit, Genesis, and the *Odyssey*', pp. 50-51. If, as most scholars believe, the book of *Jubilees* post-dates the book of Tobit, then the line of borrowing is extended. While we await further research about the nature of the relationships between the book of Tobit, Genesis and the book of Jubilees, this intriguing discovery points to another possible example of two-tier allusion.

38. MacDonald, 'Tobit and the *Odyssey*', p. 46.

1.3; cp. Job 1.1–2.10; 42.10b-17):[39] 'I, Tobit, walked in the ways of *truth* (ἀληθείας) and *righteousness* (δικαιοσύνης) all the days of my life. I performed many *acts of charity* (ἐλεημοσύνας) for my kindred and my people' (Tob. 1.3; cf. 3.2).

The occurrence of this vocabulary cluster, 'truth' (ἀλήθεια), 'right' (δικαιοσύνη) and 'alms' (ἐλεημοσύνη), would have sent Jewish hearers/ readers, so familiar with the Torah, back to the book of Deuteronomy, where these themes of 'truth,' 'right' and 'alms' occur together in contexts promoting justice (cf. Deut. 5.17-21; 10.12-19; 22-25).

The author of Tobit is clearly familiar with the Torah:[40] for example, he appeals to the law of Moses (Tob. 1.8); he uses the patriarchal names for the characters Sarah and Anna, her mother (Tob. 3.7, 17 *bis*); and he has Tobit request Tobiah to 'remember Noah, Abraham, Isaac and Jacob, our ancestors from the beginning' who took wives from among the clan (Tob. 4.12). That he draws upon Deuteronomy for his portrait of Tobit initially is confirmed when we look at his portrayal of him at the end of the book. At the end we find the same three ideals – 'truth', 'right' and 'alms' – being passed on by Tobit to his children (Tob. 14.8). Thus the author forms a literary and theological *inclusio* with the opening: 'So now, my children, I command you, serve God *faithfully* [lit., truthfully, ἐν ἀληθείᾳ]/ ... Your children are also to be commanded to do what is *right* (δικαιοσύνην) and to give *alms* (ἐλεημοσύνην), and to be mindful of God and to bless his name at all times with sincerity and with all their strength' (Tob. 14.8 // LXX 14.6-7). Moreover, the solemn expression, 'I command you' (καὶ νῦν ... ἐγὼ ὑμῖν ἐντέλλομαι) reflects also the vocabulary of Deuteronomy where it occurs no less than 36 times.[41]

There is further evidence of another literary and theological *inclusio* between the beginning and end of Tobit, which reflects the influence of Deuteronomy.[42] Temple worship is also a key requirement in Deuteronomy (cf. Deut. 12.1-14; 16.6). At the beginning of the book of Tobit, Tobit declares the importance of worship at 'the temple, the dwelling of God', to the tribes of Israel (Tob. 1.4). At the end, Tobit promises the inhabitants of the land of Israel that they 'will rebuild the temple of God' (Tob. 14.5).

The closing chapters of the book, Tobit 12–14, have been shown by scholars such as Alexander A. Di Lella (1979), Will Soll (1989) and Steven Weitzman (1996) to be modelled on Deuteronomy also. Weitzman

---

39. Soll, 'Misfortune and Exile', p. 224.

40. Weitzman, 'Allusion, Artifice, and Exile', p. 58.

41. Cf. Deut 4.2, 40; 6.2, 6; 7.11; 8.1, 11; 10.13; 11.8, 13, 22, 27, 28; 12.11, 14, 28, 32; 13.18 (19); 15.11, 15; 19.7, 9; 24.18, 20, 22; 27.1, 4, 10; 28.1, 13, 14, 15; 30.2, 8, 11, 16. See Di Lella, 'Deuteronomic Background', p. 386.

42. Di Lella, 'Deuteronomic Background', p. 385.

demonstrates how the Song of Tobit (Tobit 13) was modelled upon the Song of Moses (Deuteronomy 31–32). As an initial evidence of literary dependence, he notes the following five similarities:

1. in Tobit and Deuteronomy, God or God's angel issues a final command to the elder and his successor to write down their songs (cp. Tob. 12.20 // Deut. 31.19)
2. the two commands employ similar expressions (cp. 'And Tobit wrote a song of joy', καὶ Τωβιτ ἔγραψεν προσευχὴν εἰς ἀγαλλίασιν, Tob. 13.1 // 'Now therefore write this song', καὶ νῦν γράψατε τὰ ῥήματα, Deut. 31.19)
3. both narratives culminate with the elder's singing of his song shortly before his death (cp. Tob. 14.3 // Deut. 31.27)
4. both songs appear near the end of their respective narratives
5. finally, both are followed by an address from the dying elder to those who will succeed him (cp. Tob. 14.3-11 // Deuteronomy 33)[43]

Add to this the striking parallels of thought in both. For example, the phrase, 'he leads down to Hades in the lowest regions and there is nothing that can escape his hand' in Tob. 13.2, echoes the phrase, 'I kill and I make alive … and there is none that can deliver out of my hand' in Deut. 32.39; and the phrase, 'he … will not hide his face from you' in Tob. 13.13 echoes the phrase, 'And he [God] said, "I will hide my face from them"', in Deut. 32.20.[44]

The results of Weitzman's research further strengthens the case for the dependence of Tobit's song upon the Song of Moses. He notes these four points:

1. *Multiple Borrowing*: First, the hymn's parallels to the Song of Moses appear in the context of a number of other parallels to Deuteronomy found at the end of Tobit in Tobit's farewell address to his son (Tobit 14)
2. *Status of the Text*: Second, Deuteronomy 32 seems to have been particularly well known at the end of the Second Temple period, when Tobit was composed
3. *Analogues*: Third, a number of other narratives composed in the Second Temple and early post-Second Temple periods feature songs of praise … Judith's hymn … clearly alludes to Exodus 15 and Judges 5 … while the Magnificat in Luke 1.46-55, sung to celebrate the birth of Jesus, seems to emulate Hannah's Prayer
4. *Tradition*: Finally … Tobit's allusion to Deuteronomy 31–32 was actually recognized by at least one premodern reader[45] (italicized material added)

43. Weitzman, 'Allusion, Artifice, and Exile', pp. 53–54.
44. Weitzman, 'Allusion, Artifice, and Exile', pp. 53–54, n. 13.
45. Weitzman, 'Allusion, Artifice, and Exile', pp. 56–57.

Di Lella's analysis focuses on the last chapter of the book of Tobit. He demonstrates how the theology of the entire book of Deuteronomy is *distilled* into the Farewell Discourse in the book of Tobit (14.3–11). In the Farewell Discourse in Deuteronomy, Moses exhorts his people thus: 'I have set before you life and death ... Choose life so that you and your descendants may live' (Deut. 30.19). For the offer of the choice of 'life or death', the author only presents the reward for the choice of life – descendants (Deut. 30.19b). He omits the exhortation in the negative form, which would create literary balance – 'and do not choose death lest you and your descendants die'. The occurrence of this ellipsis increases the dramatic effect here. The author's focus is upon the positive option, 'life'.

Tobit also gives an exhortation to his children (and all) about the issue of 'life or death': 'So now, my children, see what almsgiving does [ – *it brings life*], and what injustice does – it brings death!' (14.11; italicized material added). Here too, the author has created an ellipsis. After the first clause, 'see what almsgiving does', one would expect the answering phrase, 'it brings life', to balance the phrase in the second half of the exhortation – 'it brings death!' However, it is omitted. It would appear that the author of Tobit was aware of the elliptical gap in Deut. 30.19 and fills it. His focus on the negative option (i.e., 'death') has the effect of amplifying the necessity of choosing the opposite one (i.e., 'life').

We conclude that the book of Tobit is a type of *literary mimetic 'sandwich'*: the 'filling' (Tob. 2.11–12.16) comes, primarily, from a *conflation* of the betrothal scenes of Genesis and the wedding material of Homer's *Odyssey*.[46] The 'slices' on either side are made of deuteronomized narrative (Tob. 1.1–2.15; 12.17–14.14). In this way, the author has systematically torahized his entire story.

For both the 'filling' and the 'slices' of the story of Tobit, all of the major episodes which the author draws upon in all three sources 'depict events that take place *outside* the land of Israel'.[47] The exile then appears to be the root problem among all the problems that occur in these respective narratives.[48] Soll points out: 'When we notice that the exile is the enduring misfortune underlying the particular misfortunes that are resolved in the Tobit narrative, the unity of the work impresses itself more forcibly on us.'[49] Therefore, in the author's selection and transformation

---

46. For an outline of the biblical betrothal type-scenes, see Robert Alter, *The Art of Biblical Narrative* (New York: Basic Books, 1981), p. 52.

47. Weitzman, 'Allusion, Artifice, and Exile', p. 60.

48. Soll, 'Misfortune and Exile', p. 230.

49. Soll, 'Misfortune and Exile', p. 230. Moore notes that, 'athough no poll has been taken, probably the great majority of scholars rightly regard Tobit as the product of just one author'. See Moore, *Tobit*, p. 22. See also Fitzmyer, *Dead Sea Scrolls*, pp. 135, 138.

of his source texts, the theme of 'exile' appears to be a central part of his allusive strategy.[50]

For example, Moses' Song occurs in Deuteronomy when Israel had almost ended its time in the wilderness and was about to enter the Promised Land. By placing the Song of Tobit near the end of the book and the end of his life, in imitation of the Song of Moses, the author is implying that the Jews of his own time too will see an end to their exile and return to their homeland.[51] J.C.R. Cousland summarises it thus: 'Tobit's fate prefigures Israel's. The restoration of order in the story portends the larger restoration of Israel.'[52] Thus the book of Tobit provided hope, encouragement and edification for the exiles (Tob. 13.16a).

The journey afar taken by Tobiah and Raphael, the angel-in-disguise, the safe return home (albeit still in the reality of the Assyrian exile) and the resolution of all the ills of Tobit and Sarah through the aid of Raphael reflect at a local or micro-level the hope of the Jewish people at a macro-level, that is, the resolution of all their ills. God, the divine 'Raphael of the Jews', having journeyed with them beyond the borders of Canaan, will also help them resolve their problems and bring them safely home again to Israel and to Godself. The earlier source texts are woven into a new tale that reflects 'the needs and preoccupations of the second-century Diaspora'.[53]

It is useful to restate briefly the techniques used by the author of Tobit in reworking parts of Genesis, Deuteronomy and the *Odyssey*. The more simple techniques include parallel vocabulary and themes, in parallel order, reversing the order of words or events, and filling a gap provided in a source text (i.e., ellipsis).

The more complex techniques which are dealt with briefly include the occurrence of distinctive details and narrative incongruities. The more complex techniques which are dealt with *in more detail* are as follows:

*Conflation*: In the post-wedding scene, the element of Raquel's request to Tobiah to stay for 14 days is modelled on Genesis 29. This is conflated with the idea taken from *Odyssey* 4, namely, that of using money as bait to delay the departure of the new groom for his home.

*Torahization by Distribution*: Genesis 24 provides a closer parallel to the issue of a suitable bride in the book of Tobit than Genesis 29. Moreover,

---

50. For this terminology, we are indebted to Weiztman. See Weitzman, 'Allusion, Artifice and Exile', p. 60.

51. Weitzman, 'Allusion, Artifice, and Exile', p. 61. See Cousland, 'Tobit', pp. 551–52.

52. See Cousland, 'Tobit', p. 552.

53. I. Nowell, 'The Book of Tobit: Narrative Technique and Theology' (Ph.D. dissertation, Catholic University of America, Washington DC; Ann Arbor, MI: University Microfilms International, 1985, No. 8314894), p. 360, cited in Moore, *Tobit*, p. 20.

the author of Tobit distributed elements of Genesis 24 throughout his narrative (i.e., in chs 2 through 12).

*Distillation*: The theology of the entire book of Deuteronomy is *distilled* into the book of Tobit's Farewell Discourse (ch. 14).

*Vocabulary-Cluster and Inclusio*: The vocabulary-cluster based on 'truth', 'right' and 'alms' forms an *inclusio* between the beginning and end of the book of Tobit (Tob. 1.3; 3.2; 14.8).

*Torahization by Framing*: The author of Tobit deuteronomized the opening and closing chapters of the book of Tobit. These frame the central chapters that are largely a rewriting of major sections of Genesis and of Homer's *Odyssey*.

## 2. *Paul's Use of Torah as a Source in 1 Cor 8.1–11.1*

Paul (b. first decade CE) makes extensive use of Old Testament Scripture in general, and in particular the Torah, in his letters. Here we will examine his use of the Torah as a literary source in 1 Cor. 8.1–11.1. This is the first of several New Testament texts to be analysed in this book.[54]

The aim of this section is to demonstrate, first, that the way in which Paul uses the Torah as a source is in accord with the Graeco-Roman literary conventions of his day; and, secondly, that he draws upon his sources for his theological agenda. In using the Torah in the discussion on idol food, Paul presents a radical reinterpretation (*radikal uminterpretatiert*)[55] of Jewish theology in order to reflect the radical nature of the Christ event.[56]

Paul is writing to the Christian community in Corinth about the very practical issue of whether or not the eating of food offered to idols is permissible for its members. His extensive rewriting of the Torah indicates that there were some in the community, most likely the Gentiles, who did

---

54. An analysis of the entire letter is beyond our scope here. This is a modest contribution to investigating those texts which, in Roy E. Ciampa's view, 'have been neglected'. He adds: 'The unbalanced focus on a limited selection of passages within the Pauline corpus seems to reflect an unrecognised and unexamined presupposition to the effect that a lack of scriptural citations or clear allusions obviously indicates that Scripture is not present or functioning at all.' See Roy E. Ciampa, *The Presence and Function of Scripture in Galatians 1 and 2* (WUNT, 2; series 102; Tübingen: Mohr Siebeck, 1998), p. 5.

55. Deitrich-Alex Koch, *Die Schrift als Zeuge des Evangeliums: Untersuchungen zur Verwendung und zum Verständnis der Schrift bei Paulus* (Tübingen: J.C.B. Mohr (Paul Siebeck) 1986), p. 351.

56. Stephan K. Davis, *The Antithesis of the Ages: Paul's Reconfiguration of Torah* (CBQMS, 33; Washington DC: The Catholic Biblical Association of America, 2002), p. 37.

not appreciate that Jesus Christ is one with the God and Lord spoken of in these sacred texts.

First Corinthians is an epistle, apparently the third in an ongoing correspondence between Paul and the community in Corinth. It reflects the influence of Graeco-Roman literary conventions[57] with which Paul and the communities that he addressed would have been wholly familiar.[58] In terms of function, the ancients 'considered the letter to be a sort of dialogue in written form'.[59] Paul used it as a vehicle to bear his theological and pastoral message to the communities, to which he hoped for a positive response.[60]

One can find indications of many of the explicit and implicit references to the Old Testament used by Paul in most critical bible versions and commentaries.[61] However, apart from noting correspondences between verses of Paul's letters and Old Testament Scripture, relatively little has been done by way of deeper analysis. Stockhausen makes this point: 'It is necessary to notice not only *that* Paul alludes to these various texts but *why*, and how he uses them.'[62]

Paul's use of Torah as a source in 1 Cor. 8.1–11.1 has also been chosen, first, because vis-à-vis the question of Paul's use of Old Testament Scripture, more work appears to have been done to date on sections of Paul's other major letters[63] (cf. Rom. 2.9-10,[64] 2 Corinthians

---

57. Margaret M. Mitchell, *Paul and the Rhetoric of Reconciliation: An Exegetical Investigation of the Language and Composition of 1 Corinthians* (Louisville KY: Westminster, 1991). See also Jerome Murphy-O'Connor, *Paul the Letter-Writer: His World, His Options, His Skills* (GNS, 41; Collegeville: Liturgical Press, 1995), pp. 65–86 (81).

58. See Tolbert, *Sowing the Gospel*, p. 39. Hans Dieter Betz writes: 'The fact that Paul acted as an international envoy, first on behalf of Jewish authorities (Acts 8.3; 9.1-2, 21; 22.4-5, 19; 26.10-11; Gal. 1.13, 23; 1 Cor. 15.9; Phil. 3.6), then as a Christian missionary, means that he must have received a good Hellenistic education.' See also Hans Dieter Betz, 'Paul', *ABD*, V, pp. 186–201 (187).

59. Raymond F. Collins, 'Reflections on 1 Corinthians as a Hellenistic Letter', in R. Bieringer (ed.), *The Corinthian Correspondence* (BETL, 125; Leuven: Leuven University Press, 1996), pp. 39–61 (57).

60. Collins, 'Reflections', p. 58. See also Mitchell, *Paul*, p. 257.

61. Stockhausen, *Moses' Veil*, pp. 96–101. See *idem*, '2 Corinthians 3', p. 144.

62. Stockhausen, '2 Corinthians 3', p. 155; Ciampa, *Presence*, p. 1.

63. James M. Scott, 'Paul's Use of Deuteronomic Tradition', *JBL* 112/4 (1993), pp. 645–65 (645).

64. Berkley, *Broken Covenant*; Steve Moyise, 'Intertextuality and the Study of the Old Testament in the New Testament', in Steve Moyise (ed.), *The Old Testament in the New Testament: Essays in Honour of J.L. North* (JSNTSup, 189; Sheffield: Sheffield Academic Press, 2000), pp. 14–41 (19–25).

3,[65] Galatians 3–4[66]). Secondly, the evidence for the use of this letter 'is more early, frequent, and widespread than any other New Testament writings'.[67] Thirdly, in 1 Cor. 8.1–11.1, we find, as in these other major letters, a large unit of discourse with multiple scriptural citations, references and allusions embedded in such a way that it constitutes a systematic rewriting and reinterpretation of part(s) of Old Testament Scripture.

Scholars such as Stockhausen and Hays trace the sources behind allusions to explicit citations of the Old Testament in Paul's letters. However, they do not demonstrate where Paul depends directly upon (some of) the sacred Old Testament texts, as we will do here.

Our analysis of Paul's use of the Torah as a source in writing 1 Cor. 8.1–11.1 supports the findings of Deitrich-Alex Koch (1986), upon which Stanley (1992) builds.[68] Stanley provides detailed evidence that Paul is not citing texts from memory but rather carefully assembling and working over written texts for his theological purposes.[69] However, studies such as those of Koch and Stanley focus only on Paul's explicit Old Testament citations. They do not take into account the many other clear references by Paul to the Old Testament, as we shall do here. Without the inclusion of such references, an appreciation of Paul's literary artistry and the theological import of his message is diminished.[70]

---

65. Stockhausen, '2 Corinthians 3', pp. 143–64.

66. Stockhausen, '2 Corinthians 3', pp. 149–154. Hays deals with Romans and 2 Corinthians. See Hays, *Echoes of Scripture*, pp. 34-83, 122-53. Davis examines sections of three of the great Pauline letters – Romans 9–10, Galatians 3–4 and 2 Corinthians 3. See Davis, *Antithesis*, pp. 177–214; James M. Scott, '"For as Many are Works of the Law are Under a Curse" (Galatians 3.10)', in Craig A. Evans and James A. Sanders (eds), *Paul and the Scriptures of Israel* (JSNTSup, 83; Studies in Scripture and Early Judaism, 1; Sheffield: JSOT Press, 1993), pp. 187–221. For a fuller review of Paul's use of Scripture in Galatians, see Ciampa, *Presence*, pp. 7–19. Christopher D. Stanley examines Paul's method of arguing with Scripture in his major letters – 1 and 2 Corinthians, Galatians and Romans – from a rhetorical perspective. See also Christopher D. Stanley, *Arguing with Scripture: The Rhetoric of Quotations in the Letters of Paul* (London: T&T Clark, 2004), pp. 75–170.

67. Alex T. Cheung, *Idol Food in Corinth: Jewish Background and Pauline Legacy* (JSNTSup, 176; Sheffield: Sheffield Academic Press, 1999), p. 83.

68. Other related studies recently published include: Evans and Sanders (eds), *Paul and the Scriptures of Israel*; John M. Court (ed.), *New Testament Writers and the Old Testament: An Introduction* (London: SPCK, 2002).

69. Stanley, *Paul*, pp. 77, 79, 269. Collins concurs with this view. He notes that, 'all indications are that Paul was self-consciously engaged in writing a letter as he composed 1 Corinthians' (cf. 1 Cor. 4.14; 5.11; 9.15). See Collins, 'Reflections', pp. 45–46.

70. Stanley, *Paul*, p. 255.

## a. *External Criteria Applied*

*Primary Criteria*

### 1. *Date*

First Corinthians is generally reckoned to have been written from Ephesus in the late 50s CE The reference to Galatia in 1 Cor. 16.1 indicates that it may have been written soon after the Letter to the Galatians, datable to 52/54 CE.[71] The date of 1 Corinthians does not appear then to be problematic for the claiming of its literary dependence upon the text under study here – the Torah.

### 2. *Accessibility*

The references to Paul's training at the feet of Gamaliel and his later becoming a teacher (cf. Acts 9.1-2; 22.3, 5; 26.12) indicate that he would have been utterly familiar with the texts of the Torah. Moreover, rote memorization lay at the heart of both the institutions of the Jewish synagogue and the Greaco-Roman schools.[72]

*Secondary Criteria*

### 3. *Status of Text*

In terms of status, the Torah formed part of the canon of Sacred Scripture in Paul's day and it was esteemed by the Jews everywhere.[73]

### 4. *Analogues*

Old Testament Scripture itself provides models for Paul's rewriting of the Torah. The book of Deuteronomy, for example, is largely a rewriting of the matter of the books of Genesis, Exodus, Numbers and Leviticus.[74] The book of Chronicles is usually seen as an even closer rewriting of the books of Kings.[75] We find other examples of rewriting in the literature of early Judaism, literature which forms part of the genre called 'rewritten bible' – *Testament of Abraham, Testaments of the Twelve Patriarchs, Life of Adam and Eve* – and which continued to be widely circulated in Paul's day.[76]

---

71. Betz, 'Paul', p. 191.

72. Stanley, *Paul*, p. 273. See also Peder Borgen, *Philo of Alexandria: An Exegete for His Time* (NovTSup, 86; Leiden: Brill, 1997), pp. 14–19.

73. Philip R. Davies, *Scribes and Schools: The Canonization of the Hebrew Scriptures* (London: SPCK, 1998), p. 94.

74. G. Von Rad, *Deuteronomy* (Philadelphia: Westminister, 1966), pp. 13–38; Calum M. Carmichael, *The Laws of Deuteronomy* (London: Cornell University Press, 1974), pp. 25–33.

75. Stanley, *Paul*, p. 352; S. Sandmel, *The Hebrew Scriptures: An Introduction to Their Literature and Religious Ideas* (New York: Oxford University Press, 1978), p. 471.

76. Stanley, *Paul*, p. 353.

The works of Philo of Alexandria (c. 10 BCE–45 CE), a Jew, provide a contemporaneous analogue. Peder Borgen assesses Philo's extraordinary voluminous output and concludes that, 'Philo did not only interpret small biblical units, but gave comprehensive presentations of the Law of Moses to such an extent that one might claim that he largely rewrote the Pentateuch in the set of treatises called *Exposition of the Law of Moses*.'[77]

Because of the density of citations, references and allusions to Old Testament Scripture in Paul's letters, a note on their textual history is in order. Many scholars agree that the LXX is the primary source for Paul's citations, references and allusions to Old Testament Scripture.[78] Stanley's analysis of 1 Corinthians is instructive:[79] some citations fully agree with the standard LXX (1 Cor. 6.16 // Gen. 2.24; 10.7 // Exod. 32.6); others are adaptations by Paul of the standard LXX (1 Cor. 1.19 // Isa. 29.14; 1 Cor. 1.31 // Jer. 9.23; 1 Cor. 3.20 // Ps. 93.11; 1 Cor. 15.27 // Ps. 8.6; 1 Cor. 15.24-25 // Isa. 25.8; and Hos. 13.14); others agree with or adapt a variant reading (1 Cor. 9.9 // Deut. 25.4; 1 Cor. 14.21 // Isa. 28.11-12; 1 Cor. 15.45 // Gen. 2.7; 15.55 // Hos. 13.14); and, still others find little or no support in the LXX manuscript tradition (1 Cor. 2.9 // Isa. 64.3; 1 Cor. 3.19 // Job 5.13; 9.10).[80]

The diversity of witnesses reflected in 1 Corinthians is also reflected in the other letters of Paul. While this indicates that Old Testament Scripture had not yet stabilized at the turn of the era, it also signals that Paul must have drawn his quotations directly from written sources and not from memory, because, if he had used a memorized version, one would expect him to be consistent, at least when quoting from the same Old Testament book, which, often, he is not. [81]

---

77. See Borgen, *Philo of Alexandria*, p. 63. Stockhausen's assessment of Philo is that he was 'possibly the most important of Paul's contemporaries in terms of exegetical methods and interests . . .' See Stockhausen, '2 Corinthians 3', p. 151. Stanley notes that, 'F.H. Colson, one of the editors of the Loeb edition of Philo's works, counted some 2,000 citations in Cohn and Wendland's standard critical text, of which all but fifty stem from the Pentateuch'. See Stanley, *Paul*, p. 337, n. 92. He also notes the Graeco-Roman literary influence upon Philo. He notes that, 'at least sixteen explicit quotations from Homer can be identified in the Philonic corpus . . . Philo habitually quoted the Homeric epics verbatim according to the vulgate text'. See Stanley, *Paul*, p. 326, n. 97.

78. Stanley, *Paul*, p. 68.

79. Stanley takes three of Koch's seven criteria for determining which verses count as citations: '(1) those introduced by an explicit quotation formula ("as it is written", "therefore it says", etc.); (2) those accompanied by a clear interpretive gloss (e.g. 1 Cor. 15.27); and (3) those that stand in demonstrable syntactical tension with their present Pauline surroundings (e.g., Rom 9.7, 10.18, Gal 3.12)'. See Stanley, *Paul*, pp. 56–57.

80. Stanley, *Paul*, pp. 185–215.

81. Stanley, *Paul*, p. 255.

### b. *Internal Criteria Applied*

The matter of 1 Cor. 8.1–11.1 is organized into a concentric ABA[1] structure:[82]

A:   eating idol food (idolatry), 1 Cor. 8.1-13
B:   the example of the apostle(s), 1 Corinthians 9
A[1]:  idolatry, 1 Cor. 10.1–11.1.

The B section 'functions to provide further substantiation for the main thought of the A section'.[83] Thus it may be understood as a positive digression.[84] Paul uses this structure for his argumentation several times in the letter.[85]

An overview of where the main verbal and thematic parallels between 1 Cor. 8.1–11.1 and the Torah are to be found may be simply presented as follows:

Table 3.2: *Paul's Use of the Torah as a Source*

| TEXTS | CHAPTERS | | |
|---|---|---|---|
| Genesis | 3–4 | 3–4 | - - |
| Exodus | - - | - - | 12–14; 17; 32 |
| Leviticus | - - | - - | 10–11 |
| Numbers | - - | - - | 11–25 |
| Deuteronomy | 4–6 | 23–28; 30 | 32 |
| 1 Corinthians | A: 8 | B: 9 | A[1]: 10–11.1 |

82. Joël Delobel notes that, 'the manuscript tradition is unanimous in witnessing for the three Chapters in their present form'. See Joël Delobel, 'Coherence and Relevance of 1 Cor 8–10', in R. Bieringer (ed.), *The Corinthian Correspondence* (Leuven: Leuven University Press, 1996), pp. 177–90 (178–79).

83. Cheung, *Idol Food*, p. 177. Joost Smit Sibinga notes that W. Wuellner 'has made it quite clear that a digression in an ancient text should not be considered to disrupt or disturb the context. On the contrary, it may serve and strengthen the argument and heighten its effect.' See Joost Smit Sibinga, 'The Composition of 1 Cor. 9 and Its Context', *NovT* 40 (1998), pp. 136–63 (143). See also W. Wuellner, 'Greek Rhetoric and Pauline Argumentation', in W.R. Schoedel (ed.), *Early Christian Literature and the Classical Intellectual Tradition: Festschrift R. M. Grant* (ThH, 53; Paris: Beauchesne, 1979), pp. 177–87 (186–87).

84. See Quintillian, *Inst. Or.* 4.3.4. Mitchell prefers the term 'exemplary argument' because of the negative understanding of the word digression in today's popular linguistic currency. She helpfully draws our attention to the sense that ancients such as Quintilian would have used it: 'this form of digression can be advantageously appended ... but only if the digression fits in well to the rest of the speech and follows naturally on what has preceded, not if it is thrust like a wedge parting what should naturally come together'. See Mitchell, *Paul*, pp. 249–50.

85. Cf. 1 Corinthians 5–6: A: immorality, B: court battles, A[1]: immorality; 1 Corinthians 7: A: marriage, B: circumcision, A[1]: marriage; 1 Cor. 12.1–14.49 – A: spiritual gifts, B: love, A[1] : spiritual gifts. See Cheung, *Idol Food*, p. 140.

The above scheme reveals that for section A (1 Corinthians 8) Paul draws from the beginning and end of the Torah, that is, from Genesis 3–4 and Deuteronomy 4–6. From section B (1 Corinthians 9), Paul draws upon Genesis 3–4 and Deuteronomy 23–28; and 30.[86] For section A[1] (1 Cor. 10.1–11.1), Paul again draws upon Deuteronomy 32, but also on the books *within* the Genesis–Deuteronomy frame – Exodus (12–14; 17; 32), Leviticus 10–11 and Numbers 11–25. For the entire literary unit, Deuteronomy is the only book of the Torah that Paul uses for all three sections of this literary unit of 1 Cor. 8.1–11.1.[87]

*1. Complex Rewriting: Torahization by Conflation*

Section A (1 Corinthians 8) divides naturally into two sections: part 1, 1 Cor. 8.1-6, is concerned with general principles in relation to food sacrificed to idols; and part 2, 1 Cor. 8.7-13, is an exposé on the matter of love of one's brother.

In this section, Paul sets out general principles in relation to the issue of food sacrificed to idols (τῶν εἰδολοθύτων, 8.1).

The argument is outlined as follows:

1. Even if one loves God (v. 3),
2. and knows that idols are nothing (v. 4),
3. and knows that there is no other God (vv. 4, 6),
4. and even if there are so-called gods and lords (v. 5),
5. and even if one knows that eating food is a neutral exercise (v. 8), unless eaten as food offered to an idol (v. 7),
6. Paul's instruction is not to eat meat sacrificed to idols lest it become a stumbling block for the weak ones. To cause a weak one to fall because of one's example, is 'to sin against the brothers', which is, in fact, 'to sin against Christ' (8.11-12).

The confession of monotheism in 1 Cor. 8.4 ('there is no God but one') serves as a literary flag.[88] It links us immediately with the *Sh°ma* of Deut.

---

86. Brodie concludes that, it is 'as though he accorded Deuteronomy a special role'. See Thomas L. Brodie, 'The Systematic Use of the Pentateuch in 1 Corinthians: An Exploratory Survey', in R. Bieringer (ed.), *The Corinthian Correspondence* (Leuven: Leuven University Press, 1996), pp. 441–57 (447).

87. See Brodie, 'Systematic Use', 445.

88. Stanley notes that, 'the close integration of the majority of Paul's quotations into their present argumentative contexts would likewise be more understandable if the verses in question had been selected and studied with a view to their use in just such a literary setting instead of being recalled *ad hoc* in the moment of composition'. See Stanley, *Paul*, p. 78.

6.4 that is at the very heart of Judaism. Closer examination indicates that the context of Deut. 6.4, that is, Deuteronomy 4–6, contains striking parallels with 1 Cor. 8.1-6 in terms of a vocabulary-cluster and related themes. Note the vocabulary-cluster[89] common to both, based on three words: (1) *'love'* (1 Cor. 8.3; cp. Deut. 4.47; 6.5); (2) *'know'/'knowledge'* (1 Cor. 8.1, 2, 3, 4; cp. Deut. 4.35, 39); and (3) *'God(s)'/'Lord'* (1 Cor. 8.3, 4, 5, 6; cp. Deut. 4.34, 35, 39; 5.6a; 6.4-5).

Both texts affirm that there is one God (1 Cor. 8.4, 6 // Deut. 4.35; 6.4), before whom there shall be no other (so-called) gods (1 Cor. 8.5 // Deut. 5.7), and that this is the God whom one shall love (1 Cor. 8.3 // Deut. 6.5). Thus there is continuity between the vocabulary and theology of 1 Cor. 8.1-6 and Deuteronomy 4–6.[90]

There is also radical discontinuity between these texts.[91] God's title – 'one Lord' – in Deuteronomy (4.35, 39; 5.6; 6.4, 5) is now also attributed by Paul to Jesus Christ. The preposition 'through' is significant: 'and one Lord, Jesus Christ, *through* whom are all things and *through* whom we exist' (1 Cor. 8.6b).[92] In Deuteronomy, the blessing of life comes through God ('God created human beings on the earth', Deut. 4.32). Jesus Christ *is* one with the God spoken of in Deuteronomy.[93] The way Paul has rewritten Deuteronomy here has a startling impact on the message: 'Paul [is] drawing on the Jewish *Shema* and putting Jesus right in the midst of the most fundamental assertion in early Judaism of its monotheistic faith.'[94]

89. Stockhausen speaks in terms of 'hook-word connections'. See Stockhausen, '2 Corinthians 3', p. 154.

90. See B.J. Oropeza, 'Animadversiones: Laying to Rest the Midrash: Paul's Message on Meat Sacrificed to Idols in Light of the Deuteronomic Tradition', *Bib* 79 (1998), pp. 57–68 (67).

91. Stockhausen's assessment of this characteristic of Paul is that, 'this discontinuity is due, not only to the disjunction between Paul's way of life in the customs of his fathers and his new life in Christ, but to his tendency in response to locate and exegetically reconcile passages in his traditional Scriptures which express this disjunction'. See Stockhausen, '2 Corinthians 3', p. 145. See also Neil Richardson, *Paul's Language about God* (JSNTSup, 99; Sheffield: Sheffield Academic Press, 1994), p. 307.

92. C. Marvin Pate, *The Reverse of the Curse: Paul, Wisdom and the Law* (WUNT, 2; series 114; Tübingen: Mohr Siebeck, 2000), p. 279.

93. Pate, *Reverse*, pp. 277–79.

94. Ben F. Witherington, III, *Jesus the Sage* (Philadelphia: Fortress Press, 1994), p. 316. Richardson notes that, 'the lordship of Christ *is* for Paul the expression of his (Jewish) monotheism. The literary pattern of "theological *inclusio*"–from God through Christ to God ... can be identified in several units of the Corinthian correspondence, notably 1 Cor. 1.18-25, 6.12-20, and 2 Cor. 1.18-22, 4.7-15 and 5.11-21'. See Richardson, *Paul's Language*, pp. 302–303. See also N.T. Wright, *The Climax of the Covenant: Christ and the Law in Pauline Theology* (Minneapolis: Fortress Press, 1991), pp. 127–36.

Genesis 3–4 is a context which also exhibits striking parallels to 1 Cor. 8.7-13 [and 1 Cor. 9.4-13; see section (b) below] in terms of a vocabulary-cluster and related themes. This vocabulary-cluster and related themes are centred on five words: (1) *'eating'/'food'* (1 Cor. 8.4, 8, 10, 13; 9.4, 7b, 13; cp. Gen. 3.5, 6, 11b, 12, 13b, 14, 17, 22); (2) *'know'/'knowledge'* (1 Cor. 8.1, 2, 3, 4; 9.13; cp. Gen. 3.5, 22; 4.1, 9); (3) *'God'/'Lord'* (1 Cor. 8.3, 4, 5, 6; cp. Gen. 3.5, 14, 22; 4.9); (4) *'sin'* (1 Cor. 8.12, 13; cp. Gen. 4.7, 9); and (5) *'brother(s)'* (1 Cor. 8.12; cp. Gen. 4.2, 9).

The meaning of Paul's statement that knowledge 'puffs up' (1 Cor. 8.1b) is clarified in the light of his use of Genesis 3. In Genesis 3 the woman and man are puffed up by the serpent's false promise that if they eat food that is forbidden they shall become like God/gods, *'knowing* good and evil' (3.5). Paul reverses the order of the relationship between 'eating' and 'knowledge': for him, it is *'knowledge* [which] puffs up' (1 Cor. 8.1). Those with knowledge about the neutral nature of food offered to idols have the choice of doing good or evil by the example of their eating practices. To eat idol food may cause the weak to fall into idolatry (1 Cor. 8.4, 10-11). The implicit lesson for the people of Corinth is this: 'Remember what happened in the garden and do not eat!' Thus Paul's response is the opposite to the response found in his Genesis source – an example of his method of torahization by *correction* (*correctio*).[95]

In Genesis 3, the issue of care of the weak is implicit. In spite of God's command, the woman weakens and eats. The man follows her example. As a result, they are cursed, along with the serpent, forever (Gen. 3.6-13). This issue of care of the weak is continued in Genesis 4, the narrative concerning Cain and Abel. There, it is made explicit.

In the light of Genesis 4, an anomaly in Paul's letter is clarified.[96] His sudden shifting from theoretical principle concerning the care of the weak to practical action, using himself as an example, makes hugely more sense if taken as a response to the question found in Genesis: 'Am I my brother's keeper?' (Gen. 4.9). To this rhetorical question, Paul responds with an emphatic 'Yes'. He states: '*I* will never eat meat, so that *I* may not cause one of them (*'my brother'*, ἀδελφόν μου) to fall' (1 Cor. 8.13). His

---

95. Mitchell notes that, 'the appeal to forsake one's own advantage for the sake of the common good is *the standard appeal for concord in antiquity'*. See Mitchell, *Paul*, pp. 240, 256. See Ch. 2, section 1.b. 4. above.

96. This is an example of what Davis describes as a 'surface irregularity'. He notes that, 'a skilled modern reader of post-biblical intertexture will therefore grasp for the ancient interpreter's eye or intuition for gaps, ungrammatical constructions, potential cameos of supernatural figures, unique phraseology, and other flags or "surface irregularities" in biblical texts.' See Davis, *Antithesis*, p. 34.

response to his *brother* is the absolute antithesis ('correction') of Cain's. By abstaining from meat, Paul shows himself to be truly his brother's keeper.

In terms of method, it emerges that for Section A (1 Corinthians 8) Paul has *conflated* and rewritten elements of Genesis 3–4 and Deuteronomy 4–6.[97] He does so by using some of the vocabulary, themes and theology found there, mostly in the order in which he finds them. He rewrites them 'in Christ'. This analysis concurs with F. Thielman's conclusion that his *modus operandi* is to 'build his argument in a way that allows the scandal of the gospel to find legitimacy in Israel's sacred traditions'.[98]

### 2. *Complex Rewriting: Torahization by Elaboration*

In section B (1 Corinthians 9), Paul uses Genesis 3–4 and Deuteronomy 23–28 as sources. The fact that Paul does not mention idol food or idolatry in Section B (1 Cor. 9.1-27) has seemed rather problematic for some commentators. This omission has led some to conclude that it was not part of the original unit.[99] The research above on 1 Corinthians 8 is directive here.[100] Paul's sudden shift at 1 Cor. 8.13[101] from the principle of caring for the weak to the practical commitment of caring for his brother can be explained as an elaboration of his response to the question 'Am I my brother's keeper?' (Gen. 4.9) given in 1 Cor. 8.13. However, there is a twist here that appears to have largely gone unnoticed. Paul builds his argument in Section B in the form of a response to the question in the *reverse*, that is, 'Are my brothers my keeper?'

97. Brodie notes that Genesis and Deuteronomy are combined elsewhere in this letter, notable in the section just before the unit under discussion here: 'Paul also combines Deuteronomy with Genesis. The divorce text, for instance (1 Cor. 7,10-11), seems to reflect aspects of both Gen 2,24 and Deut 24,1-4. Likewise, the reference to the one God as source of all (creation) (1 Cor. 8,1-6) may reflect aspects of both Gen 1–2 and Deut 4,5-40.' See Brodie, 'Systematic Use', pp. 447, 453–54. Gail O'Day approaches this insight when she points out that Paul's use of Jeremiah is 'multileveled'. See Gail R. O'Day, 'Jeremiah 9.22-23 and 1 Corinthians 1.26-31: A Study in Intertextuality', *JBL* 109 (1990), pp. 259–67 (260).

98. F. Thielman, 'Unexpected Mercy: Echoes of a Biblical Motif in Romans 9–11', *SJT* 47 (1994), pp. 169–81 (180). Hays speaks of Paul's method thus: 'The phenomenon of intertextuality – the imbedding of fragments of an earlier text within a later one – has always played a major role in the cultural traditions that are heir to Israel's Scriptures: the voice of Scripture, regarded as authoritative in one way or another, continues to speak in and through later texts that both depend on and transform the earlier.' See Hays, *Echoes of Scripture*, p. 14.

99. Mitchell, *Paul*, p. 250.

100. Ciampa points out that, 'the structure and interpretation of smaller units informs the analysis of the larger sections of the discourse and visa versa'. See Ciampa, *Presence*, p. 20.

101. In relation to 1 Corinthians, Mitchell notes that, 'the connection between ch. 9 and 8.1-13 is clearly made by Paul's first person reference at the end of that argument in 8.13'. See Mitchell, *Paul*, p. 239.

In this section, Paul affirms that he has the right to 'food and drink' (1 Cor. 9.4), but chooses not to avail himself of it for the sake of the weak. His argument here is an amplification[102] of his practical commitment stated in 1 Cor. 8.13.[103] Therefore, the key to understanding Paul's digression in section B (1 Corinthians 9) is found in his use of Genesis as a source. This affirms the literary unity of 1 Cor. 8.1–11.1.[104]

Alex T. Cheung notes that Paul advances five examples to demonstrate positively that his brothers are in fact his keeper in 1 Cor. 9.4-14. Paul outlines his apostolic rights 'in the Lord' (1 Cor. 9.1) in terms of the right 'to eat': (i) 'the planter of a vineyard should eat of its grapes; (ii) the tender of a flock should "eat" of its milk; (iii) the ox who treads the grain should not have its mouth muzzled; (iv) the plowman and the thresher are entitled to share in the harvest, and the sower of spiritual seed ought to reap a material harvest; and (v) the priests receive their food from the temple; the preachers of the gospel should get their living by the gospel'.[105]

The central one of these examples is based upon Paul's explicit citation of Deut. 25.9a: 'For it is written (γέγραπται) in the law of Moses, "You shall not muzzle an ox while it is treading (κημώσεις)[106] out the grain" ' (1 Cor. 9.9a).[107] Paul follows this citation with another one that has no known Old Testament textual antecedent: 'It was indeed written (ἐγράφη) for our sake, for whoever plows should plow in hope and whoever threshes [should thresh][108] in hope of a share in the crop' (1 Cor. 9.10b).[109]

---

102. Mitchell notes that, 'among its functions, (*sic*) a digression may make a comparison or often amplify a given point in an argument.' See Mitchell, *Paul*, p. 250. She cites the following examples: Cicero, *Inv. Rhet.* 1.19.27; *De Or.* 2.19.80; Quintillian, *Inst. Or.* 4.3.15. See also Mitchell, *Paul*, p. 250, n. 354.

103. See Mitchell, *Paul*, p. 243.

104. Mitchell argues for the rhetorical unity of this section based on 'Paul's reconciliatory strategy'. See Mitchell, *Paul*, p. 238.

105. Cheung, *Idol Foods*, p. 141.

106. Smit notes that 'there is very little difference in meaning between the literary φιμοῦν and the unliterary κημοῦν'. See Joop F.M. Smit, '*About the Idol Offerings*': Rhetoric, Social Context and Theology of Paul's Discourse in First Corinthians 8.1–11:1 (Leuven: Peeters, 2000), p. 102.

107. As noted above, this citation is based on an unknown variant text.

108. Smit argues against the presence of an ellipsis here. See Smit, '*Idol Offerings*', p. 102.

109. Smit notes that an even more expanded interpretation of Deut. 24.4 is found in Philo, *De Virtutibus* (145–46), in a context where Moses is presented as the model of humanity (*Virt.* 51–79), and where he gives a selection of laws which exhibit compassion for people (*Virt.* 82–124), animals (*Virt.* 125–47) and plants (*Virt.* 148–60). Moreover, Smit notes that Philo quotes explicitly, or very nearly explicitly, parts of the Torah that Paul also used in this unit (1 Cor. 8.1–11.1) – Exodus (23.19; 34.26), Leviticus (22.27, 28) and also elsewhere in Deuteronomy (14.21; 22.10). See Smit, '*Idol Offerings*', p. 111.

Both the explicit citation and its extended variation[110] are set in the middle of a context which has a series of striking parallels with Deuteronomy 23–28 in terms of vocabulary and themes. These parallels occur in the same order:[111]

Table 3.3: *Parallels between* 1 Corinthians 9 *and* Deuteronomy 23–28

| 1 Corinthians 9 | Deuteronomy 23–28 |
| --- | --- |
| 1 Cor. 9.4-5 | Deut 23.25; 24.1 |
| 1 Cor. 9.7a | Deut 24.5 |
| 1 Cor. 9.7b | Deut 24.21 |
| *1 Cor 9.8-10a* | *Deut. 25.4* |
| 1 Cor. 9.12c-14 | Deut 26.1-11 |
| 1 Cor. 9.15 | Deut 26.16–27.8 |
| 1 Cor. 9.16b | Deut 27.[9-]26 |
| 1 Cor. 9.17–18, 23 | Deut 28.1-46 |

Paul applies both a curse and a blessing to himself: 'woe to me if I do not proclaim the gospel' (1 Cor. 9.16), and, 'I do it ... so that I may share in its blessings' (1 Cor. 9.23). In the whole of the Torah, the vocabulary and theology of blessings and curses is strongest in Deuteronomy 27–28; and 30. There it is outlined that there will be blessings upon those who obey the law, and curses upon those who do not.

In terms of theology, however, Paul's is radically different. Paul and Barnabas are entitled to be fed by the brothers according to the gospel (1 Cor. 9.14), but die to this entitlement 'rather than put an obstacle in the way of the gospel of Christ' (1 Cor. 9.12b; cf. 1 Cor. 9.15a, 18, 23). This dying is a modelling of the *'life-through-death'* that has happened uniquely at the macro-level through Jesus Christ who wrought the ultimate reversal ('correction') of the curse (cf. 1 Cor. 8.11).

This blessing of 'life through death', which in Section A (1 Cor. 8.13) is for the weak, is extended in Section B (1 Cor. 9.19) to 'all' (πᾶσιν), that is, to all those within and outside the Law of Moses (cf. 1 Cor. 9.20-23; 8.6). Moreover, it is free of charge and cannot be earned, as the blessing of the Law of Moses is earned by obedience. Hence, in terms of power and

---

110. Smit notes that, 'the usual quotation formula in Paul reads: "It is written (γέγραπται)", as in v. 9. The expression: "It was written that" occurs only one other time in his letters, namely in Rom 4:23. There it functions as a connection between the preceding literal quotation and an ensuing interpretation ...' See Smit, *'Idol Offerings'*, pp. 105, 107.

111. Brodie's description is apt here. He describes the explicit citations in 1 Cor. 5.7 and 9.9 as 'tips of scriptural icebergs'. See Brodie, 'Systematic Use', p. 443, and also pp. 451–52.

scope, Paul chooses and recommends to the people of Corinth the ultimate law of Christ (1 Cor. 9.9-10, 12) over the penultimate the Law of Moses (Deuteronomy 23–28).[112]

### 3. *Complex Rewriting: Torahization by Conflation and Synthesis*

In section A[1] (1 Cor. 10.1–11.1), Paul rewrites parts of Exodus, Leviticus, Numbers and Deuteronomy (see Table 3.1 above).[113] First Cor. 10.1-11.1 is made up of three literary sub-units:

> Part 1: A Warning from the Lessons of Israel's History (10.1-13)
> Part 2: Sacrificial Feasts. No Compromise with Idolatry (10.14-22)
> Part 3: Food Sacrifices to Idols. Practical Solutions (10.23–11.1)

In part 1 (1 Cor. 10.1-13), Paul has *conflated*[114] a plethora of Scripture texts[115] taken from across a diverse range of chapters of the books of Exodus[116] and Numbers, but all of which have to do with idolatry and a new generation. His methods in using his sources vary greatly here. For

---

112.   For a note on the importance of the 'middle element' in literary units, see Kym Smith, *The Amazing Structure of the Gospel of John* (Blackwood, Aus.; Sherwood, 4th edn, 2005), pp. 8, 13, 59, 121–22. See ch. 5, section 1. below.

113.   Stanley comments that, 'First Corinthians 10.1-11 is the only place in the letter where Paul acts extensively with the Jewish Scriptures. How might the Corinthians have reacted to this sudden shift to a biblical mode of argumentation?' In the light of the above evidence, we would say that Paul uses the 'biblical mode of argumentation' throughout 1 Cor. 8.1–11.1, but deliberately intensifies it at 10.1-11. See Stanley, *Arguing with Scripture*, p. 86.

114.   Koch defines a conflated or 'mixed' citation as one that occurs when there is a 'merging portion of one verse into the text of another'. It is listed as one of seven routine adaptations to citations made by Paul, according to Koch. See Koch, *Die Schrift*, pp. 186–90. Stanley adopts Koch's term, 'mixed citation'. See also Stanley, *Paul*, pp. 252, 258.

115.   Stanley concludes that, 'finally, the fact that a number of Paul's citations are used in a sense quite foreign to their original context is easily understood if Paul is pictured as copying his citations not directly from the pages of Scripture, but rather from a diverse collection of biblical texts in which the only link with the original context is the one that is preserved in the compiler's mind. From this it follows that the investigator should approach the Pauline materials with the working assumption that Paul drew his quotations directly from written sources (i.e. a collection of passages excerpted from biblical scrolls), and not from memory unless the evidence indicates a different practice in a particular situation.' See Stanley, *Paul*, pp. 77, 79.

116.   C.J.A. Hickling notes that, 'curiously despite its important place in the Pentateuch and in Jewish tradition, it is one of the books he uses least. Paul quotes Exodus only five times out of a total of 87 quotations of the Old Testament and alludes to it only four times out of a total of 78 Old Testament allusions. (1) Two of the five quotations and all but one of the four allusions occur in the two canonical epistles to the Corinthian Christians. Was the story of Israel's origins at the back of Paul's mind when he thought of the Corinthian church?' See C.J.A. Hickling, 'Paul's Use of Exodus in the Corinthian Correspondence', in R. Bieringer (ed.), *The Corinthian Correspondence* (Leuven: Leuven University Press, 1996), pp. 367–76 (367).

example, he *cites* one verse of the Torah explicitly (1 Cor. 10.7 // Exod. 32.2: '"The people sat down to eat and drink (φαγεῖν καὶ πεῖν), and they rose up to play"' (1 Cor. 10.7).[117] He presents *variations* of other verses of Scripture (1 Cor. 10.5 // Num. 14.29; 1 Cor. 10.6 // Num. 11.14). He *conflates* two verses from different parts of the same book (1 Cor. 10.1 // Exod. 13.21; and Exod. 14.22, 29), or sometimes, (parts of) two or more verses from several books of the Torah (1 Cor. 10.4 // Exod. 17.6; Num. 21.11; and Deut. 6.16; 32.4, 15, 18, 30, 31;[118] 1 Cor. 10.9a // Exod. 17.2; and Deut. 6.16; 1 Cor. 10.9b // Deut. 21.5, 6; 1 Cor. 10.10 // Exod. 12.23; and Num. 16.49). Further, he *distils* an entire unit of Scripture into one verse (1 Cor. 10.8 // Num. 25.1-9).[119]

The themes based on the three-word vocabulary-cluster – '*knowing*', '*eating*' and '*God*'/'*Lord*' – found linking 1 Cor. 8.1-6 to Genesis 3–4; and Deuteronomy 4–6 above are also present in 1 Cor. 10.1-13: (1) 'eating': they all '*ate* ... food ... drank ... drink*' in the wilderness (10.3-4); (2) 'knowing': the happenings in the wilderness 'were written down to *instruct* us' (1 Cor. 10.11); (3) 'God'/'Lord': 'Do not become idolaters [as they did in the past] ... *God* is faithful' (1 Cor. 10.7, 13).

In part 2 (1 Cor. 10.14-22), Paul changes his method of rewriting. He uses Deuteronomy 32, the Song of Moses, as his sole model and he borrows from it in a more systematic fashion (1 Cor. 10.18 // Deut. 32.17; 1 Cor. 10.20-22 // Deut. 32.16, 21, 30-39 [*Shᵉma*]; cf. Deut. 32.1; 18.11; 31.29).[120] Hays has already noticed this. About 1 Cor. 10.14-22 he writes: 'Paul is reading the wilderness story *through the lens* of Deuteronomy 32 ...'[121] (italics added).

That Paul is borrowing from literary sources here is supported by his reference to 'things written down' (ἐγράφη) in 1 Cor. 10.13, and several distinctive details. The description of God as 'faithful' (πιστὸς δὲ ὁ θεός), found in 1 Cor. 10.13, and only in 1 and 2 Corinthians *in the whole of the New Testament* (cf. 1 Cor. 1.9; 2 Cor. 1.18), is found only in Deuteronomy

---

117. This citation is in full agreement with the standard LXX.

118. Stanley notes that, 'the distinctive literary and rhetorical artistry of Paul's combined and conflated citations shows that these texts at least were selected and shaped in advance for a particular argumentative purpose'. See Stanley, *Paul*, p. 70.

119. What Brodie says of 1 Corinthians 9, we find to be also true of 1 Cor. 10.1-11: 'He [Paul] ranges across several disparate chapters and picks out elements which seem either intrinsically important or particularly suited to his own purpose. Yet he retains some element of synthesis.' See Brodie, 'Systematic Use', p. 445.

120. Oropeza, 'Animadversiones', p. 60.

121. Hays, *Echoes of Scripture*, p. 304. Markus Bockmuehl makes an important observation: 'Just as Homer elucidated Homer, so Scripture interprets Scripture – a principle that became fundamental to Jewish and Christian biblical interpretation alike.' See Markus Bockmuehl, 'The Making of Gospel Commentaries', in Markus Bockmuehl and Donald A. Hagner (eds), *The Written Gospel* (Cambridge: Cambridge University Press, 2005), pp. 274–95 (284).

*in the whole of the Old Testament,* in the Song of Moses (Deut. 32.4) and in Deut. 7.9. Further, the reference to demons in 1 Cor. 10.20 (*bis*) and 10.21 (*bis*)[122] is found only here in 1 Corinthians, *in the whole of the entire Pauline corpus,* and only in Deut. 32.17 in the *whole of the books of the Torah.*[123]

Paul goes on to amplify his argument against those who eat and drink idol food.[124] If eating the sacrifices of the religion of Israel makes the people partners with God, so eating the sacrifices of the pagans makes them partners with demons. However, Paul does not proceed to commend the former as he denounces the latter; rather he poses a different and exclusive alternative ('correction') to *both pagan and Jewish* sacrificial practices, namely, to 'drink the cup/partake of the table of the Lord' (1 Cor. 10.21).

Here, Paul reflects Aaron's correction of Moses in Leviticus 10.[125] The matter in Leviticus 10 concerns laws about sacrificial eating and drinking. The law prohibits the drinking of wine or strong drink forever so that '[you] may not die' (Lev. 10.9). Moses scolds Aaron's sons for not eating sacrificed meat (Lev. 10.17). Aaron's response indicates that he recognizes the emptiness of the prescribed sacrifice: 'See, today they offered their *sin* offering and their burnt offering before the Lord; and yet such things as these have befallen me! If I had eaten the *sin* offering today, would it have been agreeable to the Lord?' (Lev. 10.19). This issue is paralleled in Paul. Paul asks: 'What do I imply then? That food sacrificed ... is anything?' (1 Cor. 10.19). Moreover, the vocabulary of 'sin' in Leviticus 10 is also found in 1 Cor. 8.12: 'But when you thus *sin* ... you *sin* against Christ'.

What is happening here? Paul draws upon Leviticus 10 at this point of his letter. He uses one Scripture text to *correct* another text from the Torah: Leviticus 10 ('Israel's sacrifices are empty') corrects Exod. 32.6 ('They ... offered burnt offerings', Exod. 32.6b, which Paul quotes, 1 Cor. 10.7b). Moreover, he *corrects* both Scripture texts in the light of the Christ

---

122. It is interesting to note that the only other occurrence among all the Pauline letters is found in 1 Tim. 4.1 (δαιμονίων), which is contextually close to the only other occurrence of the citation of Deut. 25.4 (which Paul cites in 1 Cor. 9.9) in 1 Tim. 5.18.

123. Regarding 1 Cor. 10.1-11 and 2 Cor. 3.7-18, Hickling concludes that, 'Paul appears ... as a professional, dare we say?—interpreter of the Torah'. See Hickling, 'Paul's Use of Exodus', pp. 369–70.

124. This concurs with Cheung 'two-stage argument' theory. See Cheung, *Idol Food,* pp. 108, 116. See also Stanley, *Arguing with Scripture,* p. 85.

125. Tolbert notes that, 'in the rhetorical fashion of the first century one very effective way of refuting one's opponents was to incorporate their arguments in one's own presentation and then demonstrate how faulty their conclusions were'. See Tolbert, *Sowing the Gospel,* pp. 28–29. Further, she adds: 'Paul, in fact employs this strategy frequently in his letters. The opening chapters of 1 Corinthians provide several examples of Paul quoting the views of the Corinthians and then refuting their conclusions. See, for example, 1 Cor. 1.10-17; 3.1-9, 18-23; 4.6-13; 5.9-13; 6.12-20.' See also Tolbert, *Sowing the Gospel,* p. 29, n. 13.

event.[126] The unique sacrifice of Jesus upon the cross, remembered at 'the table of the Lord' (1 Cor. 10.21), replaces all other previous sacrifices, pagan *and* Jewish.

What of part 3 (1 Cor. 10.23–11.1)? Here, Paul does not draw explicitly on the books of the Torah. Rather he recapitulates or synthesizes all that has already been said in his own argument.

That 'all things are lawful' (1 Cor. 10.23 *bis*) is mentioned twice at the beginning of this section. It reflects the two explicit citations of the Law of Moses given already at 1 Cor. 9.9; and 10.7. However, the point that all things which are lawful do not 'build up' (1 Cor. 10.23) forms an *inclusio* with section A, part 1, where Paul has told us that it is 'love [which] builds up' (1 Cor. 8.1).[127] For Paul, love is superior to the law.

In the final part (1 Cor. 10.23–11.1), Paul gives two further practical examples of the principle of caring for the weak set out in section A, part 2 (1 Cor. 8.7-13) and Section B (1 Corinthians 9): (1) care for your unbelieving brother or sister by eating what is set before you 'without raising any question' about the source of the food (1 Cor. 10.25, 27); and (2) *if* someone informs you that it has been offered in sacrifice, care for that person's conscience by not eating, and care for your own monotheistic belief (1 Cor. 10.28).

Because of the brevity of Paul's conclusion, scholars have sometimes missed the power of his message and his literary creativity: 'Be imitators of me, as I am of Christ' (1 Cor. 11.1). Already alerted to Paul's use of Leviticus 10, we find the principle of imitation in Lev. 11.44: [God says] 'be holy, for I am holy (καὶ ἅγιοι ἔσεσθε ὅτι ἅγιός εἰμι ἐγὼ κύριος ὁ θεὸς ὑμῶν)'. This reference to holiness in imitation of God occurs in Leviticus in the context of laws about eating and drinking, and defilement and monotheism (Lev. 11.31-47; ἐγώ εἰμι occurs 4 times in two verses, 11.44, 45, and 22 other times in Leviticus).

That Paul is rewriting this element of Leviticus 11 here is confirmed by a distinctive detail. In Leviticus 11, the people are twice commanded thus: 'do not defile (μιακίνω) yourselves' (Lev. 11.43, 44). Nowhere else *in the whole of the Torah* is the issue of defilement phrased thus, such that it indicates the people's responsibility for their own defilement. Only in 1 Cor. 8.7b (μολύνω), *in the whole of Paul's letters*, is there a reference to people as being 'defiled', albeit by a different verb form.[128] This detail affirms Roy E.

---

126. Davis, *Antithesis*, p. 37. Regarding Paul's method of working with a 'text-group', Stockhausen observes that, 'thus the Torah narrative is brought into Paul's contemporary world in such a way that Paul can pass a critical judgment on it on the basis of other scriptural passages and accepted interpretative procedures'. See Stockhausen, '2 Corinthians 3', p. 158.

127. Gregory W. Dawes, 'The Danger of Idolatry: First Corinthians 8.7-13', *CBQ* 58 (1996), pp. 82–109 (102).

128. Dawes, 'Danger of Idolatry', p. 105.

Ciampas's conclusion about Paul's use of Old Testament Scripture, namely, that, 'at times an echo may be condensed into a significant word'.[129]

The analysis given in this chapter regarding the use of the Torah in 1 Corinthians accords with Koch's analysis of the way in which Paul uses the Old Testament in general: 'On the basis of a fundamentally changed horizon of understanding because of the eschatological acting of God in Christ, Paul claims the texts anew as evidence of the gospel ... '.[130]

On the issue of eating idol food, Paul writes to the Corinthian community in order to correct misconstrued theology and pastoral practice. This section of 1 Corinthians indicates there were some in the community who did not yet understand the radical nature of the sacrifice of Jesus, renewed at the table of the Lord. The highly sensitive and exhortative manner in which Paul handles the subject indicates that it was a highly sensitive and emotive issue in the community. The sacrifice of Jesus replaces all previous religious sacrifices. Until such time as they do understand this, and, concomitantly, that idol food and idol worship is useless in itself, Paul exhorts them not to scandalize those who do not yet understand this relativity by eating idol food socially. Such restraint is an act of love (1 Cor. 8.1, 3).

It is useful to restate briefly the techniques used by Paul in rewriting parts of the Torah in 1 Cor. 8.1–11.1.

In the above sample of complex rewriting, the more simple techniques used include parallel vocabulary and themes, in parallel order. A more complex technique dealt with briefly includes some distinctive details shared between Paul's letter and parts of the Torah. The more complex techniques which are dealt with in more detail are as follows:

*Torahization by Conflation*: Paul torahizes Section A (1 Cor. 8.1-13) by conflating words (vocabulary-clusters) and themes in his rewriting of Genesis 3–4; and Deuteronomy 4–6. He torahizes Section A[1] (1 Cor. 10.1-13) by conflating several Scripture references, sometimes from different sources, in the creation of his own text. His references to the Torah are thematically related. They centre on the issue of Israel's idolatry in the wilderness. All are taken from the central books of the Torah – Exodus (12–14; 17; 32); Leviticus (10–11); and Numbers (11–25).

*Elaboration*: The whole of Section B (1 Corinthians 9) is an elaboration of the commitment given by Paul in Section A (1 Cor. 8.13) to abstain from eating meat for the sake of his weak brother(s).

---

129. Ciampa, *Presence*, p. 28
130. Koch, *Die Schrift*, p. 352.

*Torahization by Correction*: Paul uses Leviticus 10 as a source for his argument in Section A$^1$, part 2 (1 Cor. 10.14-22), to correct the issue regarding the efficacy of Israel's sacrifices as presented in Exodus 32. Such sacrifices are ineffective, according to Aaron (Lev. 10.19). Paul draws upon this correction in order to correct the people of Corinth on the issue of the eating of idol food. Paul corrects not only those who think pagan sacrifices are valid; he also corrects those who think Jewish sacrifices are valid. Only partaking at the table of the Lord is acceptable now, according to Paul.

*Synthesis*: Section A$^1$, part 3 (10.23–11.1) is a synthesis of all that has gone before (1 Cor. 8.1–10.22).

*Systematic Rewriting*: While the techniques by which Paul rewrites the Torah vary in this unit, he is consistent in continuously drawing upon some part of the Torah in a systematic way, most especially Deuteronomy, which he draws on for the entire unit.

## 3. *Conclusion*

The aim of this chapter has been to demonstrate that the methods and techniques used by Graeco-Roman authors to incorporate earlier sources into their works are also found reflected in Jewish sacred works.

To this end we examined evidence from two texts of different genres and eras – the book of Tobit, a Jewish romance (300–200 BCE), and Paul's First Letter to the Corinthians (c. 55 CE). In both cases, we first applied and satisfied the primary external criteria outlined above. Then we applied the internal criteria for demonstrating literary dependence based on the evidence of the text.

In the texts selected, we find that some techniques are used by both authors to achieve their literary and theological purposes. These include: parallel vocabulary, themes and events, in parallel order; distinctive details in the form of shared particular words; conflation and vocabulary-clusters. Other techniques used by one or other author include: abbreviation, correction, distillation, distribution, elaboration, framing, *inclusio* and synthesis.

As with some of the Graeco-Roman texts examined above (Virgil's rewriting of Homer's epics in the *Aeneid* and Livy's rewriting of part of Polybius for his *History of Rome*), we found evidence of systematic rewriting in both sacred Jewish texts examined.

In each case, an increased awareness of *how* and *why* an author uses his earlier source(s) increased our understanding of his literary agenda. Of the two Jewish works sampled, the shared key effect of the rewriting was the Torahization of the text, albeit for different purposes. In Tobit,

Torahization was used to boost a community in exile; in 1 Corinthians, it was used to correct the theology and practice of a community in relation to eating idol food.

The above provides the contemporary hearer/reader of texts from the Jewish world with an insight into the wonderful skill, creativity and, sometimes, complex use of sources by ancient authors.

Part 2

MATTHEW'S USE OF MARK AS A SOURCE

# Chapter 4

## MATTHEW'S USE OF MARK AS A SOURCE

Matthew's use of Mark as a literary source is a thesis far more often presumed than demonstrated by scholars.[1] Despite detailed research on the matter of the similarities and differences between Matthew and Mark as is found in commentaries such as those of Ulrich Luz,[2] there has been little in-depth research into and analysis of Matthew's overall literary and theological agenda reflected in his rewriting of Mark.[3]

The aim of this chapter is, first, to examine the issue of the genre of Matthew and his Markan source as this affects greatly our understanding of *how* and *why* Matthew uses Mark; and secondly, to provide initial evidence of Matthew's use of 'Greco-Roman rather than strictly Palestinian Jewish literary conventions' in his rewriting of this source.[4]

These matters will be examined under the following headings:

1. Matthew and Mark: The Same Genre and Sub-Genre
2. Matthew Rewrites Mark

---

1.  Lohr noted, several decades ago that, 'the form-critical method ... has had the disadvantage of shifting our interest from Mt, Mk, and Lk to the isolated, individual units of the synoptic material. As a result, comparatively little attention has been paid to the process by which the synoptic Gospels were given their eventual form. This is mainly due to ... the view that it is sufficient to have distinguished Mk and Q in order to understand the composition of Mt and Lk. This neglect is, I believe, unwarranted, because the individual message of each Gospel can only be understood in function of its total structure.' See Lohr, 'Oral Techniques', pp. 403–404.

2.  Ulrich Luz, *Matthew 1–7: A Commentary* (trans. Wilheim C. Linss; CC; Minneapolis: Fortress Press, 1989); *idem*, *Matthew 8–20: A Commentary* (trans. James E. Crouch; HCHCB; Minneapolis: Fortress Press, 2001).

3.  Richard C. Beaton notes this: 'However one dissects Matthew, a comparison with the written souces to which we have access deomonstrates that Matthew's interest is to compose a new gospel. While this may not be clear when examining the minute adjustments, it becomes evident when one considers the consistent thematic changes.' We find this to be true, as you will see below. See Richard C. Beaton, 'How Matthew Writes', in Bockmuehl and Hagner (eds), *Written Gospel*, pp. 116–34 (134).

4.  Keener, *John*, I, p. 25, and n. 212.

## 1. *Matthew and Mark: The Same Genre and Sub-Genre*

We turn first to the issue of the genre of Matthew. Any examination of the genre of a text must be 'set in its historical context'.[5] The generic expectations of that context must be discerned because such expectations are indispensable to the proper interpretation of a text. This is so most especially in relation to texts that come from a very different period and environment than our own.[6]

A genre, by definition, cannot be wholly unique – or else it would be un-interpretable.[7] Charles H. Talbert explains why:

> It is the particular text's participation in the universal type or genre that gives it a first level of meaning. The particular text's transformation of the genre is then seen as a further way of saying something about the meaning of the document as a whole. An author communicates not only through a system of shared conventions (a genre), but also through modifications of those conventions. [8]

The closest literary analogues to Matthew in terms of genre are the other Gospels.[9] We concur with the earliest and perhaps the most consistent

---

5.  Burridge, *What Are the Gospels?*, p. 48.

6.  Burridge, *What Are the Gospels?*, pp. 61, 255; P.L. Shuler, 'The Genre(s) of the Gospels', in David L. Dungan (ed.), *The Interrelations between the Gospels* (BETL, 95; Leuven: Leuven University Press, 1990), pp. 459–83 (459). See also Tolbert, *Sowing the Gospel*, p. 48.

7.  The view of R. Bultmann, *The History of the Synoptic Tradition* (trans. John Marsh; Oxford: Blackwell, 1963), that the Gospel form was a unique (*sui generis*) literary genre devised by the evangelists is now generally disregarded because he compared the Gospels with modern rather than ancient biographies. More recently, Tolbert writes: 'However, without that theological impetus [New Hermeneutic of the 1950' and 1960's] and with a clearer understanding of the sociological function of genre in providing the common ground necessary to make texts intelligible to readers, the assertion of a totally new, or unique genre for the Christian Gospels has little to recommend it.' See Tolbert, *Sowing the Gospel*, p. 56. See also M. Eugene Boring, 'Matthew', in E. Keck Leander *et al.* (eds), *The New Interpreters Bible* (Nashville: Abingdon, 1995), VIII, pp. 87–505 (109); R.A. Burridge, 'About People, by People, for People: Gospel Genre and Audiences', in Bauckham (ed.), *Gospel for All Christians*, pp. 113–45 (121); Shuler, 'Genre(s)', pp. 463–64; Michael E. Vines, *The Problem of Markan Genre: The Gospel of Mark and the Jewish Novel* (SBLAB, 3; Atlanta: SBL, 2002), p. 8.

8.  Charles H. Talbert, *What Is a Gospel?: The Genre of the Canonical Gospels* (Macon, GA.: Mercer University Press, 2nd edn, 1985), p. 11. Cox posits a wise caution: 'In order to define the genre of Graeco-Roman biography, we must abandon the notion that an intricate, standard biographical form was developed and passed through the centuries'. See Cox, *Biography*, p. 54.

9.  Klyne Snodgrass summary of the use of the term 'gospel' in the Gospels is helpful: 'Matthew uses *euangelion* only four times, twice in summary statements and twice reporting sayings of Jesus [4.23; 9.35; 24.14; 26.13], and *euangelizesthai* only once (in a statement from Jesus). Mark uses *euangelion* seven times (excluding 16.15), five in sayings of Jesus and does not use the verb at all. Luke does not use the noun at all (although he uses it twice in Acts but

scholarly hypothesis: Matthew and the other canonical Gospels belong to the broad[10] Graeco-Roman category of *ancient bioi* (Lt., *Vitae*).[11] This is how Jewish Christian readers would have understood 'works concerning primary characters'.[12]

Studies now show that the genre of ancient *bioi* was 'an extremely flexible one'.[13] It can be seen at times to overlap with several other evolving ancient genres such as poetry, drama and, in particular, historiography.[14] Talbert provides a good working definition of the genre of ancient *bioi*: 'ancient biography is prose narration about a person's life, presenting supposedly historical facts which are selected to reveal the character or essence of the individual, often with the purpose of affecting the behaviour of the reader'.[15]

uses *euangelizesthai* ten times, four of which are sayings of Jesus. John uses neither the noun nor the verb.' See Klyne Snodgrass, 'The Gospel of Jesus', in Bockmuehl and Hagner (eds), *Written Gospel*, pp. 31–44 (31–22). See also John R. Donahue and Daniel J. Harrington, *The Gospel of Mark* (SPS, 2; Collegeville, MN.: Liturgical Press, 2002), pp. 13–14.

10. David Aune, *The New Testament in Its Literary Environment* (Philadelphia: Westminster, 1987), pp. 46–76. For an extensive list, see Keener, *John*, I, p. 11, n. 87. Even among scholars who regard the Gospels as belonging to the genre of ancient biography, there are differences as to which particular category of this genre they belong. For example, Helmut Koester regards the Gospels as aretalogical biographies. See Helmut Koester, 'Romance, Biography, and Gospel' (Working Paper for the Task Force on the Genre of the Gospels; SBL, 1972), p. 147, cited in Talbert, *What Is a Gospel?*, p. 9, n. 34. See also Moses Hadas and Morton Smith, *Heroes and Gods: Spiritual Biographies in the Greco-Roman World* (New York: Harper & Row, 1965); Morton Smith, 'Prolegomena to a Discussion of Aretalogies, Divine Men, the Gospels, and Jesus', *JBL* 90 (1971), pp. 174–99. P.L. Shuler regards them as encomium biographies. See P.L. Shuler, *A Genre for the Gospels: The Biographical Character of Matthew* (Philadelphia: Fortress Press, 1982), and *idem*, 'Genre(s)', p. 462.

11. C.W. Votaw, 'The Gospels and Contemporary Biographies in the Greco-Roman World', *AJT* 19 (1915), pp. 45–49; J. Drury, 'What Are the Gospels?' *ExpTim* 87 (1976), pp. 324–28; Tolbert, *Sowing the Gospel*, p. 58, and n. 33; Talbert, *What Is a Gospel?*, pp. 15–17; Donald A. Hagner, *Matthew 1–13* (WBC, 33A; Dallas, TX: Word Books, 1993), p. lvii; G.N. Stanton, 'Matthew: ΒΙΒΛΟΕ ΕΥΑΓΓΕΛΙΟΝ ΒΙΟΕ?', in F. van Segbroeck, C.M. Tuckett, G. van Belle, and J. Verheyden (eds), *The Four Gospels 1992: Festschrift Frans Neirynck* (3 vols.; Leuven: Leuven University, 1992), II, pp. 1187–1201 (1201); David E. Aune, 'Greco-Roman Biography', in David E. Aune (ed.), *Greco-Roman Literature and the New Testament: Selected Forms and Genres* (SBLSBS, 21; Atlanta: Scholars Press, 1988), pp. 107–26; Burridge, 'About People', p. 123; Craig S. Keener, *A Commentary on the Gospel of Matthew* (Grand Rapids: William B. Eerdmans, 1999), p. 2.

12. Keener, *John*, I, p. 4; Shuler, 'Genre(s)', p. 465.

13. Pelling, 'Plutarch's Adaptation', p. 139. See Burridge, *What Are the Gospels?*, pp. 68, 188.

14. Keener, *John*, I, p. 13; Brodie, 'Greco-Roman Imitation', p. 27.

15. Talbert, *What Is a Gospel?*, p. 17. Burridge notes that Plutarch, in his famous introduction to the *Alexander* (1.1–3), distinguishes clearly between history (ἱστορία) and *bioi*. However, an analysis of this work and his other lives shows that in practice Plutarch himself does not implement it. See Burridge, *What Are the Gospels?*, pp. 63–64.

One comment on the above definition is in order. The qualification of 'historical facts' with 'supposedly' may lead one to think that because ancient biographers invented (*inventio*) some *historical-like* facts,[16] they had little regard for actual historical facts. This has not been found to be the case. Craig S. Keener explains:

> [And] given the Gospel's basic genre, Matthew's literary method is inseparable from his presuppositions as a biographer/historian. Because ancient biography normally included some level of historical intention, historical questions are relevant in evaluating the degree to which Matthew was able to achieve the intention his genre implies. This does not require us to demand a narrow precision regarding details, a precision foreign to ancient literature, but to evaluate the general fidelity to substance.[17]

The importance of the historical dimension of *bioi* must be taken seriously.[18] It moves us to qualify the naming of the generic nature of the Gospels with the term 'historical', such that they may be described as a type of ancient *historical bioi* (cf. Acts 10.36-37).[19]

Burridge provides perhaps the most definitive analysis of the genre of the Gospels in recent times. In order to settle the question of whether or not the Gospels can be classified as ancient *bioi*, he sets up a clear methodology to address the matter.[20] He searches for the most common generic characteristics of the genre from ten well-known sample *bioi* texts. He takes five such texts that date from the emergence of the genre to just before the arrival of the Gospels, and five that date from immediately after the Gospels. He categorizes his research under the following four headings: (1) Opening Features; (2) Subject; (3) External Features; and (4)

---

16. Keener, *John*, I, pp. 16–17.

17. Keener, *Matthew*, p. 2. See Cox, *Biography*, p. 8; and Aune, 'Biography', p. 125.

18. P. Stuhlmacher clearly does not appreciate the degree of overlap among the ancient genres of *bioi* and historiography when, in critiquing P. Shuler's work on the genres of the Gospels, he writes: 'It is difficult to conceive how these conventions of "history" and "doctrine/teaching" can be brought together with the genre of the Βίος.' See P. Stuhlmacher, 'The Genre(s) of the Gospels: Response to P.L. Shuler', in David L. Dungan (ed.), *The Interrelations between the Gospels* (BETL, 95; Leuven: Leuven University Press, 1990), pp. 484–94 (487–88).

19. Keener, *John*, I, pp. 25, 34. See *idem*, *Matthew*, pp. 8–36, 51–68.

20. Burridge, *What Are the Gospels?*, pp. 241–42. The objective of Burridge's work is not 'primarily taxonomic' as Vines would have us believe. Labels, well used, distil in one or a few words what may be unpacked subsequently in pages or volumes. Burridge provides ample evidence to warrant his terminology. See Vines, *Markan Genre*, p. 29. Our thesis that the Gospels can be regarded as ancient *bioi* does not exclude the fact that elements or aspects of them may *also* be otherwise regarded.

Internal Features. He then analyses the Gospels according to his findings, and the cumulative evidence yields a positive result.[21]

Here we will provide an overview of Burridge's findings. We will also supplement these.[22] A clear understanding of the nature of the texts leads to a clearer understanding of the way in which Matthew uses Mark as a source. Obviously, not every feature will be found in every text to the same degree in the *bioi* compared.

1. Opening Features: Like most Graeco-Roman *bioi*, Matthew (so Mark) places the name of the subject at the very start – Jesus Christ (Mt. 1.1; cf. Mk 1.1).[23] Like Plutarch, he goes straight into the subject's ancestry (Mt. 1.1-17; Plutarch, *Cato Yng.* 1.1; *Ant.* 1.1; *Eum.* 1.1).[24]

2. Subject: The dominance of the focus upon one subject is the *key* element that distinguishes *bioi* from other genre types.[25] An analysis of the subjects of the verbs in Matthew demonstrates the dominance of one main subject, namely, Jesus. In Matthew, Jesus is subject of 17.2 per cent of the verbs (cp. Mark, 24.4 per cent), as compared to the other main characters, for example, 8.8 per cent, for the disciples (cp. Mark, 12.2 per cent) and 4.4 per cent for the priests, scribes and Pharisees (cp. Mark, 5 per cent).[26] This is comparable to the results of other ancient *bioi*. For example, in Xenophon's *Agesilaus*, the main subject's name, Agesilaus, is the subject of 18.7 per cent of the sentences. In Plutarch's *Caesar*, Caesar appears in 34.4 per cent and Pompey in 13.9 per cent; while in the *Pompey*, Pompey occurs as the subject of 35.8 per cent, with Caesar occurring in only 10.9 per cent.[27] Such evidence demonstrates that 'the freedom to select and edit sources to produce the desired picture of the subject is another feature shared by both the Gospels and the Graeco-Roman Βίοι.[28]

---

21. As with the criteria outlined above for establishment of an author's use of sources, Burridge notes that some criteria are primary and indispensable whereas others are secondary or optional. See Burridge, *What Are the Gospels?*, pp. 44, 111–12.

22. For an introduction to the issue of the genre of the Gospels, see Graham N. Stanton, *The Gospels and Jesus* (Oxford: Oxford University Press, 2nd edn, 2002), pp. 13–18.

23. Burridge, *What Are the Gospels?*, pp. 113, 134, 161–62.

24. Burridge, *What Are the Gospels?*, pp. 162, 194–95.

25. See ch. 2, section 3. b. 2. above. See Burridge, *What Are the Gospels?*, p. 141; and Talbert, *What Is a Gospel?*, p. 16.

26. Burridge, *What Are the Gospels?*, pp. 196–97.

27. Burridge, *What Are the Gospels?*, p. 163.

28. Burridge, *What Are the Gospels?*, p. 205. Gerd Theissen, who had considered the genre of Graeco-Roman *bios* to be 'alien to Jewish literature' (1999), appears to have revised his position (2003). In a later publication, he suggests that the Gospel is a relative of the genre of *bioi*. See Gerd Theissen, *A Theory of Primitive Christian Religion* (London: SCM Press, 1999), p. 169, and *idem*, *Introduction to the New Testament* (Mineapolis: Fortress Press, 2003), pp. 1–13.

In terms of the allocation of space, Burridge points out that the issue of the relatively small attention given to the early life of Jesus and then the large concentration of space given to the passion and death of Jesus (Matthew, c. 15 per cent) can no longer be used as an argument against the Gospels being classified as ancient *bioi*, as similar dominance is found in several such texts. In Xenophon's *Agesilaus*, the first forty years of the chief subject's life before he became king is covered in one paragraph (1-4) while in Plutarch's *Cato the Younger* the end of Cato's life gets the greatest attention in terms of volume of narrative – over a sixth (17.3 per cent).[29]

3. External Features: The following, Burridge found, are among the dominant external generic features of ancient *bioi*: mode of representation, size and length, language, structure or sequence, literary units, use of sources, and methods of characterization. All of these features are clearly discernible in Matthew.

In terms of mode, Matthew (so all the Gospels) is written in the mode of continuous prose narrative like ancient *bioi*.[30] In terms of length, ancient *bioi* range usually between 10,000 to 20,000 words in length.[31] Such medium-length scrolls or books, by ancient standards,[32] would have taken about two hours to be heard/read in a single sitting.[33] Matthew has 19,417 words (Mark 11,984; Luke 20,633).[34] Xenophon's *Agesilaus* has 7,558 words. While Plutarch's parallel *Lives* average in length at about 10,000 or 11,000 words,[35] his *Anthony*, *Alexander* and *Pompey* have about 19,000 to 20,000 words, and so are very close in size to Matthew.[36]

According to P. Stuhlmacher, 'the literary and rhetorical ability needed for the composition of *vitae* in the Hellenistic period could be acquired only in the highest levels of the Greek educational system'.[37] While the structure used by Matthew reflects a high degree of sophistication (as we shall see below), his language (so all the Gospels) is found to be 'within the range of contemporary Koiné'.[38] The use of less sophisticated Greek may be accounted for by the literary style of the author and/or his aim to reach

29.   Burridge, *What Are the Gospels?*, pp. 137, 139, 164–65, 197.

30.   Burridge, *What Are the Gospels?*, p. 199 and pp. 117, 138, 168, 199.

31.   Burridge, *What Are the Gospels?*, pp. 139, 200.

32.   Burridge notes that after the Alexandrian library reforms, an average scroll was from 30 to 35 feet and could hold up to 25,000 words of a text of any given genre. See Burridge, *What Are the Gospels?*, p. 118 and n. 29.

33.   Burridge, *What Are the Gospels?*, p. 139.

34.   This count based on the Gospels in NA[27]. See Burridge, *What Are the Gospels?*, p. 199.

35.   Burridge, *What Are the Gospels?*, pp. 169, 200.

36.   Burridge, *What Are the Gospels?*, p. 169.

37.   Stuhlmacher, 'Genre(s)', p. 486.

38.   Burridge, *What Are the Gospels?*, p. 210, and see also pp. 147, 180–81.

as widespread an audience as possible.[39] Such an aim is affirmed by Matthew's choice of the codex format.

Wayne Meeks' research shows that the Gospel of Matthew and all of the Gospels emerged in the context of urban Christian communities that included a broad range of social strata, excluding the most upper and lower levels.[40] Burridge confirms that such communities were certainly not outside the reach of the genre of *bioi*.[41]

Matthew's structure follows the typical convention of *bioi*, that is, it has an 'exterior framework of a chronological sequence with topical material inserted'.[42] Xenophon's *Agesilaus* is organized in two parts, as noted above: part 1 is a chronological account of the words and deeds of the subject's life (πράξεις) and part 2 is a treatment of his character or essence (ἦθος) arranged by topics.[43] While subsequent authors of *bioi* did not strictly adhere to the division,[44] the two elements are found in the works of biographers, such as Plutarch and Suetonius up to the imperial era.[45] For Plutarch, chronology formed the main organizing framework for most of his *bioi* (dubbed 'chronological biography').[46] However, for Suetonius, the extent of the chronological data was minimal, often including either vague or inaccurate details.[47] He arranged the materials

---

39. *Contra* Stuhlmacher, 'Genre(s)', pp. 486–87. Martin Hengel notes that, 'non-literary, simple Greek knowledge or competency in multiple languages was relatively widespread in Jewish Palestine including Galilee, and a Greek-speaking community had already developed in Jerusalem shortly after Easter ... [and] "Hellenists" driven out of Jerusalem, soon preached their message in the Greek language'. See Martin Hengel, 'Eye-Witness Memory and the Writing of the Gospels', in Bockmuehl and Hagner (eds), *Written Gospel*, pp. 70–96 (89).

40. Wayne A. Meeks, *The First Urban Christians: The Social World of the Apostle Paul* (New Haven: Yale University Press, 1983), pp. 51–73.

41. Burridge, *What Are the Gospels?*, p. 214. Cicero notes the popularity of history among the uneducated in his day (*Cael.* 71). See Woodman, *Rhetoric*, pp. 254–55.

42. Burridge, *What Are the Gospels?*, p. 202.

43. See Ch. 2, section 3. b. 2. above. See also Burridge, *What Are the Gospels?*, pp. 139–40.

44. Cox makes a helpful distinction between structure and literary units: 'The hero's acts are depicted through the use of a variety of specific literary units (anecdotes, maxims, discourses, and catalogs). Structure has become not a literary pattern or skeleton but a pastiche of literary forms that the biographer uses to coordinate the elements of his ideal with the activities of his hero.' See Cox, *Biography*, pp. 57–58.

45. Cox, *Biography*, pp. 8–9.

46. Burridge, *What Are the Gospels?*, p. 170

47. This sometimes led to a mix of tenses. Hence it counters the position of Judith Lieu, who states that 'the mix of present and future tenses [in John] (e.g. 14.17-24; 15.18-27) ... challenges the historiographical conventions of the *bios* genre with which the Gospels are now frequently aligned'. See Judith Lieu, 'How John Writes', in Bockmuehl and Hagner (eds), *Written Gospel*, pp. 171–83 (174).

topically within a 'birth-to-death envelope'[48] type of chronological frame (dubbed 'topical biography').[49]

In chronological biography, authors followed the convention of placing the period of the subject's most outstanding achievements (*akmē*) in the mature period of his life. The subject's brilliance was perceived to be the culmination of the factors that shaped the earlier part of his life. In topical biography, the entire life of the subject was demonstrated to reflect some unique single trait from birth to death.[50]

Matthew presents the deeds (*praxeis*) and the essence (*ēthos*) of the chief subject, Jesus, in a more systematic way than Mark, but not quite in the bi-part mode of Xenophon. He orders his material topically, for example, grouping the miracles (e.g., chs 8–9) and similar teachings of Jesus (e.g., ch. 10, Missionary Discourse; ch. 18, Community Discourse). He adds a mythic-type infancy narrative, not present in his model Mark, thus creating the 'birth-to-death envelope'[51] that is typical of ancient topical *bioi*. He presents Jesus as *the* supreme Wisdom figure[52] and miracle worker,[53] whose outstanding achievement (*akmē*) – salvation through the cross – was evident from his birth (Mt. 1.23; 26.39).[54] Thus in terms of content, Matthew's transformation of Mark brings him closer to the Seutonian-type topical biography genre than his model, Mark.[55]

Finally, in terms of literary units, Burridge notes that as a result of the work of scholars such as M. Dibelius, V. Taylor and R. Tannehill, we can be sure that the combination of several types of literary units such as stories, *logia* and discourses found in the Synoptic Gospels is very similar to the basic literary units used by ancient *bioi*.[56]

---

48.   Cox, *Biography*, pp. 54–57. Gavin B. Townend notes that, 'the *Caesars* differ from earlier works, as from the nearly contemporary *Lives* of Plutarch, in being arranged *per species* rather than chronologically: after a section on the subject's ancestors, a chronological passage outlines his life from birth to accession; then his activities and characteristics are treated as if under a series of rubrics, varied according to the individual and illustrated with a number of relevant anecdotes; and the chronological sequence is resumed for an account of his death, sometimes followed by a description of his physical and other personal peculiarities'. See Gavin B. Townend, 'Suetonius Tranquillus, Gaius', *OCD* (2nd edn), pp. 1020–21.

49.   Townend, 'Suetonius', p. 1020.

50.   Cox, *Biography*, pp. 56–57.

51.   Cox, *Biography*, pp. 54–57.

52.   Keener, *John*, I, p. 51 and n. 450.

53.   Smith, 'Prolegomena', pp. 174–199.

54.   Jack Dean Kingsbury notes that Matthew 'consistently designates Jesus the new-born King as "the child" (*to paidion*; cf. Matt 1.8-9, 11, 13-14, 20-21)'. See Jack Dean Kingsbury, *Matthew: Structure, Christology and Kingdom* (London: SPCK, 1975), p. 12.

55.   Burridge, *What Are the Gospels?*, pp. 249, 254. See M. Eugene Boring, 'Matthew', in E. Keck Leander *et al.* (eds), *The New Interpreters Bible* (Nashville: Abingdon, 1995), VIII, pp. 87–505 (111). Kingsbury, *Matthew: Structure*, pp. 37–38; Keener, *John*, I, p. 13.

56.   Burridge, *What Are the Gospels?*, pp. 141–42, 172–73, 202–204.

4. Internal Features: The following are among the dominant internal generic features of ancient *bioi*: geographical setting, topics, atmosphere, quality of characterization, authorial intention or purpose, and social setting or occasion.

Matthew reflects most of the internal generic features of ancient *bioi*. In Matthew, as in ancient *bioi*, geographical settings, for example, are not the chief focus of the units in which they occur. They serve to reveal something more about the chief subject (Mt. 2.1-23; 4.23-25; 16.21; 17.22-23; 20.17-19; Plutarch, *Cato Yng.* 9-15, 34-39; Tacitus, *Agr.* 18, 29-38, 43).[57] Matthew also reflects the chief *topoi* associated with the genre: ancestry (Mt. 1.2-17; cp. Xenophon, *Ages.* 1.2-4; Philo, *On Moses* 1.5), birth (Mt. 1.18–2.23; cp. Philo, *On Moses* 1.8-17),[58] great words and deeds (Matthew 5–7, 'Words'; 8–9, 'Deeds'; Xenophon, *Ages.* 1.7–2.31; Plutarch, *Cato Yng.* 4-73), virtues (e.g., Mt. 9.36; 11.28-30; 12.1-14; Xenophon, *Ages.* 3-9), and, finally, death and its consequences (Matthew 26–28; Xenophon, *Ages.* 10.3-4; 11.16; Philo, *On Moses* 2.291).[59]

The 'atmosphere' of most ancient *bioi* – derived from the tone, mood, attitude and values portrayed – tends to be mostly 'respectful and serious' (e.g., Xenophon, *Ages.*; Philo, *On Moses*; Plutarch, *Cato Yng.*). Such is also found to be the case in Matthew's Gospel.[60] This is intimated from the outset with his solemn presentation of the genealogy of the chief subject, Jesus Christ 'the son of David, the son of Abraham' (Mt. 1.1-17).

The *quality* of characterization in ancient *bioi* tended toward the typical, and even the stereotypical, while at the same time conveying the essence of the real subject. Concerning Suetonius' works, Patricia Cox notes that, 'the individual personality was not entirely subsumed by the type since he personalized his portraits of the emperors by reporting distinguishing traits and habits' (cf. Plutarch, *Pom.* 8).[61] Matthew, using Mark, reflects what was typical about Jesus, while at the same time he selects, organizes and supplements this source in order to reveal something of his own unique sense of the essence of Jesus.

Authors of *bioi* were generally concerned 'to establish precise ranking on the scale' of the divinity of those subjects whom, because of their wisdom or miraculous powers, they considered to be sons of god.[62] In terms of the degree of Jesus' divinity, Matthew amplifies Mark's message

---

57. Burridge, *What Are the Gospels?*, pp. 177–78, 206–207.

58. Some *bioi* do not have birth narratives, such as Xenophon's *Agesilaus*, Satyrus' *Euripedes* and Nepos' *Atticus*. Therefore, this cannot be used to exclude the Gospel of Mark from this genre type. See Burridge, *What Are the Gospels?*, p. 146.

59. Burridge, *What Are the Gospels?*, pp. 146–47, 207–208.

60. Burridge, *What Are the Gospels?*, pp. 147, 182, 211.

61. Cox, *Biography*, p. 13; see also p. 12 and n. 31.

62. Cox cites Plutarch's *De Defectu Oraculorum* as an example. See Cox, *Biography*, p. 34.

that Jesus Christ is the superlative divine being – the 'Son of God' (Mt. 8.29).[63] The nature of the divinity of Matthew's subject is wholly and utterly unique (so all the Gospels).[64] Thus in terms of the nature of the subject, Matthew (so all the Gospels) may be considered peculiar among ancient *bioi*.

The nature or essence of Jesus Christ is described in terms of Christology.[65] Matthew's focus on his subject's essence is such that Christology appears to have provided the 'conceptual foundation'[66] of his text. Matthew's *bios* is 'christology in narrative form'.[67] Moreover, as with Mark, his use of the genre of ancient biography is 'at the service of the portrayal of mystery-filled history'.[68] Matthew, however, amplifies both the Christological and historical dimensions of the material about his subject that he takes from his model, Mark.[69] Relative to Mark, he portrays a more 'Jewish Jesus in continuity with Israel, the "new Moses"

63. So strong is the portrait of Jesus as 'Son of God' that Jack Dean Kingsbury writes: 'Our thesis is that, taken together [that is, the form and meaning of Matthew], they reveal Matthew to be, above all, the Gospel of the Son of God.' See Jack Dean Kingsbury, 'Form and Message of Matthew', *Int* 29 (1975), pp. 13–23 (13). Robert Tannehill writes of Mark that, 'every detail of this narrative has been selected and expressed in such a way that you might accept its fundamental Christological belief, that Jesus is the Christ'. See Robert Tannehill, 'The Gospel of Mark as Narrative Christology', p. 57, cited in Stibbe, *John as Storyteller*, p. 17.

64. Boring writes: 'The Gospels are different from Hellenistic biographies in that they presuppose and mediate a christological understanding of their central character that is different from the Hellenistic heroes and gods. This perspective on the nature of the Gospels is important for interpretation, whether or not one considers the Gospel genre unique.' See Boring, 'Matthew', p. 110. Adela Yabro Collins notes that, 'the earliest datable instance of this use of the "gospel" as a literary form is in the writings of Justin Martyr. Even when "gospel" seems to refer to a document, for example *Did.* 15.3-4 and *2 Clem.* 8.5, the reference seems to be to content rather than a literary form.' See Adela Yarbro Collins, *Is Mark's Gospel a Life of Jesus?: The Question of Genre* (The Père Marquette Lecture in Theology 1990; Milwaukee: Marquette University Press, 1990), pp. 9–10.

65. D. Moody Smith, *Johannine Christianity: Essays on Its Setting, Sources, and Theology* (Edinburgh: T&T Clark, 2nd edn, 1987), p. 175.

66. Donald Senior, 'Directions in Matthean Studies', in David E. Aune (ed.), *The Gospel of Matthew in Current Study: Studies in Memory of William G. Thompson* (Grand Rapids: William B. Eerdmanns, 2001), pp. 5–21 (15–16). See Kingsbury, *Matthew: Structure*, p. 36; Burridge, 'About People', p. 124.

67. Burridge, 'About People', p. 124. Burridge elsewhere notes that, 'the hermeneutical consequences of their biographical genre are essentially Christological'. See Richard A. Burridge, 'Who Writes, Why, and For Whom?', in Bockmuehl and Hagner (eds), *Written Gospel*, pp. 99–115 (113). Senior, following Davies and Allison, and Luz, stresses 'the profound christological focus of Matthew's Gospel'. See Senior, 'Directions', p. 15 and n. 19

68. Thomas L. Brodie, *The Crucial Bridge: The Elijah-Elisha Narrative as an Interpretative Synthesis of Genesis-Kings and a Literary Model for the Gospels* (Collegeville: Liturgical Press, 1999), p. 87.

69. Hagner, *Matthew 1–13*, pp. lxi, lxv-lxxv.

who delivers his teaching from the Mount and then reinterprets the Law'.[70]

Finally, in terms of authorial intention or purpose, 'βίοι are written to fulfil many different intentions'.[71] Some appear to have multiple purposes. All purposes, however, ultimately function to communicate something of the subject with a view to evoking a positive response from the hearer/reader. Plutarch's peripatetic parallel *Lives* served as popular pedagogical and propagandist tools directing the hearers/readers toward the political, religious and moral ideals and virtues exemplified by his chosen heroes.[72] Suetonius' *Lives of the Caesars* was more concerned with the hero's inherent greatness than his particular political or moral ideals. Informing people of the greatness of heroes of their past was a way to edify them in the present to aspire upward to the practice of the good.[73]

Matthew also seeks to edify his readers/hearers and direct them to aspire upward to the good. To this end, Matthew reflects the purposes of several *bioi*: exemplary (Matthew 10 and 18; cp. Xenophon, *Ages.* 10.2), informative (Mt. 1.18; 6.25; 13.52; cp. Philo, *On Moses* 1.1), didactic (Matthew 5–7; cp. Philo, *On Moses* 2.292), apologetic and polemical (Matthew 23; cp. Xenephon, *Ages.* 2.21; 4.4; 5.6; 8.7).[74]

There is, however, also something peculiar about the purpose of the Gospel of Matthew. The account is not only offered for exemplary, informative, didactic, historical and informational purposes. It is also and ultimately designed to evoke a *faith* response in Jesus Christ as agent of God, the ultimate good (cf. Mt. 1.1; 28.19). Such a response requires one to imitate the subject in word and deed, and, through the power of the Spirit (promised), to lead others to do the same (Mt. 28.19). This is a unique dimension not found in the non-Gospel ancient *bioi*.[75]

Matthew and the Gospels, in general terms, 'belong within the overall genre of βίοι.[76] However, in particular, because of their shared content

---

70. Burridge, *What Are the Gospels?*, p. 211; see also, pp. 148–49, 182–84.

71. Burridge, *What Are the Gospels?*, p. 188 and p. 51.

72. Cox, *Biography*, pp. 12, 16; Burridge, *What Are the Gospels?*, p. 150.

73. Talbert, *What Is a Gospel?*, p. 17.

74. Burridge, *What Are the Gospels?*, pp. 214–17; see also, pp. 149–52, 185–88.

75. Burridge, *What Are the Gospels?*, p. 216; Shuler, 'Genre(s)', pp. 466, 471; Martin Hengel, *The Four Gospels and the One Gospel of Jesus Christ: An Investigation of the Collection and Origin of the Canonical Gospels* (London: SCM Press, 2000), pp. 85–87.

76. Burridge, *What Are the Gospels?*, pp. 218–19; Craig A. Evans, 'How Mark Writes', in Bockmuehl and Hagner (eds), *Written Gospel*, pp. 135–48 (148). *Contra* David P. Moessner who writes: 'Accordingly, the Third Gospel *cannot* be adequately construed as a "biography", since all the emphasis upon Jesus' character is subsumed and integrally, intertextually!, interwoven with the characters and events of Israel's past and future hopes of God's reign.' See David P. Moessner, 'How Luke Writes', in Bockmuehl and Hagner (eds), *Written Gospel*, pp. 149–70 (161).

about the unique nature of the chief subject, Jesus Christ, they 'form their own subgenre', appropriately called βίοι 'Iησοῦ.[77]

We will now apply the external criteria outlined above to Matthew.[78] We will then provide initial evidence for Matthew's use of Mark as a source

### a. *External Criteria Applied*

*Primary Criteria*

Primary criteria are about date and accessibility: is Mark's date earlier than Matthew's? Were copies of Mark accessible/available? First, we examine the issue of the date.

### 1. *Date*

Our analysis of the external evidence available to us supports the chronological priority of Mark over Matthew.

*The Dating of Mark: Evidence for a Date in the Late 60s*

The text of Mark, as is the case with each of the Gospels, does not provide us with an explicit date of completion. The earliest external inference comes from Papias' commentary, *Interpretation of the Lord's Sayings* (Λογίων κυριακῶν ἐξηγήσεως) (c. 100-30 CE, *apud* Eusebius, *Hist. Eccl.* 3.39.15, 323 CE).[79] He records that Mark composed his Gospel 'after Peter died'.[80] Papias ascribes his information to an earlier source, 'the Elder'. This evidence indicates that the tradition originated in the last decades of the first century CE.[81] This tradition appears to be supported explicitly by several other witnesses: Justin Martyr, *Dialogue with Tripho* (106, c. 150 CE),[82] the Anti-Marcionite Prologue of Mark (c. 160–80 CE),[83] and Irenaeus, *Against Heresies* (3.1.1-2, c. 180–200 CE).[84]

---

77. Burridge, *What Are the Gospels?*, pp. 246–47, 258.

78. See ch. 1, section 3. above.

79. Papias was bishop of Hierapolis, in Southern Phyrgia in the Province of Asia. See Ben Witherington III, *The Gospel of Mark: A Socio-Rhetorical Commentary* (Grand Rapids: William B. Eerdmans, 2001), p. 22. See also Hagner, *Matthew 1–13*, p. xliv; Davies and Allison, *Matthew*, I, p. 14. For a response to the objections to the tradition of Papias, see Robert H. Gundry, *Mark: A Commentary on His Apology for the Cross* (Grand Rapids: William B. Eerdmans, 1993), pp. 1026–44.

80. Witherington, *Mark*, p. 24.

81. See Seán P. Kealy, *Mark's Gospel: A History of Its Interpretation: From Beginning until 1979* (New York: Paulist Press, 1982).

82. Justin Martyr states that Jesus described James and John as 'sons of thunder', a phrase which occurs only in Mark 3.17 among the Gospels. Outside of Papias, Justin gives us the only other early reference to the Gospel of Mark as Peter's 'memoirs' (*apomnemoneumata*). See Kealy, *Mark's Gospel*, p. 13.

83. F. Howard, 'The Anti-Marcionite Prologue', *ExpTim* (1936), pp. 534–38.

84. Kealy, *Mark's Gospel*, pp. 11–20.

Other slightly later witnesses, however, reflect the tradition that Peter was alive when Mark wrote – Clement of Alexandria (*Hypo.*, c. 180 CE, *apud* Eusebius, *Hist. Eccl.* 6.14.6-7; 2.15.1-2), Origen (c. 200 CE, *apud* Eusebius, *Hist. Eccl.* 6.25.5), Ephraem (d. 373 CE, *Com. Diatess.*), and Jerome (c. 393–95 CE, *On Famous Men*).[85] R.T. France accounts for the inconsistency by pointing out that the references to the 'passing on' of Peter in the Anti-Marcionite Prologue of Mark (*post excessionem Petri*) and Irenaeus (μετὰ τὴν ἔξοδον) may refer to 'relocation rather than death'. [86]

Let us turn to an extract from a letter of Clement, third bishop of Rome (after the apostles), to the Christians at Corinth (c. 96 CE). He states that, 'by reason of jealousy and envy the greatest and most righteous pillars of the church were persecuted and contended even unto death' (*1 Clem.* 5.2).[87] Galatians 2.9 supports the characterization of Peter and Paul as pillars: 'and when James and Cephas and John, who were acknowledged *pillars*, recognized the grace that had been given to me ...' Unfortunately, Clement does not state the date of the occurrence, but his qualification that it was a time when a 'great multitude' was also persecuted in Rome is instructive.[88]

Cornelius Tacitus (c. 55–117 CE), the great Roman historian, describes the brutal persecutions of the Roman Christians by Nero who falsely blamed them for the burning of Rome in 64 CE, in order to suppress rumours that he himself was responsible for it (c. 115 CE, *Annals* 15.44.2-9).[89] Although the persecution of Christians[90] and Jews[91] had already begun before the great fire and lasted for several years after, it was at its most intense just after the occurrence of the great fire in 64 CE.

Scholars discern ample internal evidence in the Gospel of Mark that

---

85. R.T. France, *The Gospel of Mark: A Commentary on the Greek Text* (Grand Rapids: William B. Eerdmans, 2002), pp. 37–38.

86. France, *Mark*, p. 37.

87. Cited in Donahue and Harrington, *Mark*, p. 44.

88. Donahue and Harrington, *Mark*, p. 44.

89. See Suetonius (*Ner.* 16.2). See also Bas M.F. van Iersel, *Mark: A Reader-Response Commentary* (JSNTSup, 164; Sheffield: Sheffield Academic Press, 1998), p. 41.

90. Stephen was persecuted in 37 CE, and James in 62 CE. Cf. Acts 11.19 and 12.2. See van Iersel, *Mark: A Reader-Response*, p. 41.

91. Witherington notes that Nero's portioning the blame on Christians for the fire, and not Jews, suggests that he was the first Roman ruler to distinguish between them. Witherington also notes that a number of prominent Graeco-Romans expressed strong feelings of revulsion towards Judaism and its offshoot which they regarded as *superstitio*, for example, Cicero, Tacitus, Martial, Juvenal, Ovid, Quintilian, Seneca and Plutarch. See Witherington, *Mark*, pp. 34–35. Donahue and Harrington note that, 'since Christianity was perceived by the Romans as either a Jewish sect or an offshoot from Judaism the negative feelings that Romans had toward Jews (and vice versa) at the time were very likely a factor in the persecution of Christians'. See Donahue and Harrington, *Mark*, p. 44.

connects its origin to a situation of persecution.[92] The texts of Mk 8.34-38; 9.42-48; and 13.9-13 reflect aspects about the interrogation and arrest of individual disciples of Jesus by officials *because* they are part of the group that followed him (cf. Mk 4.17; 10.30; Rom. 8.35-36). Bas van Iersel notes that the records concerning the persecution of Jews outside Rome in the works of the Jewish historian, Flavius Josephus (c. 37–100 CE, *J. Ant.*, *J. War*), do not make any reference to the charge of apostasy on account of membership in the Jesus movement.[93] Josephus' accounts tell, rather, of the many persecutions of Jewish civilians by other Jewish civilians for multiple reasons *other* than apostasy.[94] Moreover, at the time of Josephus' writing the followers of Jesus were still regarded as being within Judaism in Palestine.

Thus the background to Mark's references to persecution in texts such as Mark 13 does not point to the situation of Palestine in the 60s CE. Tolbert notes of Mark in general that, 'the occasional attempt by the Gospel to explain, with notable lack of clarity, Jewish customs and practices (e.g., Mk 7.3-4), suggests that the intended audience, and perhaps the author as well, were at some distance from the more established practices of Judaism'.[95]

Most likely the references in Mark 13 point towards Rome (cf. 1 Pet. 5.13). Tacitus records that under the Neronian persecutions in Rome, 'those who confessed that they were members of the Christian sect were arrested first, and then, on their disclosures, a great many others were convicted, not of arson but of hatred of mankind' (*Ann.* 15.44).[96] This echoes very closely the prophecy placed on Jesus' lips in Mk 13.12: 'Brother will betray brother to death, and a father his child, and children will rise against parents and have them put to death'. The charge of hatred of mankind would be understandable in the light of the reality of Mk 13.12. Moreover, Mark has the same charge as Tacitus, 'hatred ... by all'. The roles of victims and protagonists, however, are found in reverse order:

92.   Donahue and Harrington, *Mark*, pp. 43, 382; France, *Mark*, pp. 513–19; Eduard Schweizer, *The Good News according to Mark* (trans. Donald H. Madvig; London: SPCK, 1987), pp. 215, 284; Francis J. Moloney, *The Gospel of Mark: A Commentary* (Peabody, MA: Hendrickson, 2002), pp. 260–61.

93.   Van Iersel cites from Josephus, *J. Ant.* 18.376-79; 20.1-9; *J. War* 2.19-20, 266-70, 284-92, 407-19, 457-68, 477-98, 559-65; 3.9-28; 7.41-62, 437-44. See van Iersel, *Mark: A Reader-Response*, p. 40. See also Hengel, *Four Gospels*, p. 79.

94.   This data does not concur with the attempt of a number of scholars since the 1950s to locate the composition of Mark further east and associate it with events in Palestine during the first Jewish Revolt (66–70 CE). For a list of such scholars, see Donahue and Harrington, *Mark*, p. 44.

95.   Tolbert, *Sowing the Gospel*, p. 36.

96.   Cited in van Iersel, *Mark: A Reader-Response*, p. 41.

in Mark, it is the Christians who are hated by all [humankind], because of Jesus' name (Mk 13.13a).

The beginning of the end of the persecutions in Rome came in 69 CE under the rule of General Vespasian, after the rise and fall of three pretender emperors. He was also responsible for the Roman victory over the Jews in Jerusalem by 73 CE. Some scholars see a reference to this in Mk 13.7: 'when you hear of wars and rumours of wars'. The hearing of wars suggests a more imminent reality, while the phrase 'and rumours of wars' suggests realities that are at a distance. In 68 CE the Romans were three times at civil war, overturning three successive post-Neronian leaders. Along with the trouble in Jerusalem, the Romans were also dealing with 'the concurrent revolts of the Batavians, and other Germanic and Gallic tribes, and the unrest in Britain, Africa, Pontus and on the Danube frontier'.[97] Rumours of the success or otherwise of these wars would have circulated in Rome.

Thus Mk 13.7 best fits the Rome situation of the late 60s CE. Moreover, a Roman provenance for the origin of the Gospel of Mark is supported by the density and location of the references to Peter,[98] and the occurrence of Latinisms that have been found to be unique among Greek texts of the first century.[99]

The cumulative evidence from the extant external witnesses (the patristic texts and Josephus' writings) is corroborated by the internal witness of the Gospel of Mark. Both point towards a dating of the writing of the Gospel of Mark to a general time of persecution and, most likely, to Rome at the time of the 'wars and rumours of wars' in 68 CE. More exact than this we cannot be.[100]

---

97. Van Iersel, *Mark: A Reader-Response*, p. 42. Moreover, van Iersel adds: 'That we have contemporary reports about earthquakes in Italy and hunger riots in Rome may provide an extra-textual confirmation of v. 8b' (p. 42, n. 24).

98. Hengel provides a good summary of the significance of Peter in Mark: Simon Peter is named as a disciple first and last in the Gospel, forming an *inclusio* (1.16; 16.7); of the 43 times Mark mentions the 'disciples', Simon/Peter is mentioned 25 times, 'i.e., as often as in Matthew, which is 70 per cent longer, and where the term "disciples" of Jesus appears around seventy times'. See Hengel, *Four Gospels*, pp. 82–84. Hengel also notes that Peter is cited first in the list of disciples, and is the only one to be given the title Πέτρος and to have a conversation with Jesus, to be addressed by Jesus, to follow Jesus to the palace of the high priest. Hengel adds: 'Moreover a survey of the mentions of Peter in Mark shows that they accumulate at key points in the Gospel: at the beginning of Jesus' activity (ch. 1), at the denouement (chs 8 and 9) and in the passion narrative (ch. 14)' (p. 84).

99. Hengel, *Four Gospels*, pp. 68, 78; van Iersel, *Mark: A Reader-Response*, pp. 33–39.

100. Raymond E. Brown, *An Introduction to the New Testament* (ABRL; New York: Doubleday, 1997), p. 127.

*The Dating of Matthew: Evidence for c. 80 CE*

Our earliest external evidence of the dating of Matthew also comes from
Papias' record of 'the Elder' (*apud* Eusebius).[101] This provides a *terminus
ad quem* for Matthew, as well as Mark.[102] Matthew must have also been
completed by the last decades of the first century CE.

Papias first comments on Mark thus: 'Mark became Peter's interpreter
and wrote accurately (ἀκριβῶς) all that he remembered, not, indeed, in
order (οὐ τάξει), of the things said or done by the Lord' (*apud* Eusebius,
*Hist. Eccl.* 3.39.16). He immediately notes that, 'Matthew for his part
compiled the oracles (τὰ λογία συνετάξατο) in Hebrew dialect and everyone
[interpreted or] translated them as he was able' (3.39.16). The inference
from the order of Papias' comments is that Mark's account preceded
Matthew's. While no Hebrew copy of Matthew remains extant, Papias'
account of Mark as Peter's 'interpreter' who wrote down accurately,
though not in order, and of Matthew as 'compiler', is wholly in accord
with the literary conventions of Graeco-Roman antiquity, as shown above
(cf. Mt. 13.52).[103] Moreover, the detail that 'everyone' made interpret-
ations/translations of Matthew's composition fits the context of book
production in first-century Rome, as noted above.

Later witnesses disagree with the thesis of the priority of Mark among
the Gospels. Clement of Alexandria (150–215/16 CE) states that, 'those
Gospels were written first which include genealogies' (*apud* Eusebius, *Hist.
Eccl.* 6.14.5; cf. Augustine, 345–430 CE, *De Cons. Evang.* 1.2.4.).[104]

How do we evaluate this disagreement among the early witnesses? In
the same context as the above, Eusebius notes that Clement of Alexandria
also says that Peter had authorized the Gospel of Mark to be read in the
churches. This indicates that Clement understood the Gospel of Matthew
to have been composed before Peter died (c. 64/5 CE). This would mean
that the Gospels with the genealogies (Matthew and Luke) would have
had to be written, at the latest, by the early 60s. There is scant evidence to

---

101. Hagner, *Matthew 1–13*, p. xliv. See France, *Mark*, p. 8.

102. According to Eusebius, Papias had become well known during the time of Ignatius
(d. c. 107 CE) and Polycarp (c. 70–155 CE). Moreover, that the historian presents his account
of Papias before the account of the persecutions by Trajan (98–117 CE) leads scholars such as
Davies and Allison to conclude that, 'Papias *may* therefore, have written ca. 100 or before, in
which case Matthew would have to be dated even earlier.' See Davies and Allison, *Matthew*,
I, pp. 128–29.

103. See ch. 1, section 2. above. See also F.G. Downing, 'A Paradigm Perplex: Luke,
Matthew and Mark', *NTS* 38 (1992), pp. 1–28; *idem*, 'Compositional Conventions and the
Synoptic Problem', *JBL* 107 (1988), pp. 69–85; *idem*, 'Redaction Criticism: Josephus'
*Antiquities* and the Synoptic Problem', *JSNT* 8 (1980), pp. 46–65; *idem*, 'Redaction Criticism:
Josephus' *Antiquities* and the Synoptic Problem', *JSNT* 9 (1980), pp. 28–48.

104. Kealy, *Mark's Gospel*, pp. 27 and 243, n. 51.

support this conclusion, although, for several reasons[105] it held sway until the nineteenth century CE.[106]

For internal evidence regarding the dating of Matthew, historical critics point us to the parable of the wedding banquet – Mt. 22.1-14, especially 22.7, which is unparalleled in Mark: 'The king was enraged. He sent his troops, destroyed those murderers, and burned their city'.[107] The account – with its use of the past tense, the brief successive phrases that gives a sense of a series of events that happened intensely and in quick succession, and the movement of the parabolic narrative immediately to the issue of paying taxes to the emperor (Mt. 22.17) – betrays a striking similarity to the events which occurred in Palestine in the late 60s CE.[108] Boring notes that, 'the war of 66–70, and the consequent destruction of Jerusalem, is almost certainly reflected in 22.7. Yet Matthew does not seem to be overwhelmed by the catastrophe, which seems some distance away in both space and time.'[109] Therefore, Matthew may be dated to sometime after the fall of Jerusalem (70 CE), and thus after Mark.

### 2. Accessibility

The Gospel of Mark 'must have circulated widely within ten to twenty years of its origin'.[110] Bauckham demonstrates that the levels of 'mobility and communication in the first-century Roman world were exceptionally high'.[111] In fact, movement by land and sea of people and goods[112] was

---

105. Benedict T. Viviano cites two reasons: 'The Gospel early acquired prestige not only because of its intrinsic merits (e.g., the Sermon on the Mount, chs 5–7) but because it bore the name of the apostle (mentioned 9.9; 10.3).' See Benedict T. Viviano, 'The Gospel according to Matthew', *NJBC*, pp. 630–74 (630). See also Hengel, *Four Gospels*, p. 67.

106. Kealy, *Mark's Gospel*, p. 27.

107. Keener, *Matthew*, p. 43.

108. Davies and Allison conclude that, 'when all has been said, Mt 22.7, while it does not demand a date after AD 70, does strongly imply one'. See Davis and Allison, *Matthew*, I, p. 132. Hagner cites a number of others, along with himself, who support a pre-70 CE dating. He argues that because the language is hyperbolic, as is that of Mt. 24.15-28 (par. Mk 13.14-23), it cannot encode a historical reference. See Hagner, *Matthew 1–13*, pp. lxxiii-iv.

109. Boring, 'Matthew', p. 105. Davies and Allison support this conclusion. See Davies and Allison, *Matthew*, I, pp. 131–32.

110. Gamble, *Books and Readers*, p. 102.

111. Richard Bauckham, 'For Whom Were the Gospels Written?', in Bauckham (ed.), *Gospel for All Christians*, pp. 9–48 (32). Keener notes, following Davies and Allison (*Matthew*, III, p. 700), that 'first century couriers could get a letter from Rome to London in a week ...'. See Keener, *Matthew*, p. 47, n. 143. See also Lionel Casson, *Travel in the Ancient World* (London: George Allen & Unwin, 1974), p. 221.

112. In the assessment of Tolbert, 'the ability of that milieu to establish a common language, *koine* Greek, and a common sensibility, Greek *paideia*, (9) throughout many disparate regions of the known world had revolutionary consequences, three [mobility, insecurity and rhetoric] of which may affect our understanding of the Gospel of Mark', and all the New Testament Scriptures, we may add. See Tolbert, *Sowing the Gospel*, p. 38.

the order of the day across the first-century CE Roman Empire, including Judea.[113]

Evidence of the movement and trading of books, specifically, can be traced back to the fifth century BCE.[114] This exchange was driven chiefly by the requirements of the great Hellenistic libraries,[115] the administrative requirements of the Hellenistic period and the Roman empire,[116] the religious requirements of the Jewish Diaspora,[117] and, in the first century CE, the newly founded Christian movement.[118] Books were a highly marketable commodity, which required the skills of authors, recorders and copyists.

What was peculiar about the literature of the new Jesus-movement was that, while most of the literature of the period took the form of scrolls, including the Jewish Scriptures, it was produced in codex format,[119] a practice that 'originated most probably in the Church of Rome'.[120] Not surprising, when one considers that first-century Rome saw an explosion of commercial book production, as noted above.

The codex was a form of notebook that had been in use for the purpose of everyday secular administration, and commercial and literary memoranda. Its advantage over the scroll was that it was more easily produced and much more portable, especially over long distances.[121] It was also far more adaptable for reading and checking references than the bulkier scroll.[122] Original copies of texts were often composed from authors' memoranda or auditors' notes of oral teaching.[123] Further, multiple copies were made for dissemination by means of direct copying by copiers,

---

113. The routes of ancient Israel have been documented by D.A. Dorsey, *The Roads and Highways of Ancient Israel* (ASORLBNEA; Baltimore: Johns Hopkins University Press, 1991). For a map of the grid of fine roads of Israel at the time of Jesus, see Ninian Smart (ed.), *Atlas of the World's Religions* (Oxford: Oxford University Press, 1999), p. 139.

114. Frederic George Kenyon and Colin Henderson Roberts, 'Books, Greek and Latin', *OCD* (2nd edn), p. 173.

115. Kenyon and Roberts, 'Books', p. 175.

116. Alexander, 'Book Production', p. 89.

117. Gamble, *Books and Readers*, p. 196; Keener, *John*, I, pp. 145-46 and 146, n. 48.

118. Gamble, *Books and Readers*, pp. 95–108. Cf. Acts 2.9-11.

119. Kurt Aland and Barbara Aland, *The Text of the New Testament* (Grand Rapids: William B. Eerdmans, 1989), p. 75. See also David J. Neville, *Mark's Gospel – Prior or Posterior?: A Reappraisal of the Phenomenon of Order* (JSNTSup, 222; Sheffield: Sheffield Academic Press, 2002), p. 124 and n. 37.

120. Alexander, 'Book Production', p. 88.

121. Bauckham, 'For Whom Were the Gospels Written?', p. 29.

122. Alexander, 'Book Production', p. 76.

123. See ch. 3, section 2. b. above. Alexander, commenting on Papias' reference to Mark's method of composition, notes that, 'there are good ancient parallels to the practice of circulating written texts based on author's memoranda or auditors' notes of oral teaching'. She cites, 'Papias *apud* Euseb. *Hist. Eccl.* 3.39; Clem. Alex. *Adumbrationes ad I Petr.* 5.13'. See Alexander, 'Book Production', p. 100 and also n. 84.

a practice which was widespread at the time.[124] Thus what is clear is that a codex such as the Gospel of Mark could have been easily produced, and multiple copies of it made for dissemination, in an environment such as Rome.

How sure are we that Matthew could have access to it? First, Michael B. Thompson explains that, 'many churches were less than a week's travel away from a main Christian network. We know of Jewish precedents for the dissemination of pastoral correspondence between the Jewish authorities and diaspora Jews.'[125] It would thus not take long for the word to spread eastward from Rome that Mark had produced an account about Jesus, especially if it was associated with Peter's preaching.[126] Secondly, where people travelled, texts were transported. The Gospel of Mark was transported to various places, among them, Antioch in Syria where both Matthew and Luke used it as a source.[127] Moreover, John Mark, most likely the author of Mark,[128] had contact with the church in Antioch in Syria[129] ('one of the three or four largest cities in the ancient world'),[130] as had Paul. This adds further weight to the plausibility that Matthew had access to a copy of Mark.[131]

We know from the Letters of Paul that many churches knew what was happening within other churches in other cities (cf. Rom. 1.8; 1 Cor. 11.16; 14.33; Eph. 6.21-22; Col. 4.7-9; 1 Thess. 1.7-9). Missionaries carried such news (cf. Rom. 15.26; 2 Cor. 8.1-5; 9.2-4; Phil. 4.16; 1 Thess. 2.14-16; cf. 3 Jn 5-12). Paul had assumed that each of his letters, while addressed

---

124. Neville, *Mark's Gospel*, p. 119 and also n. 21.

125. Michael B. Thompson, 'The Holy Internet: Communication between Churches in the First Century Generation', in Bauckham (ed.), *Gospel for All Christians*, pp. 49–70 (57). Keener notes that urban Christians travelled (1 Cor. 16.10, 12, 17; Phil. 2.30; 4.18) and relocated to other places (Rom. 16.3, 5). See Keener, *John*, I, p. 42.

126. Thompson, 'Holy Internet', p. 68. See Bauckham, 'For Whom Were the Gospel's Written?', p. 30.

127. Bauckham, 'For Whom Were the Gospel's Written?', p. 12. See Keener, *John*, I, p. 43; Gamble, *Books and Readers*, p. 103.

128. Cf. Acts 12.12, 25; 15.37, 39; Col. 4.10; 2 Tim. 4.11; Phlm. 1.24; 1 Pet. 5.13.

129. Witherington, *Mark*, pp. 24–26; Gundry, *Mark*, pp. 1029–34.

130. Thompson, 'Holy Internet', p. 54.

131. B.H. Streeter, *The Four Gospels* (New York: Macmillan, 1924), pp. 500–23. See Davies and Allison, *Matthew*, I, pp. 143, 147; John L. McKenzie, 'The Gospel according to Matthew', *JBC*, pp. 62–114 (15, 65); Donald Senior, *Matthew* (ANTC; Nashville: Abingdon, 1998), p. 21; Hagner, *Matthew 1–13*, p. 6; Boring, 'Matthew', p. 105; C.K. Barrett, 'The Place of John and the Synoptics within the Early History of Christian Thought', in Denaux (ed.), *John and the Synoptics*, pp. 63–79 (75); Rudolph Schnackenburg, *The Gospel of Matthew* (trans. Robert R. Barr; Grand Rapids: William B. Eerdmans, 2002), p. 5. For a more extended list, see Keener, *Matthew*, p. 41 and n. 122.

to a specific community, would reach others (cf. Rom. 1.7; 16.1-2, 21-23; 1 Cor. 16.19; 2 Cor. 1.1; Gal. 1.2; Phil. 2.25; 4.22; Col. 4.16.).[132] In at least one case, the letter was clearly intended to reach *all* in the community (cf. 1 Thess. 5.27).[133] There is no evidence that it would not have been likewise for Mark.

The New Testament epistles and Luke's Acts indicate the existence of an extensive Christian diaspora-based network from Judea to Rome, as noted above. We know of the hospitality afforded to the travelling preachers, messengers, disciples and texts[134] prior to the time of Mark being written (cf. Acts 2.9-11; Rom. 12.13).[135] The account of the speedy circulation of the letters of Ignatius of Antioch coupled with the evidence of Clement of Rome's ministry of sending out literature to the churches indicates that the tradition of circulating Christian literature continued into the second century CE.[136] It is, therefore, most unlikely that this was any different during the time in between Paul and Ignatius, when Mark would have been circulating.[137]

In the light of the above evidence, it is reasonable – along with scholars, such as C.K. Barrett, Bauckham and Keener – to conclude that Matthew could have used Mark as a major source and could have possessed or had access to a written copy of it.[138]

### Secondary Criteria

Secondary criteria are about establishing the status of a source text and other examples of its use: did Mark enjoy the kind of status that would attract Matthew? Are there analogous instances of the use of gospels? First, the question of the status of Mark.

### 3. *Status of Text*

The likelihood of one text being dependent on another is increased if the former text was held in high regard or was popular in the tradition of the later author. Matthew, bent on writing his own account of the life of Jesus, would have been very interested in acquiring a copy of Mark and

---

132. Keener, *John*, I, p. 42.
133. Thompson, 'Holy Internet', pp. 64–65.
134. Bauckham, 'For Whom Were the Gospels Written?', p. 38.
135. Cf. Rom. 15.23-24; 16.1-2, 23; 1 Cor. 16.6-7, 11; 2 Cor. 7.15; 1 Thess. 4.10; Tit. 1.7-8; Phlm. 1.22; 1 Pet. 4.9; Heb. 13.2.
136. Bauckham, 'For Whom Were the Gospel's Written?', p. 43.
137. Keener, *John*, I, pp. 42–43.
138. Barrett, 'Place of John', p. 68; Bauckham, 'For Whom Were the Gospels Written?', p. 12; Keener, *John*, I, p. 34.

most especially if he knew of its association with Peter (cf. 1 Pet. 5.13)[139] and Paul.[140]

Moreover, the great number of textual witnesses for Mark's Gospel indicates that it was a highly popular text.[141] A list of these witnesses may be found in such catalogues as that of S.C.E. Legg, *Novum Testamentum Graece: Evangelicum Secundum Marcum* (1935).[142]

### 4. *Analogues*

The existence of the Gospel of Luke (c. 80–90 CE) is the most indisputable analogue to Matthew's use of Mark as a source. Tatian's *Diatessaron* (c. 170 CE) is evidence of the continuation of the tradition of compiling a gospel from earlier gospel sources.

## 2. *Matthew Rewrites Mark*

Matthew's use of Mark as a source is an elaborate example of systematic rewriting from the Jewish world of the Roman imperial era. While redaction-critics have done much by way of tracing the additions, omissions and extensive modifications of Matthew's and Luke's rewriting of Mark in order to discern the evangelists respective theological purposes, they say little about *how* Matthew incorporates his Markan source, that is, the ancient literary techniques that he uses. Here we will address (albeit quite briefly) this lacuna.

To this end we will apply to Matthew the internal criteria for establishing literary dependency outlined above.[143] In this section we will examine Matthew's use of Mark under two sub-headings. a. Parallels; and b. Simple Rewriting.

In the next chapter entitled 'Matthew's Judaization of Mark', we will analyse several examples of Matthew's more complex rewriting of Mark.

---

139.  Kealy, *Mark's Gospel*, p. 11. Cf. 1 Tim. 1.5; 5.14; 1 Pet. 5.1, 5.

140.  Donahue and Harrington point to similarities in terminology: for example, the term 'Gospel of God' (cf. Mk 1.14 // Rom. 1.1; 15.16); mention of 'Rufus' (cp. Mk 15.21 // Rom. 16.13); theology (e.g., soteriology, cp. Mk 10.45 // Rom. 3.24); community concerns and structures (e.g., 'clean and unclean', cp. Mk 7.14-23 // Rom. 14.1-23); 'houses' (cp. Mk 10.3 // Rom. 16.1-16). See Donahue and Harrington, *Mark*, pp. 40 and 13–14. See also France, *Mark*, p. 25.

141.  Kealy notes that Marcion's ejection from the church at Rome (c. 144 CE) because of his disapproval of the Gospel of Mark, in favour of Luke and Paul's letters, is a further witness to the fact that Mark's Gospel was highly regarded by the church in Rome at that time. See Kealy, *Mark's Gospel*, p. 13.

142.  S.C.E. Legg, *Novum Testamentum Graece: Evangelicum Secundum Marcum* (Oxford: Clarendon Press, 1935).

143.  See Ch. 1, section 3. above.

### a. *Parallels*

The Gospel of Matthew contains a systematic rewriting of Mark. When one aligns the whole of Matthew beside the whole of Mark one can appreciate immediately that their respective narratives exhibit great similarities in terms of order, vocabulary, themes and events. The synopses or parallel models of the Gospels, such as Kurt Aland's *Synopsis of the Four Gospels* (1982)[144] and the large one-poster type graphic model of the Synoptic Parallels, such as Allan Barr's *A Diagram of Synoptic Relationships* (1976),[145] are helpful aids in noting the similarities and differences between the Gospels.

The high degree of similarity between Matthew and Mark indicates that Matthew was basically a conservative author by ancient standards.[146] Ben Witherington provides a general picture of Matthew's use of Mark:

> [Matthew] takes over more than 90 per cent of his Markan source (606 out of 661 Markan verses), while Luke takes over only a little over 50 per cent. The difference in degree of word for word appropriation of Mark in the pericopae and sayings that Matthew and Luke take over is minimal. Luke uses about 53 per cent of Mark's exact words in the material culled from that source, while the First Evangelist uses about 51 per cent of Mark's exact words of the 606 verses he appropriates.[147]

Matthew mostly follows Mark's order. There are, however, *six* exceptions: all of these are taken from Mark 1–6, and all are used in Matthew 4–12. In each case the transfer is clearly understandable in terms of Matthew's literary and theological agenda (see Table 4.1 below).[148]

---

144. Kurt Aland, *Synopsis of the Four Gospels* (English edn; United Bible Societies, 1982). See Burton H. Throckmorton, Jr., *Gospel Parallels: A Synopsis of the First Three Gospels* (Nashville: Thomas Nelson, 4th edn, 1979); Reuben J. Swanson, *The Horizontal Line Synopsis of the Gospels* (Dillsboro, NC: Western North Carolina Press, 1975).

145. Allan Barr, *A Diagram of Synoptic Relationships* (Edinburgh: T&T Clark, 1976).

146. See Ch. 1, section 2. above.

147. Ben Witherington III, *Jesus the Sage* (Philadelphia: Fortress Press, 1994), p. 214. Richard C. Beaton provides the following data: 'Matthew is conservative in his treatment of his Marcan source. Matthew excludes only seven sections from Mark (1.23-28, 35-39; 4.26-29; 7.32-37; 8.22-26; 9.38-40; 12.41-44), thereby reproducing roughly 80 per cent of the gospel, much of it in close verbal agreement.' See Beaton, 'How Matthew Writes', p. 120. See Burridge, 'Who Writes, Why, and For Whom?', p. 82.

148. As pointed out in Ch. 1, the issue is not whether there are differences, because of course there will be differences between the source text and the later text; the issue is whether the differences are intelligible. See Ch. 1, section 3 above.

Table 4.1: *Matthew's Distribution of Mark 1–6*[149]

| Mark | Matthew |
|---|---|
| 1.1-20 | 3.1–4.22 |
| (1.21) | (4.23-25; 5.1-2) |
| 1.22 | 7.28-29 |
| | 8.2-4 |
| 1.29-34 | 8.14-17 |
| *1.40-45* | |
| | 8.18-34 |
| 2.1-22 | 9.1-17 |
| | 9.18-26 |
| | 9.35 |
| | 10.1-16 |
| 2.23–3.12 | 12.1-16 |
| *3.16-19* | |
| 3.22-30 | 12.24-32 |
| *3.31-35* | 12.46-50 |
| *4.1-34* | 13.1-35 |
| *4.35–5.20* | |
| *5.21-43* | |
| 6.1-6a | 13.53-58 |
| *6.6b* | |
| *6.7-11* | |

Davies and Allison provide a very satisfactory interpretation of Matthew's six transpositions of Mark 1–6:

1.  *Healing of the Leper* (Mt. 8.2-4 // Mk 1.40-45): In the account of the Healing of the Leper, the requirement of Jesus that the cured leper go 'and offer the gift that Moses commanded' (Mt. 8.4b) fits well thematically just after Matthew's first discourse which portrays Jesus as the definitive Moses and exhorts the upholding of the Torah (Matthew 5–7). It also serves to complete the first of three units – 8.1-22, 8.23–9.17 and 9.18-34 – which are formed in the typically Matthean triadic structural pattern[150] in Matthew's

149.  Based on a table provided by Frans Neirynck. See Frans Neirynck, 'The Synoptic Problem', *NJBC*, pp. 587–95 (588). See Davies and Allison, *Matthew*, I, pp. 100–101.

150.  The recognition of the pervasiveness of the triadic patterns in Matthew has largely been the work of Davies and Allison's three-volume commentary on Matthew. To fit a triadic pattern, Davies and Allison regard Mt. 9.18-26 as one miracle account. Mt. 9.18-26 records

collection of miracles in chs 8 and 9. Each of the three units consists of three consecutive miracle stories plus a comment.[151]

2.  *Call of the Twelve* (Mt. 10.1-16 // Mk 3.16-19): Mark's account of the Call of the Twelve is also moved for thematic reasons and serves as suitable introductory material to Matthew's Missionary Discourse.

3.  *Two Miracles* (Mt. 8.18-34 // Mk 4.35–5.20): The miracles of the Calming of the Storm and the Curing of the Gardarene Demoniacs are used by Matthew to create his grand collection of miracle stories and serve to complete the second of the three triadic units mentioned above, namely, Mt. 8.23–9.17.

4.  *Two Healings* (Mt. 9.18-26 // Mk 5.21-43): The two healings stories – of the Woman with the Haemorrhage, and Jairus' Daughter – are also transposed to create Matthew's great miracle collection and to complete the third of the three triadically organized units in this collection mentioned above, namely, Mt. 9.18-34.

5.  *Introduction to the Mission of the Twelve* (Mt. 9.35 // Mk 6.6b): The element about Jesus' noticing the great needs of the people found at the beginning of the Mission of the Twelve in Mark is *elaborated* upon by Matthew. In its new Matthean context it forms an appropriate introduction to the issue of the urgency of harvesting the mission.

6.  *Mission of the Twelve* (Mt. 10.1-16 // Mk 6.7-11): Mark's account of the Mission of the Twelve is also transposed (and *conflated* with Mk 3.16-19) because of its thematic suitability for Matthew's Missionary Discourse.[152]

We begin to notice two key elements of Matthew's literary style – the deliberate creation of an organized literary structure and the gathering together of thematically similar material.

### b. *Simple Rewriting*

Here we will present four examples of the more simple techniques by which Matthew rewrites Mark – omission, variation, addition and conflation – and to what effect.

*Positivization by Omission*: By *omitting* Mark's references to Jesus' emotions – for example, 'after sternly warning him' (Mk 1.17) – Matthew positivizes Mark's portrait of Jesus (Mt. 1.43; cf. also Mt. 1.41; 3.5; 6.6;

---

two miracles but it describes only one of them. Thus Matthew 8–9 may be regarded as both a ninefold and tenfold unit. It is evidence of Matthew's use of poly-structures in the fashioning of sections of his Gospel.

151. Davies and Allison, *Matthew*, I, p. 102. See also II, *idem*, *Matthew*, pp. 6, 66–68, 122–23.

152. Davies and Allison, *Matthew*, I, pp. 101–103.

8.12; 10.14, 21; 14.33).[153] Matthew also omits phrases in Mark that reflect Jesus' inability, ignorance, impatience, or madness: for example, 'he [Jesus] asked him, "Can you see anything?"' (Mk 8.23), and, 'people were saying, "He has gone out of his mind"' (Mk 3.21; see also Mk 1.45; 5.9, 30; 6.5, 38, 48; 7.24; 8.12, 23; 9.16, 21, 33; 11.13; 14.14).[154]

*Positivization by Variation*: By altering a word or phrase of his Markan source, Matthew positivizes Mark's portrait of both Jesus and the disciples: for example, Mark's 'and he cured *many* who were sick' (1.34a) becomes in Matthew, 'and [he] cured *all* who were sick' (8.16b; cf. Mt. 12.15 // Mk 3.10; Mt. 19.17 // Mk 10.18; Mt. 26.61 // Mk 14.58).[155] Matthew modifies Mark's query about the disciples' inability to understand – 'and he said to them, "Do you not understand this parable? Then how will you understand all the parables?"' (Mk 4.13) – into an expression of their ability to 'see', that is, understand: 'But blessed are your eyes, for they see, and your ears, for they hear' (Mt. 13.16; cf. Mt. 14.33 // Mk 6.52).[156]

*Amplification by Addition*: Matthew also retains some of Mark's portrayal of the deficiency of the disciples' response (Mk 8.17 // Mt. 16.8), and occasionally amplifies it in order, ultimately, to amplify the power of Jesus: for example, Matthew amplifies the deficiency of the disciples' response in the Markan account of Jesus' walking on the water by *adding* the striking account of Peter's inadequate response in order to amplify Jesus' power over creation (14.28-31).[157]

*Amplification by Conflation*: The extent of Matthew's literary creativity has often not been fully appreciated because he uses so much of his

153. Some details of Jesus' emotions remain. Regarding the final two healing miracles in Matthew 8, John P. Meier notes: 'Likewise Markan and un-Matthean is the rough description of Jesus' emotions ("sternly charged", literally, "snorted"). Perhaps Mt allowed the silence-motif and the rough language here because the blind men have addressed Jesus as Son of David, a messianic title too easily interpreted in a political and nationalist sense.' See John P. Meier, *Matthew* (NTM, 3; Dublin: Veritas, 1980), p. 99.

154. Davies and Allison, *Matthew*, I, pp. 104–105; Werner Georg Kümmel, *Introduction to the New Testament* (London: SCM Press, 1975), p. 108.

155. Davies and Allison, *Matthew*, I, p. 105.

156. Matthew retains some of Mark's portrait that demonstrates the failure of the disciples. He does so, for example, in the pericope on the issue of what is clean and unclean (Mt. 15.15-16 // Mk 7.17b-18), and in particular, in the pericope about Peter's confession of faith (Mt. 16.22-23 // Mk 8.32b-33). In the latter pericope, Matthew's retention of the negative portrait of Peter highlights that suffering and the cross is the way of Jesus, and that the fulfilment of this way is only possible through Jesus' power (cf. Mt. 26.32; 28.13-20). See Bauer, *Structure*, p. 107, and also pp. 62–63.

157. Kümmel, *New Testament*, p. 108.

Markan source and much of it in parallel order.[158] Boring notes well that 'his use of Q and Mark is at the farthest pole from a "cut-and-paste" use of them as "sources"'.[159]

Matthew's *conflation* of Mark's accounts of the cursing of the fig tree and the withered fig tree (not found in Luke or John) provides a very good brief example of the extent of his creative artistry (Mt. 21.17-22 // Mk 11.11-14, 20-24).

In Mark, the two fig tree pericopae are interwoven between Jesus' visits to the Temple. More specifically, these pericopae frame the account of the cleansing of the Temple (Mk 11.15-19). Interweaving stories and framing are typically Markan techniques. When used, they indicate that the interpretative key to each incident may be found by examining its relationship to the other (see Table 4.2 below).

Table 4.2: *Matthew's Re-Ordering of Markan Pericopae*[160]

| Mk 11.15-19 | Mt. 21.12-22 |
| --- | --- |
| A Jesus' First Visit to the Temple (11.11) | A Cleansing of the Temple (21.12-17) |
| B Cursing of the Fig Tree (11.12-14) | |
| A Cleansing of the Temple (11.15-19) | |
| B The Withered Fig Free (11.20-25) | B Cursing of the Fig Tree (21.18-22) |
| A Jesus' Return Visit to the Temple (11.27) | |

Mark interlocks the accounts of the Jesus' visits to the Temple with that of his cursing of the fig tree. The act of the destruction of the fig tree prepares the reader for the prophetic act of the destruction of the Temple of Jerusalem. Matthew, however, *conflates* Mark's two pericopae concerning the fig tree into one (Mt. 21.18-22), and places the new condensed unit *after* the account of the cleansing of the Temple and Jesus' return to Bethany (Mt. 21.12-17).

This *re-ordering* has the effect of amplifying Mark's portrait of the

---

158.  Davies and Allison, *Matthew*, I, p. 95.
159.  Boring, 'Matthew', p. 96.
160.  This table is based on that of France. See France, *Mark*, p. 436.

power of Jesus,[161] and, secondly, it equally amplifies the charge of fruitlessness against the chief priests and the scribes in Jerusalem.[162]

## 3. *Conclusion*

The aim of this chapter has been, first, to examine the issue of the genre of Matthew and his Markan source in order to present a fundamental understanding of *why* Matthew uses Mark; and, secondly, to provide initial evidence that the methods and techniques used by Graeco-Roman authors to incorporate earlier sources into their works are also found reflected in Matthew's use of Mark as a source.

To this end, evidence that Matthew and Mark (so all the Gospels) belong within the genre of ancient historical βίοι and to the subgenre of βίοι 'Iησοῦ is presented. The central purpose of this genre is the establishment of the essence of the subject. In Matthew (so all the Gospels) the uniqueness of the subject, Jesus Christ, Son of God, is presented. This essence, which in theology is discussed in terms of Christology, is reflected throughout Matthew (so all the Gospels).

The external criteria for establishing literary dependency outlined above (ch. 1) are applied and satisfied. The case for the chronological priority of Mark is made. Evidence for the dating of the Gospel of Mark to c. 68 CE, and Matthew, to c. 80 CE is presented. A case is made for the plausiblity of the thesis that Matthew could have had access to a copy of Mark, given the level of book production in Rome, the movement of texts throughout the Graeco-Roman empire, and the established network of Christian communities at the time he was writing. Mark's association with Peter would have made the circulation of his Gospel all the more likely.

The internal criteria for establishing literary dependence outlined and applied above (chs 1–3) are applied to selected texts from Matthew. Some initial evidence of Matthew's rewriting of Mark is presented. In terms of parallel vocabulary, themes and events, 90 + per cent of Mark appears in Matthew, 51 per cent of which reflects Mark's exact words. In the first half of his Gospel, Matthew creatively re-orders the pericopae taken from his Markan source. In the second half, he follows the Markan order exactly.

Some of the more simple techniques by which Matthew rewrites Mark are then examined. Matthew uses the techniques of *omission* and *variation* for the purpose of positivizing his portrait of Jesus and the disciples, and the techniques of *addition* and *conflation* for the purpose of amplifying his Christology, relative to his Markan source.

---

161. France, *Mark*, p. 442. See Witherington, *Mark*, p. 312.

162. R.H. Gundry, *Matthew: A Commentary on His Handbook for a Mixed Church under Persecution* (Grand Rapids: William B. Eerdmans, 2nd edn, 1994), p. 415.

# Chapter 5

## MATTHEW'S JUDAIZATION OF MARK

It has long been recognized that Matthew's Gospel has a more strongly Jewish flavour than Mark's. In fact it is this 'judaization'[1] that is the most distinctive hallmark of Matthew's meticulous rewriting of his Markan source.[2] Matthew, much more so than Mark (or Luke), reflects a far greater engagement with Judaism,[3] Pharisaism[4] and Rabbinism.[5]

The aim of this chapter is, first, to present a more in-depth analysis of Matthew's overall literary and theological agenda of judaization which is reflected in his rewriting of his Markan source; and, secondly, to provide further evidence that the methods and techniques used by Graeco-Roman authors to incorporate earlier sources into their works are also found reflected in his use of Mark as a source.

This section examines Matthew's judaization of Mark under the following headings:

1. Matthew's Restructuring of Mark as Based on Key Numerals of Judaism

---

1. Speaking of Matthew as a Jewish Gospel is a misnomer. All the Gospels, although written in Greek, may be considered Jewish as they recount the event of the life, death and resurrection of Jesus, a Jew among fellow Jews in Israel. Speaking about this, Boring quite rightly points out that, 'Jewish Christianity was not a monolith, but a spectrum of groups with a variety of stances toward the law. It is thus somewhat simplistic to think of Matthew as a Jewish Gospel, particularly since it has considerable elements that reflect an alienation from Judaism.' See Boring, 'Matthew', p. 97. By claiming that Matthew judaizes Mark, we wish to emphasize the literary process by which Matthew, in rewriting Mark, increases the density of explicit and implicit references to Judaism and OT Scripture.

2. With regard to Matthew's use of language, Keener writes: 'sometimes he *re-Judaizes* his language ("kingdom of heaven/God"; Matt 19.3 // Mark 10.2, 11-12)' (italics added). See Keener, *Matthew*, p. 10; Kümmel, *New Testament*, pp. 112–13.

3. Cf. Mt. 9.13; 12.7 (M). See Davies and Allison, *Matthew*, I, p. 133. Senior summarizes the comparison thus: 'none of the Gospels is more thoroughly Jewish in perspective than Matthew'. See Senior, *Matthew*, p. 22. See also Frederick J. Murphy, 'The Jewishness of Matthew: Another Look', in Alan J. Avery-Peck, Daniel Harrington and Jacob Neusner (eds), *When Judaism and Christianity Began: Essays in Memory of Anthony J. Saldarini* (Fest. Anthony J. Saldarini; JCB; SupJSJ, 85; Leiden: Brill, 2004), II, pp. 377–403.

4. Keener, *Matthew*, p. 42.

5. See Davies and Allison, *Matthew*, I, p. 134; Keener, *Matthew*, p. 42.

## 2.   Matthew's Reworking of Mark as Based on Judaism's Torah

### 1. *Matthew's Restructuring of Mark as Based on Key Numerals of Judaism*

One of the concerns of literary criticism is to discern the literary markers, explicit and implicit, which point to the literary structure of a text.[6] As seen above, 'no narrative is natural; a choice and a construction will always preside over its appearance'.[7] Authors in antiquity designed a variety of structural markers, often ingeniously, to facilitate their literary and ideological or theological goals and reflect their intended interpretation of the text.[8] Matthew includes a high density of such markers of very varied kinds – ranging from temporal, geographical and theological, as well as other phenomena such as form, repetitions of words or themes, and topical arrangements.[9]

Scholars upholding the priority of Mark agree that Matthew takes over the Markan framework and employs it as the base (Lt., *edificatio*) for his own narrative.[10] We will begin by examining the marco-structure into which Matthew sets 90 + per cent of his Markan source.[11]

Scholars often comment on how fascinated Matthew seems to be with

---

6.   We borrow the term 'marker' from Ziva Ben-Porat. See Ziva Ben-Porat, 'The Poetics of Literary Allusion', *JDPTL* (1976), pp. 105–28.

7.   Taveton Todorov, 'Primitive Narrative', in *idem, The Poetics of Prose* (trans. R. Howard; Oxford: Basil Blackwell, 1977), pp. 53–65 (55), cited in Tolbert, *Sowing the Gospel*, p. 1.

8.   Christopher R. Smith, 'Literary Evidences of a Fivefold Structure in the Gospel of Matthew', *NTS* 43 (1997), pp. 540–51 (541). Literary markers were very important in antiquity, as Paul J. Achtemeier points out: 'The written page consisted entirely of lines each containing a similar number of letters, lines that ended and began irrespective of the words themselves. Documents were written without systematic punctuation, without indications of sentence or paragraph structure, indeed without separation of the letters into individual words.' See Paul J. Achtemeier, '*Omne Verbum Sonat*: The New Testament and the Oral Environment of Late Western Antiquity', *JBL* 109 (1990), pp. 3–27 (10–11). See Gamble, *Books and Readers*, pp. 66–81.

9.   For a summary of such markers, see Boring, 'Convergence', pp. 591–97.

10.   Kümmel, *New Testament*, p. 106.

11.   We disagree with Bauer's claim that, 'it is methodologically inappropriate to begin an examination of literary structure with an investigation into Matthew's use of Mark'. See Bauer, *Structure*, p. 35. Our contention is that both methods can be instructive, that is, studying Matthew apart from any other text, and studying it in relation to other texts. In the examination of an author's uses of sources, comparisons are most instructive. Imagine studying the structure of Virgil's *Aeneid* without recourse to Homer's epics, *Iliad* and *Odyssey*? Or, Deuteronomy without reference to Exodus? Our analysis would indeed be the poorer. Moreover, Bauer appears to contradict what he said earlier, namely, that, 'this convergence of theological conclusions based on the application of different methods to the text of the Gospels underscores the validity of these conclusions'. See Bauer, *Structure*, p. 20.

numbers in general.[12] Scholars who link this phenomenon with the structure of Matthew usually argue for a structural outline based on one or other number, mostly, three or five. Our contention is that Matthew, in fact, purposefully creates a complex *poly-structural*[13] text that accentuates key numerals which were used theologically in Judaism – two, three, five, seven and twelve.[14] His use of such numerals is one of the ways in which he judaizes his Markan source.

Craig R. Koester provides a good criterion for testing the significance of a number in a text, which we will apply here: 'it is useful to ask whether the meaning would change if the text cited a different number or made a more general statement about quantity'.[15] Apart from using this criterion, we must also appeal to the available knowledge of the literary use of numbers in antiquity, and for our purposes here, particularly in the Old Testament and New Testament.

The use of numerals by authors for structuring literature in both Graeco-Roman and Jewish antiquity is well documented.[16] In recent decades, scholars have been discerning ancient theories about numbers from analysing patterns in (units of) texts based on the quantitative analysis of syllables, words, size of units, and the numerical relationships between proportions of (units of) whole texts. Scripture scholars too have been unlocking aspects of Old and New Testament[17] texts by using such

12. Donald Senior, *The Gospel of Matthew* (IBT; Nashville: Abingdon, 1997), p. 26; Davies and Allison, *Matthew*, I, pp. 85–86.

13. Among the scholars who choose one structure for Matthew, see Gundry, *Matthew*, p. 11; Davies and Allison, *Matthew*, I, p. 72; Keener, *Matthew*, p. 37; Hagner, *Matthew 1–13*, p. 1; Boring, 'Convergence', pp. 590–91, 598. We concur with Kingsbury's assessment that, 'however the Gospel is outlined, it should be done in such a fashion that classification leaves each grouping intact'. See Kingsbury, *Matthew: Structure*, p. 25. Some Markan scholars have also begun to notice the poly-structural nature of Mark. Donahue and Harrington write: 'It might be best to think of Mark as a series of overlays that comprise multiple structures and modes of composition.' See Donahue and Harrington, *Mark*, p. 47.

14. B.C. Birch, 'Number', *ISBE*, III, pp. 556–61.

15. Craig R. Koester, *Symbolism in the Fourth Gospel: Meaning, Mystery, Community* (Minneapolis: Fortress Press, 2nd edn, 2003), p. 266.

16. For an overview of the use of numerals by authors for (poly-)structural purposes in the literature of both Graeco-Roman and Jewish antiquity, see the opening chapter of M.J.J. Menken, *Numerical Literary Techniques in John: The Fourth Evangelist's Use of Numbers of Words and Syllables* (NovTSup, 55; Leiden: E.J. Brill, 1985), pp. 1–41.

17. The following scholars analyse Matthew's use of numbers in structuring (units of) his Gospel: J.C. Fenton, 'Inclusio and Chiasmus in Matthew', in *Studia Evangelica* (TU, 73; Berlin: Akademie-Verlag, 1956), I, pp. 174–79; Lohr, 'Oral Techniques' pp. 403–35; Kingsbury, *Matthew: Structure*, pp. 1–39; J. Smit Sabinga, 'Matthew 14:22-33 – Text and Composition', in Jay Eldon Epp and Gordon D. Fee (eds), *New Testament Textual Criticism: Its Significance for Exegesis: Essays in Honour of Bruce. M. Metzger* (Oxford: Clarendon Press, 1981), pp. 15–33; idem, 'The Structure of the Apocalyptic Discourse, Matthew 24 and 25', *ST* 29 (1975), pp. 711–79.

methods. Schnackenburg observes this in Matthew. He writes: 'Matthew the "systematician" has a preference for certain numbers in the composition of his material; indeed, he employs an underlying *number symbolism*.'[18]

By his use of numbers and other markers, Matthew emulates Mark's structure in order to accentuate aspects of Jewish theology and to present Jesus Christ as having both fulfilled and surpassed the Old Testament scriptures.[19] Therefore, 'the structure of Matthew should be thought of in a more dynamic, interactive way, as a complex of interlocking structures with more than one movement present in the text at the same time, as though there were multiple layers of outline; as a result, any one element may be involved in the dynamics of more than one movement'.[20]

We shall now look at the fundamental turning points in the narrative, which divide the Gospel into major units, in terms of number, location, type, function and effect.[21] Matthew's Gospel reflects some of the same type of structural markers as Mark's, although in a more elaborate and striking fashion.

The structural model provided by Boring provides a very helpful visual aid when analysing the issue of structure in Matthew (see Table 5.1 below). We take it as a point of departure. In line with the genre type of Matthew outlined above, that is, ancient historical *bios*, we regard the Gospel as 'a narrative with inserted speeches, which themselves become part of the narrative, not a collection of speeches with a narrative framework'.[22]

The model 'speaks loudly' (See Table 5.1 below).[23]

---

18. Schnackenburg, *Matthew*, p. 4.

19. Stibbe quite rightly notes that, 'one of the things which has been omitted by narrative critics is a careful consideration of the relationship between theological purpose and the narrative form'. See Stibbe, *John as Storyteller*, p. 12.

20. Boring, 'Matthew', p. 114.

21. Boring, 'Convergence', p. 589. Kingsbury notes that, 'Matthaean research has thus far achieved no consensus of opinion on either the broad structure of the first Gospel ... [moreover] there are fewer still who have endeavoured to let the structure of the Gospel be their guide as they determine its portrait of Jesus'. See Kingsbury, *Matthew: Structure*, p. 1.

22. Boring, 'Convergence', p. 588; *idem*, 'Matthew', p. 112. *Contra* Peter F. Ellis who regards the narratives as secondary and supportive of the discourses. See Peter F. Ellis, *Matthew: His Mind and His Message* (Collegeville: Liturgical Press, 1974), pp. 16–17.

23. See 'Figure 3' in Boring, 'Matthew', p. 117, Lohr writes: 'Chiastic and symmetrical repetition ... is well known in both the Greek and the Semitic traditions'. See Lohr, 'Oral Techniques', pp. 424–25. See also G.E. Duckworth, 'The Architecture of the *Aeneid*' in Hardie (ed.), *Virgil*, IV, pp. 13–25.

Table 5.1: *Matthew's Macro-Structure*

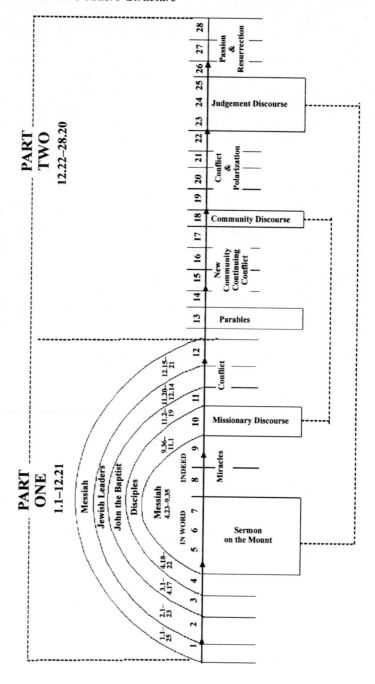

## a. *Twofold Structure*

Matthew may be divided in two parts – part 1, 1.1–12.21, and part 2, 12.22–28.20 (see Table 5.1 above). What is the basis for this? The strongest literary clues are that, first, *up to Mt. 12.21*, Matthew creatively *reorders* his Markan source, but, *from Mt. 12.22*, Matthew consistently *follows the order* of his Markan source;[24] and, secondly, he ceases ordering of his material triadically at Mt. 12.21, except for his additions to the Markan speeches.[25] A satisfactory explanation has largely eluded scholars.[26] We concur with Boring that this feature is far 'too striking to be coincidence and requires some explanation'.[27]

Matthew's change of method of composition comes just after the seventh and longest fulfilment citation in his Gospel, Isa. 42.1-4; 41.9: 'Here is my servant ... my beloved ... he will proclaim justice to the Gentiles ("nations", τοῖς ἔθνεσιν )' (Mt. 12.18-21). *Seven* in Jewish theology is a mark of completeness (cf. Gen. 2.2-3; 8.4; Exod. 12.15-16; Lev. 13.5-6; Num. 8.2; 12.14-15; Deut. 16.3-15).[28] Here, as a literary marker, it indicates implicitly that a section of the narrative is complete. As a theological marker, it indicates that a dimension of the portrait of Jesus is complete – he is the promised messianic servant of all the nations.

We can be sure that Matthew intends this to be the *end of part 1* because Matthew's *conflation* of Isa. 41.9 and 42.1-4, two quotations concerning 'the nations' (v. 18, τοῖς ἔθνεσιν; v. 21, ἔθνη), links us forward to the *end of part 2* of Matthew where Jesus confers this mission to his disciples to: 'Go therefore and make disciples of all the nations' (ἔθνη) (Mt. 28.16-20). Moreover, there is a clue that the next pericope, concerning Beelzebul, acts as a *beginning of the second part* because Matthew's reference to David ('Can this [Jesus] be the Son of David?', Mt. 12.23), mirrors the

24.  The author is indebted to Boring for noticing the precise juncture where Matthew resumes Mark's order. See Boring, 'Convergence', pp. 598–99 and n. 24.

25.  For example, Mark 4 // Matthew 13; Mark 13 // Matthew 24–25. See Boring, 'Convergence', pp. 596, 601.

26.  Gundry, in his large commentary on Matthew, devotes one page to 'The Structure of Matthew' in which he notes that, 'at first Matthew freely rearranged his Markan materials in addition to inserting other materials (often shared with Luke)'. Then, he presents this conclusion regarding Matthew's use of Mark: '*But editorial fatigue set in*, so in the latter half of his gospel he stuck close to Mark's order even when continuing to insert other materials' (italics added). See Gundry, *Matthew*, p. 10.

27.  Boring, 'Convergence', p. 601. Beaton comments: 'It must be noted, however, that he uses considerably less of Mark in the first half than in the second, *an oddity that has yet to be satisfactorily explained*' (italics added). See Beaton, 'How Matthew Writes', p. 120. Senior notes that, 'it may not be coincidence that the first thirteen chapters, where the majority of the fulfilment texts are to be found, are also that part of the gospel where we discover Matthew's most intense editorial work in relation to his sources Mark and Q'. See Senior, *Gospel of Matthew*, p. 37.

28.  See Bauer, *Structure*, p. 78.

reference to David at the *beginning of the first part* of the Gospel, 'Jesus Christ, son of David' (Mt. 1.1).

Scholars have long divided Matthew's model, Mark, into two parts – 1.14–8.30 and 8.31–16.8.[29] In part 1, Mark gradually builds up to Peter's correct recognition of Jesus as 'the Christ' (Mt. 8.29). (We shall discuss Matthew's use of the parallel to Mk 8.29, that is, Mt. 16.16, under *Three-fold Structure*).

The structural midpoint of Matthew (Mt. 12.21, where he returns to following the exact Markan order) also occurs at a key moment of recognition: the Pharisees incorrectly recognize Jesus as Beelzebul (a claim which they make *three* times in all), while all the people are astounded by his cure of the dumb man, and so wonder if he is the Son of David (Mt. 12.22-28; cf. Mt. 9.34; and 10.25).[30]

In Mark, Peter's great profession of Jesus' identity (Mk 8.30) occurs just before Peter's rejection of Jesus' prophecy of his passion (Mk 8.31-33).[31] Jesus recognizes the nature of the force at work in Peter and says to him: 'Get behind me, Satan!' (Mk 8.33). Matthew *transfers* the matter of satanic power from Peter to the Pharisees by having Jesus declare that his power is not from Satan, and questioning rhetorically the source of theirs: 'And if it is through Beelzebul that I cast out devils, through whom do your own experts cast them out?' (Mt. 12.27).

The effect of Matthew's striking change of methodology serves to alert the hearer/reader familiar with his Markan source to the acute change in the attitude of some toward Jesus that will last throughout the entire second half of the Gospel: the meek beloved Jesus, God's favourite son (Mt. 3.17), in whom the nations put their hope (Mt. 12.18), and who is recognized by all as 'Son of David' (Mt. 12.23), is now rejected by the misguided Pharisees as Beelzebul, 'Prince of Devils' (Mt. 12.24; cf. Matthew 23).

---

29. Brown, *Introduction*, p. 127; Edward J. Malley, 'The Gospel according to Mark', *JBC*, pp. 21–61 (22); D.L. Baar, 'The Drama of Matthew's Gospel: A Reconsideration of Its Structure and Purpose', *TD* 24 (1976), pp. 349-59 (350); Witherington, *Mark*, p. 38. Scholars who divide Mark otherwise, for example, into three, five, or seven parts structurally also recognize Mk 8.29 as a significant literary and theological juncture. See Robert A. Guelich, *Mark 1–8:26* (WBC, 34A; Dallas: Word Books, 1989), p. xxxvi; Bas M.F. van Iersel, *Reading Mark* (Edinburgh: T&T Clark, 1989), p. 20; Daniel J. Harrington, 'The Gospel according to Mark', *NJBC*, pp. 596–629 (598); Witherington, *Mark*, p. 38; Donahue and Harrington, *Mark*, pp. 47–48; France, *Mark*, pp. 1–14.

30. The Beelzebul pericope is one of the few pericopae common to both Mark and the so-called Q source.

31. Veron Robbins notes that, 'much ancient writing attached particular importance to texts' beginning, middle, and end'. See Veron Robbins, *The Tapestry of Early Christian Discourse: Rhetoric, Society and Ideology* (London: Routledge, 1996), p. 22. See also Brodie, *Crucial Bridge*, p. 89. See Ch. 2, n. 114 above.

The fact that Matthew's mid-point change of methodology occurs in a scene of recognition (Mt. 12.23-24) betrays his awareness of the mid-point recognition scene in his Markan source (Mk 8.30).

### b. *Threefold Structure*

The threefold dimension of the structure of Matthew is more easily recognizable, and consequently has been far more commented upon, than its twofold structural dimension.

As a point of departure we begin by noting that, on the macro-level, Matthew's use of three geographical markers broadly reflects his Markan source (a Galilean section, Matthew 1–18 // Mk 1.1–8.21; a journey to Jerusalem, Matthew 19–20 // Mk 8.22–10.52; and a Jerusalem section, Matthew 21–28 // Mk11.1–16.8).[32] In both Gospels, geography is full of theological symbolism – Galilee, a symbol of Jesus' mission, ministry and resurrection appearances; Jerusalem, a symbol of his suffering and death.[33]

On the micro-level, Matthew presents Jesus as having being tempted in the desert by Satan *three* times (Mt. 4.1-11 // Mk 1.12-13 par.). He parallels Mark's use of *three* passion predictions in the corresponding locations (Mt. 16.21 // Mk 8.31; Mt. 17.22-23 // Mk 9.30-33; Mt. 20.17-19 // Mk 10.32-34), and adds a fourth (Mt. 26.2). Here, largely, the three-fold parallels between the macro-structure of Matthew and Mark end. Davies and Allison have drawn our attention to Matthew's extraordinary propensity ('mania') for arranging his literary units into triads.[34] The extraordinary degree to which he re-structures his Markan material into triadic units reflects the work of deliberate literary composition, rather than the effects of oral formation.

In the Old Testament Scripture, the numeral *three* is usually used as an indication of perfection, in the sense of a time of perfect or complete readiness of a person or people (cf. Gen. 40.10, 12, 16, 18; 40.12-23; Deut. 16.16).[35] The greatest moment of revelation for the people of Israel, for example, happened on Sinai:

---

32. France, *Mark*, pp. 11–14. Tolbert, however, discerns a two-fold geographical divide in Mark, the preaching tour in Galilee (1.14–10.52), and the events in Jerusalem (11.1–16.8). See Tolbert, *Sowing the Gospel*, pp. 107, 120.

33. Keener, *John*, I, pp. 231–32; Harrington, *Gospel of Matthew*, p. 5.

34. For a brief summary where 44 examples of the use of the number *three* in Matthew are cited, see Davies and Allison, *Matthew*, I, pp. 86–87. See also Fishbane, *Interpretation*, pp. 450–451.

35. Schnackenburg, *Matthew*, p. 4. See David P. Wright, 'Numbers', *HCBD*, p. 763–764; Jöran Friberg, 'Numbers and Counting', *ABD*, IV, pp. 1139–46 (1145); Gerhard Delling, 'τρεῖς', *TDNT*, VIII, pp. 217–18; Birch, 'Numbers', III, p. 558.

On the *third* new moon after the Israelites had gone out of the land of Egypt, on that very day, they came into the wilderness of Sinai. And he [Moses] said to the people, 'Prepare for the *third* day; do not go near a woman'. On the morning of the *third* day there was thunder and lightning, as well as a thick cloud on the mountain, and a blast of a trumpet so loud that all the people who were in the camp trembled (Exod. 19.1, 15-16; cp. Mt. 27.45-54, 63; 28.1-4).[36]

A reference to 'three' is made here *three* times, and the final time an additional reference is given, 'on the morning', to add emphasis as the narrative builds up to a dramatic climax. (Exodus is a book with which Matthew was demonstrably familiar, as we shall see below.)

In speaking of Jonah, Matthew adds the temporal detail: 'For just as Jonah was *three* days and *three* nights in the belly of the sea monster, so for *three* days and *three* nights the Son of Man will be in the heart of the earth' (Mt. 12.40; cf. 12.39, 41; 16.4, 17; Jon. 1.17; 3.3; Mk 8.12; Lk./Q = 11.30).[37] This is not found in Mark's (or Luke's) presentation. It demonstrates Matthew's deliberate use of *three* for temporal and theological purposes.[38]

In terms of macro-structure, it is repetition of the phrase, 'from that time Jesus began to ...' (ἀπὸ τότε ἤρξατο ὁ Ἰησοῦς + infinitive + a summary of the message)[39] at 4.17; and 16.21 which, most scholars agree, provides the most explicit turning points dividing the account of the life of Jesus into three temporal phases.[40] These phases may be outlined as follows:

---

36. Keener notes that, 'when dealing with short periods of time, a "third day" was common'. He cites many examples from the OT. However, this is to interpret the reference only as a temporal indicator, rather than both as a temporal and theological one. See Keener. *John*, p. 497, and n. 48.

37. Allison, *New Moses*, p. 167.

38. Delling, 'τρεῖς' VIII, pp. 221–24.

39. This distinctive phrase is found only on two other occasions in the NT: Mt. 26.16; and Lk. 16.16. Bauer dismisses the occurrence of the phrase at Mt. 26.16 as a structural marker because of its asyndetic character. He fails to notice that in a series of three, the third and final element is climactic (as noted above), hence Matthew's addition of 'and' (καί) at the beginning of his third use of this phrase: '*And* from that moment ...' Because Jesus is not the main subject in Mt. 26.16, Bauer says that the phrase is not linked explicitly with Jesus. Not so. Jesus is no longer the subject, but is linked explicitly with the phrase as the object of the sentence – 'he [Judas] began to look for an opportunity to betray him [Jesus]'. See Bauer, *Structure*, pp. 44, 88.

40. Hagner notes that the significance of these phrases had early been noted by J.C. Hawkins (*Horae Synopticae*; Oxford: Clarendon Press, 1899). See Hagner, *Matthew 1–13*, p. li. Two proponents of the primacy of these similar phrases as structural markers in Matthew are Kingsbury and Bauer. Of Mt. 4.17; and 16.21, Bauer notes quite rightly that, 'many commentators remark that the formula indicates a turning point in the ministry of Jesus, but for reasons usually left unexplained they fail to draw structural conclusions from this observation'. See Bauer, *Structure*, p. 85 and p. 157, n. 17. See Kingsbury, *Matthew: Structure*, p. 7.

1. The preparation of Jesus (1.1–4.16)[41]
2. The ministry of Jesus to Israel and Israel's rejection of Jesus (4.17–16.20)[42]
3. The journey of Jesus to Jerusalem and his passion, death and resurrection (16.21–28.20).[43]

David R. Bauer, *The Structure of Matthew's Gospel* (1989), demonstrates convincingly how each section unfolds as an expansion of its opening statement (1.1; 4.17; and 16.21),[44] and how the first section provides the background for the second, and the second for the third – building up to the ultimate literary and theological climax at the end (Mt. 28.16-20).[45]

Bauer outlines how Matthew's macro-triadic structure functions to support his Christological purpose. Matthew arranges the narrative so that in each of the three phases there is a build up to an explicit Christological declaration: (1) In Mt. 1.1–4.17, it occurs at the baptism when God calls Jesus 'the Beloved' (Mt. 3.17) and where Jesus wishes to do the perfect thing, that is, 'all that righteousness demands' (Mt. 3.15); (2) in Mt. 4.18–16.21, it occurs when Peter declares Jesus to be the Messiah: 'You are the Christ' (Mt. 16.15 // Mk 8.29). In fact, Matthew has Peter give a longer and more perfect confession than Mark. By way of clarification, Matthew *adds* to Peter's confession the words: 'the son of the living God'. Further, Jesus is presented as greater than John the Baptist, Elijah, Jeremiah or any of the prophets (Mt. 16.13-17);[46] (3) and finally, in Mt. 16.22–28.20, the Roman centurion, a representative of 'all the nations' (Mt. 12.18c), recognizes that the description of Jesus as 'God's son', was indeed a perfect one ('*In truth*', Ἀληθῶς, *NJB*, 27.54). This contrasts with the imperfect recognition of 'some of those who stood there' and thought that Jesus needed Elijah 'to come to save him' (Mt. 27.47-50). Moreover, following the chronological movement of the

---

41. Some scholars note a turning point at Mt. 3.1, with the phrase 'in those days'. Matthew begins to use his Markan source at this point. Others argue that the element of continuity is more dominant, that is, that the δέ in 3.1 acts as a connective linking the ministry of John the Baptist with the previous infancy narratives. We see this as a technique of 'overlapping' where endings are also beginnings, and vice versa. It is part of Matthew's literary genius.

42. At Mt. 6.1-18, Matthew lists *three* kinds of piety.

43. At Mt. 26.30-35, 69-75, Peter's *three* denials prophesised by Jesus come to pass.

44. Bauer acknowledges that he takes his lead here from Kingsbury, *Matthew: Structure*. See Bauer, *Structure*, pp. 40-45. Boring's assessment of Bauer's work is that his divisions 'belong more appropriately under the "chronological" heading rather than the "topical" one, since "from that time on" is the key phrase'. See Boring, 'Convergence', p. 589, n. 5.

45. Bauer, *Structure*, p. 73.

46. T.W. Buckley, 'The Christology of Matthew', *ChicStud* 40 (2001), pp. 251–60 (256).

narrative, there is in the final section a double-climax.[47] Not only does a
Gentile declare Jesus' true identity, so does the risen Jesus himself. At the
very end, Jesus can promise to be with his disciples always because he is
one with God (ἰδοὺ ἐγὼ μεθ' ὑμῶν εἰμι, 28.20).

Matthew models his threefold geographical arrangement upon his
Markan source. He organizes much of his Markan source material
triadically. By his use of the Jewish numeral *three*, he judaizes Mark. This
evidence betrays something of his overall purpose – to portray that the
time of the longed-for Messiah to which Judaism had looked forward had
arrived with the coming of Jesus.

### c. *Five–Seven–Twelvefold Structure*

B.W. Bacon's *Studies in Matthew* (1930)[48] marked the launch of the
modern discussion of the fivefold structural dimension of Matthew. In a
chapter entitled 'Matthew's Use of Mark', Bacon draws our attention to
the way in which Matthew arranges the words of Jesus topically, creating
five great discourses whose endings are marked by a similar summary
phrase: 'Now when Jesus had finished saying these things, the crowds were
astounded at his teaching, for he taught them as one having authority,
and not as their scribes' (Mt. 7.28; cf. Mt. 11.1; 13.53; 19.1; 26.1;[49] see
Table 5.1 above).[50]

Bacon's work has influenced many, and his insight has been helpful in
generating intense and fruitful debate among scholars as to the significance of these five structural markers.[51] His weakness, however, and that
of those who have followed his lead, is in concluding that Matthew's five-

---

47.  Bauer rightly notes that, 'Matthew has a proclivity toward emphasizing the final
element, and what is true for individual pericopae is true also for the Gospel as a whole'. See
Bauer, *Structure*, p. 37.

48.  B.W. Bacon, *Studies in Matthew* (New York: Henry Holt, 1930). See *idem*, 'The "Five
Books" of Matthew against the Jews', *ExpTim* 15 (1918), pp. 56–66.

49.  Matthew's addition of 'all' in Mt. 26.1 highlights the deliberateness of these five
markers: 'Jesus had now finished *all* he wanted to say ...' Allison notes that while the
repetition of a transitional formula throughout a Jewish book is 'a well attested
phenomenon', the diction of three of Matthew's five formula – τοὺς λόγους τούτους – in
7.28; 19.1; 26.1, reflects two of the three formula at the end of Deuteronomy, that is, Deut.
31.1, 24, but not Deut. 32.45. See Allison, *New Moses*, pp. 192–93. Gundry notes that, ' "all"
may reflect Deut 34.45 and carry forward Matthew's portrayal of Jesus as the greater Moses
...' See Gundry, *Matthew*, p. 517.

50.  Kingsbury notes that, 'this formula is found five times in the first Gospel and, except
for Luke 7.1 in D, exclusively here. For this reason, it can properly be construed as a
thoroughly Matthaean idiom'. See Kingsbury, *Structure*, p. 6. See also Boring, 'Matthew', p.
111.

51.  For a list of scholars who follow Bacon's lead in seeing in Matthew's five-fold
structure an allusion to the Pentateuch, see Keener, *Matthew*, p. 37. Smith states that he
prefers the five-fold structure based on the work of redaction critics, because 'Bauer's

fold structure is modelled on the Pentateuch *alone* (so Papias), and in failing to recognize the dynamic poly-structural nature of Matthew's text.[52]

Some scholars, such as Donald A. Hagner and Keener, dismiss the conclusion of Bacon *et al.* because a fivefold structure can be found in other canonical Old Testament writings – for example, the book of Psalms, Proverbs, and Ecclesiastes.[53] According to our analysis, both groups of scholars are correct. The fivefold structural dimension of Matthew's Gospel is part of Matthew's judaizing strategy to point to the Old Testament at large, and, in particular, the books of the Torah, which were popularly called the Five Books of Moses.

Because of the status of the Five Books of Moses, the numeral *five* came to be associated primarily with the Torah in Jewish theology.[54] The Hebrew word 'Torah' literally means 'teaching, doctrine'.[55] In Exodus, God gives the great teaching, the Decalogue, at the greatest moment of revelation for Israel on Sinai (5 x 2; Exod. 20.1-21; cf. Deut. 5.1-22).[56] Here, teaching is associated with the revelation of God. It is striking that, in the five structural markers outlined above, Matthew's focus is initially *exclusively* on Jesus as 'teacher'.[57] *Five* times he is presented as having

---

analysis ... is not able to account, by literary critical means, for the presence of the discourses'. See Smith, 'Literary Evidences', p. 551. As demonstrated above, the three-fold model is not the *only* possible conclusion to the fascinating issue of the structure of Matthew.

52.   Goulder observes that Matthew's correspondence with Leviticus and Numbers is much weaker than with the other books of the Torah. See Goulder, *Midrash*, pp. 171–72.

53.   Hagner, *Matthew 1–13*, p. li. Keener also notes the presence of this structure in other Jewish sacred literature – Megilloth; the prototype of 2 Maccabees; *1 Enoch, 2 Enoch; Pirqe 'Abot*. See Keener, *Matthew*, pp. 37–38.

54.   David H. Stern, a Jewish scholar commenting on Matthew, points out that, 'in Judaism the word "Torah" may mean: (1) *Chumash* (the Pentateuch, the five books of Moses); or (2) That plus the Prophets and the Writings, i.e., the *Tanakh* (known by Christians as the Old Testament; see 4:4–10N); or (3) That plus the Oral *Torah*, which includes the Talmud and other legal materials; or (4) That plus all religious instruction from the rabbis, including ethical and aggadic (homiletical) materials'. However, he points out that when 'the Law and Prophets' are mentioned together as in Mt. 5.17 (cf. 7.12; 22.40), 'the Law' then corresponds to number one above. See David H. Stern, *Jewish New Testament Commentary* (Clarksville, MD: Jewish New Testament Publications, 1992), p. 25. See also Birch, 'Numbers', III, p. 559.

55.   Stern notes that, 'it is rendered in both the LXX and the New Testament by the same Greek word—"*nomos*" which means "law"'. See Stern, *New Testament*, p. 25.

56.   Note the doubling of the number *seven, three* times in Matthew's genealogy. Allison notes that the number *ten* can also indicate 'fullness, completeness, perfection'. He cites several scriptural examples. See Allison, *New Moses*, p. 208, n. 164. See Friberg, 'Numbers and Counting', IV, p. 1145.

57.   Mt. 11.1 is the only one of the five markers that mentions that Jesus preaches, as well as teaches.

finished: 'Now when Jesus had finished' (ἐτέλεσεν)[58] what he wanted to say to/teach the people (Mt. 7.28; 11.1; 13.53; 19.1; 26.1).

Matthew's deliberate use of the numeral *five* for his theological purposes is affirmed by examples of his use of it on the micro-level: for example, he uses *five* Old Testament formula citations in the infancy narratives (chs 1–2), and, in the Gospel, he provides *five* witnesses to Jesus' identity in the opening narrative (Mt. 1.1, 20; 2.2; 3.11, 17; cf. Gen. 1.1–2.3).[59]

Can we say then that Matthew's setting of his Markan source within a fivefold structure may be understood as an act of literary and theological emulation? Further, is there evidence to support the thesis that Matthew's fivefold structure is also in the service of his portrait of Jesus' identity with the God who taught/spoke on Sinai? Is the Jesus of Matthew the 'Last Word', the fulfilment of the Torah to which Judaism had looked forward? We answer these questions in the affirmative with confidence.

Scholars, from Papias to the present day, have noted how pedagogically effective Matthew's improved topical arrangement of his sources, including Mark, is for catechesis. In terms of genre, it has led some scholars to classify it as a catechetical document.[60]

Many scholars of recent years have noticed the extensive use that Mark makes of the framing or 'sandwiching' technique, a popular literary device in Graeco-Roman antiquity, in terms of his micro-structuring. Scholars, such as van Iersel,[61] have discerned the presence of this technique at the macro-level. He outlines a fivefold chiastic (concentric)[62] structure within Mark:

---

58. The verb τελέω is used in these structural markers in the sense of 'to complete an activity or process, *bring to an end, finish, complete something*'. See J.H. Moulton and G. Milligaw, 'τελέω', *GELNTECL*, p. 997–998.

59. The five witnesses in Matthew are as follows: (1) Matthew himself declares that Jesus is *three* things, the 'Christ', 'Son of David' and 'Son of Abraham' (1.1); (2) the angel addresses Joseph as 'son of David', and so Jesus, indirectly (1.20); (3) the wise men look for 'the king of the Jews' (2.2); (4) John the Baptist declares that Jesus is 'the Christ' (3.11); and finally, (5) God, himself, declares that Jesus is his 'beloved Son' (3.17). Menken, following P. Beauchamp, relates this to the occurrence of *five* utterances of God in both parts of Gen. 1. 1-31 (Gen. 1.3, 6, 9, 11, 14, and 1.20, 24, 26, 28, 29). See Menken, *Literary Techniques*, p. 16 and n. 87.

60. Schnackenburg, *Matthew*, p. 4.

61. Van Iersel, *Reading Mark*, p. 20. For a similar outline see Augustine Stock, *The Method and Message of Mark* (Wilmington, DE: Michael Glazier, 1989). For more detailed analysis of Mark's micro-structural use of chiasm, see Joanna Dewey, *Markan Public Debate: Literary Technique, Concentric Structure and Theology in Mark 2.1–3.6* (SBLDS, 48; Chico, CA: Scholars Press, 1977).

62. We find George Mlakuzhyil's distinction between chiastic and concentric structures helpful. He notes that, 'for while chiasmus has two inverted parallel panels (e.g. A B // B' A'/ A B C // C' B' A'; etc.), the concentric structure has a unique central element around which

*Title* (1.1)
**(A1) In the desert** (1.2-13)
              (y1) first hinge (1.14-15)
     **(B1) In Galilee** (1.16–8.21)
              (z1) blindness → sight (8.22-26)
         **(C) On the way** (8.27–10.45)
              (z2) blindness → sight (10.46-52)
     **(B2) In Jerusalem** (11.1–15.39)
              (y2) second hinge (15.40-41)
   **(A2) At the tomb** (15.42–16.8)

Mark thus reflects a precedent that is found accentuated in Matthew. Bacon draws attention to the fivefold nature of Matthew based on the great discourses. More recently, Boring has outlined Matthew's penchant for five in his analysis of Mt. 1.1–12.21. He outlines how Matthew has created a fivefold structure by means of thematic shifts and repetitions within part 1 of Matthew's twofold structure – 1.1–12.21//12.22–28.20 – in order to teach us that Jesus is the long-awaited Messiah (see Table 5.1 above).[63] By his thematic arrangement, Matthew has placed the issue of Jesus' identity very strongly at the beginning, middle and end of part 1 (Messiah of extra-ordinary origin, 1.1-25; Messiah in word and deed, chs 5–9;[64] Messiah of the nations, 12.15-21). Jesus, the Christ, is both the Alpha and Omega, *and* the heart of the fullness of Judaism.

We believe that what Boring points out as true of part 1 of Matthew, is also true of the entire Gospel. Scholars have often noted the thematic links between the first and fifth discourses (chs 5–7 and 23–25), and between the second and fourth (chs 10 and 18).[65] The narratives are also linked, although not as strongly (chs 1–4 and 26–28; chs 8–9 and 19–22; chs 11–12 and 14–17). Presented thus, we see another dimension of the poly-structural nature of Matthew. The fivefold structure may *also* be seen as 'a three-fold discourse structure *within* a threefold-narrative structure' (see Table 5.2 below).

---

other elements are arranged in a parallel manner (e.g., A B A'; A B C B' A'; etc.)'. See George Mlakuzhyil, *The Christocentric Literary Structure of the Fourth Gospel* (AnBib, 117; Rome: Biblical Institute Press, 1987), pp. 125–26.

63.  Boring, 'Convergence', pp. 605–11. As noted above, Matthew places *five* fulfilment quotations in the infancy narrative, Matthew 1–2.

64.  Many scholars note the structural/transitional role of Mt. 4.23-25; and 9.35, the two summaries that Matthew takes from Mark to frame his portrait of Jesus as Messiah in word and deed (Matthew 5–9). See Boring, 'Matthew', p. 112.

65.  Lohr, 'Oral Techniques', pp. 427–30; Viviano, 'Matthew', p. 633.

Table 5.2: *Matthew's Threefold Structure within a Threefold Structure*

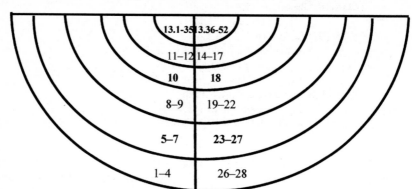

Matthew puts the mystery of God at the very centre of the whole narrative in ch. 13, where he has grouped *seven* parables about the kingdom of heaven.[66]

As has already been noted, Matthew begins to follow Mark's exact pericope order at Mt. 12.22. From that point on he includes almost all of the remainder of his Markan source – Mk 3.22–16.8. Commenting on Matthew's discourses, Boring draws our attention to the fact that Mark has already placed *four* speeches in this long Markan section, two before the great Christological juncture at Mk 8.29 (Mk 4.3-32; and 6.8-11) and two after it (Mk 9.39-50; and 13.5-37).[67] What does Matthew do? He increases the number of discourses to *five*, lengthens them, and sets them

---

66. Menken notes several examples of the outstanding significance of the middle section of a text in both the classics: for example, Isocrates, *Panegyricus* (99), 'where the claim of Athens to leadership in the war against the Persians culminates, is the middle of the entire oration'; and Plato's *Republica* (8.1–9.3), where Plato 'gives a certain splendour to the middle by symbols or symbolic thoughts'. See Menken, *Literary Techniques*, pp. 7–8. H.J. de Jonge provides an example of the importance of the central element from the Gospel of Luke. He observes that in Lk. 2.41-51a, a 170-word pericope, the word μέσῳ in 2.46 is the eighty-fifth word; and the phrase ἐν μέσῳ τῶν διδασκάλων forms the mathematical centre of the pericope. See H.J. de Jonge, 'Sonship, Wisdom, Infancy: Luke 2.41–51a', *NTS* 24 (1977–78), pp. 317–54; 337–39 (338), n. 5. See Ch. 2, n. 114 above.

67. Boring, 'Convergence', p. 610. Van Iersel outlines how Mark's first and last discourses may be considered part of a five-fold chiastic substructure within the Gospel. Both discourses are framed within the Galilee and Jerusalem sections of the narrative respectively. See van Iersel, *Reading Mark*, pp. 24–25, 74, 110–13.

symmetrically, balancing the length of the corresponding ones (chs 5–7 match chs 23–24 in length approximately; ch. 10 matches ch. 18; ch. 13 forms the centre).[68]

Matthew's fivefold structural arrangement, indicated by the five similar formulae synopsizing Jesus' ministry, is directive. Kingsbury writes:

> Now when we recall that it is a major objective of Matthew to depict Jesus as the promised Messiah through whose words and deeds God reveals himself to his people (cf. 11.25-30; 12.28; 17.5; 28.18-20), we recognize that the theological function of this formula is to undergird the twin truths that specifically Jesus Messiah is the one who presents each discourse demarcated by the formula and that these 'words' or 'parables' or 'instructions' of his have the status of divine revelation.[69]

Bacon's neglect of the narrative material in his fivefold structural arrangement of Matthew has not gone unnoticed. Some scholars point out the continuity between the narratives and the discourses that follow.[70] They note the presence of one or several hook-words or themes that link them together.[71] When we take this into account, we can still trace a five-fold narrative-discourse *within* an infancy and passion-resurrection frame.[72] The net effect is a *sevenfold* (concentric) structure, as some scholars suggest:

---

68. Ellis, *Matthew*, pp. 12–13; J. Smit Sabinga comments that, consciously and consistently, the author of the First Gospel 'arranged his text in such a way, that the size of the individual sections is fixed by a determined number of syllables'. This comment, made in a communication to the 'Journée Bibliques' of Louvain (1970), is cited in Menken, *Literary Techniques*, p. 21: see also, n. 115.

69. Kingsbury, *Matthew: Structure*, pp. 6–7.

70. For a list of other such scholars, see Bauer, *Structure*, p. 33, and p. 153, n. 32. Streeter, in contrast, regards the five formulae at the end of the discourses as transitions or bridges to the *following* narrative material. See Streeter, *Four Gospels*, p. 262.

71. Boring, 'Matthew', p. 117; Smith, 'Literary Evidences', p. 545. Bauer provides a list of other such scholars. See Bauer, *Structure*, p. 37, n. 24.

72. *Contra* Lohr who states that, 'the Gospel cannot be divided into five books each of which is made up of sermon plus narrative, or vice versa, because whichever way it is taken, there is one narrative section left over'. Lohr, 'Oral Techniques', p. 428. Brown cautions that, 'to give them [infancy narratives] less value than other parts of the Gospels is to misread the mind of the evangelists from whom the infancy narratives were fitting vehicles of a message they wanted to convey'. See Raymond E. Brown, *The Birth of the Messiah: A Commentary on the Infancy Narratives in Matthew and Luke* (Garden City: Doubleday, 1977), p. 38.

$$\text{A} \qquad \text{B} \qquad \text{C} \qquad \text{B}^1 \qquad \text{A}^1$$

**[(1) 1–2 | (2) 3–7[73] | (3) 8–10 | (4) 11–13[74] | (5) 14–18 | (6) 19–25 | (7) 26–28]**

The number *seven* in Jewish theology refers to the completion of something that is required (cf. Gen. 1.1–2.4a; 7.2–8.12; 29.18; 41.26-27; Zech. 4.2-3; 6.1-7).[75] Matthew's text reflects deliberate usage of this numeral also (double *sevens* of the genealogy, 1.1-17; *seven* petitions of the Lord's prayer, 6.9–13; *seven* parables in ch.13; *seven* woes in ch. 23). Some scholars, for example, John R. Donahue and Daniel J. Harrington,[76] discern a *sevenfold* structure in Mark that is not chiastic.

Still other scholars argue for the discontinuity between the narratives and discourses in Matthew. Terence J. Keegan, for instance, points out that the recurring phrase, 'the disciples came to him' (προσῆλθαν [αὐτῷ] οἱ μαθηταί) which occurs at the beginning of four of the five discourses (Mt. 5.1; 13.10; 18.1; 24.1), does not appear in the Mission Discourse because it is more appropriate for Jesus to call (and send) the disciples himself

---

73. 'See Boring, 'Convergence', pp. 605–10, In keeping with Matthew's poly-structural approach, there is an element of continuity marked by the connective δέ in 3.1, as noted above. However, the fact Matthew places the *fifth* of the five fulfilment quotations used in chs 1–2 (the introduction that he adds to his Markan source) at the end of ch. 2 indicates an element of discontinuity there also.

74. Scholars differ as to whether the turning point of the chiasm occurs at ch. 11 (so H.B. Green, *The Gospel according to Matthew*, 1975, cited in Senior, *Gospel of Matthew*, p. 27) or at 13.35-36 (so Peter F. Ellis, Terence J. Keegan). We concur with the findings of Ellis and Keegan. Keegan writes insightfully that, 'in the first two and a half discourses Jesus is speaking before an assembly including both disciples and the crowds. At the centre of the Gospel, in the middle of the parable discourse (13.36) Matthew has Jesus change locations, symbolically entering the house. The disciples come to Jesus signalling a new beginning and from that point forward Jesus addresses his major discourses to the disciples alone.' See Terence J. Keegan, 'Introductory Formulae for the Matthean Discourses', *CBQ* 44 (1982), pp. 415–30 (423–24). Cp. Mt. 5.2 // Mt. 4.25; and 7.8; Mt. 10.1 // 9.36; and Mt. 13.2 // 13.10. See also Ellis, *Matthew*, p. 13.

75. For example, the completion of creation in Gen. 1.1–2.3 is indicated numerically by the use of *seven*. Menken, citing U. Cassuto, observes that, 'Gen 1,1 has a size of 7 words, that Gen 1,2 has a size of 14 (= 2 × 7) words, and that the seventh paragraph of this unit, about the seventh day (2,1-3), has a length of 35 (= 5 × 7) words; this paragraph contains, moreover, three successive clauses, in which the expression "the seventh day" occurs, of 7 words each (2,2a.2b.3a)'. See Menken, *Literary Techniques*, pp. 16 and 37, n. 86. See also Fishbane, *Interpretation*, pp. 450–51. See also Friberg, 'Numbers and Counting', IV, pp. 1144–45; Birch, 'Numbers', III, p. 558; Robert A. Kraft, 'Philo's Treatment of the Number Seven in *On Creation*' (Paper presented for the SBL Philo Group; New Orleans, 1996).

76. Donahue and Harrington indicate that they recognize the poly-structural nature of Mark. However, they do not develop the concept: 'It might be best to think of Mark as a series of overlays that comprise multiple structures and modes of composition ...' See Donahue and Harrington, *Mark*, p. 47 and also pp. 46–50; Harrington, 'Mark', pp. 597–98.

(Mt. 10.1).[77] Keegan also points out the presence of distinctive terminology at the beginning of each discourse that distinguishes each one from the preceding narrative.[78] The net effect of this analysis is that Matthew may also be viewed as having a *twelvefold* (chiastic) structure.[79] The numeral *twelve* is reminiscent of the twelve tribes of Israel,[80] that is, *all* of Israel (cf. Mt. 19.28; Gen. 25.16; 49.28).[81] As noted above, Jesus Christ, son of David, son of Abraham, came to *all* nations/races of the earth (Mt. 12.18, 21; 20.19).[82]

1. Infancy narratives: 1–2
    2. First Narrative: 3–4
        3. *First Discourse: 5–7*
    4. Second Narrative: 8–9
        5. *Second Discourse: 10*
    6. Third Narrative: 11–12
        7. *Third Discourse: 13*
    8. Fourth Narrative: 14–17
        9. *Fourth Discourse: 18*
    10. Fifth Narrative: 19–22

77. Keegan, 'Introductory Formulae', p. 422.

78. Keegan's research counters scholars, such as Senior, who argue that Matthew 11 should be part of the second great discourse, or that Matthew 23 should not be part of his fifth and final discourse. See Keegan, 'Introductory Formula', p. 428. See also Senior, *Matthew*, p. 26. Ellis finds two minor speeches (3.8-12; 28.18-20) as well as the five major ones in Matthew, that is, seven speeches in all. See Ellis, *Matthew*, p. 13.

79. M.S. Enslin had early discerned this structure. See M.S. Enslin, ' "The Five Books of Matthew": Bacon on the Gospel of Matthew', *HTR* 24 (1931), pp. 67–97. For a list of scholars who hold the unity of Matthew 1–4, and thus divide Matthew chiastically into eleven parts see Hagner, *Matthew 1–13*, pp. lii–liii. The ambiguity between the presence of an elevenfold or twelvefold structure is clear from Boring's table above (see Table 5.1 above). His outline marks out eleven subsections up to 12.21, which is the end point of part one in the Matthew's twofold structure. It does not take account of Mt. 12.22-50. However, if one looks at the five/seven/twelvefold macro-structural dimension of Matthew with ch. 13 as its centre, it is clear from Boring's table that there are 12 sub-units from ch. 1 to the end of ch. 12.

80. For an example of the literary use of the combination of the numbers *twelve* and *seven* for theological purposes, see Exod. 15.27: 'Then they came to Elim, where there were *twelve* springs of water and *seventy* palm trees; and they camped there by the water' (cf. Num. 33.9; Jdt. 7.2). For examples of the literary-theological use of the number *twelve* alone, see Exod. 24.4; 28.21; Josh. 4.8; 1 Kgs 18.31; and 1 Chron. 6.33.

81. The theological use of numbers is used up to the time of Augustine (354–430 CE). For Augustine's view on the numerals *five*, *six*, *seven* and *twelve*, see John E. Rotelle (ed.), *On Genesis: A Refutation of the Manichees Unfinished Literary Commentary on Genesis: The Literal Meaning of Genesis* (trans. Edmund Hill; WSA, I; New York: New City Press, 2002), pp. 242–45.

82. Jesus gives the disciples the ministry of teaching when he commissions them (Mt. 28.20). Before his passion, death and resurrection, they are sent only to heal and preach, the other two chief ministries of Jesus.

11. *Fifth Discourse: 23–25*
12. Passion and Resurrection Narrative: 26–28

Mark uses the numerals *seven* and *twelve* quite extensively.[83] However, there appears to be little or no evidence to link Matthew's sevenfold and twelvefold structural dimensions directly to his source's structure. Matthew appears both to have accentuated the more significant structural markers reflected in his Markan source and added others. Not all structural markers in Matthew are of equal importance. Some are stronger than others. However, we cannot attend more fully to that issue here.

This examination of Matthew's use of Jewish numerals in his rewriting of Mark is a case in point in which the 'convergence of criteria of diverse natures can guarantee greater objectivity than can dependence on a single norm which might mesmerize a scholar and lead him [or her] to subjective conclusions'.[84]

By creating a high density of different types of structural markers – change of methodology, Christological junctures, temporal/chronological markers, summary statements, chiastic and concentric arrangements – according to the ancient key Jewish numbers, Matthew *emulates* Mark. In terms of literary style Matthew's *poly-structure* surpasses that of Mark's; in terms of Christology, Matthew's numerically based poly-structure serves to steep the narrative of Jesus, as found in Mark, in an ocean of Jewish theological overtones.[85]

In terms of structure and theology, we may say that Matthew puts 'new wine [i.e., *the account of Jesus Christ*] into fresh skins [i.e., *Judaized poly-structure*] and both [i.e., *the Jewish origin of Jesus and faith in him as the Christ*] are preserved' (Mt. 13.17; italicized material added).

## 2. *Matthew's Reworking of Mark as Based on Judaism's Torah*

We will now examine how Matthew's judaizes Mark by another means, namely, his use of the Old Testament.[86] Mogens Müller observes correctly

---

83. The number *twelve* occurs 15 times (= 5 × 3) in Mk: 3.14, 16; 4.10; 5.25, 42; 6.7, 43; 8.19; 9.35; 10.32; 11.11; 14.10, 17, 20, 43. The number *seven* occurs 9 times (= 3 × 3) in Mk: 8.5, 6, 8, 20 *bis*; 12.20, 22, 23; 16.9.

84. Mlakuzhyil, *Literary Structure*, p. 87.

85. See Robert H. Gundry, 'Matthew: Jewish-Christian or Christian-Jewish? At an Intersection of Sociology and Theology', in Robert H. Gundry (ed.), *The Old Is Better* (NTESTI; WUNT, 178; Tübingen: Mohr Siebeck, 2005), pp. 111–19.

86. Boring provides an excellent summary of the distribution of OT citations in Matthew: 'Matthew directly quotes the Scripture forty times with an explicit indication, such as "it is written" (e.g., Matt 4:4 = Deut 8:3). Matthew also contains several other direct citations not explicitly so identified (e.g., 27:46 = Ps 22:1; their exact number depends on how strictly one

that, 'in the Gospel of Matthew, which is otherwise adequately described as a rewritten and expanded Gospel of Mark, the use of the Old Testament is much more comprehensive and intensive'.[87] Of Matthew's ten so-called fulfilment quotations (Mt. 1.23; 2.15, 17-18, 23; 4.14-16; 8.17; 12.17-21; 13.35; 21.4-5; 27.9),[88] only one, 21.4-5, arises out of Mark's narrative.[89] All of them diverge from the LXX,[90] while the other quotations taken from Mark retain the LXX.[91] This reflects deliberateness about Matthew's selection and use of Old Testament scriptural quotations.[92]

Matthew's literary and theological agenda concerning his sustained use of the Old Testament has been well expressed by Müller: 'At first the task had been to legitimise the Christ faith by reference to Scripture. But in this

---

distinguishes between quotation and allusion). The current edition of the Nestle-Aland Greek New Testament identifies twenty-one such quotations, making a total of sixty-one direct quotations in twenty-eight chapters. Of the sixty-one quotations, twenty-four are taken over from Mark and nine from Q. Twenty-eight citations, however, are peculiar to Matthew. Ten of these quotations are Matthean additions to Markan contexts, three are added to Q contexts, and fifteen are in peculiarly Matthean material. Thus Matthew introduces almost as many quotations as he takes over from his sources, and often adds quotations to his sources. Matthew never omits a biblical quotation from the Markan or Q material he incorporates, and he preserves most of the allusions as well. As in the other Gospels and the New Testament as a whole, Matthew cites most often the Psalms, Isaiah, and Deuteronomy. No direct quotations are taken from apocryphal and pseudepigraphical books, but there may be allusions to them.' See Boring, 'Matthew', p. 151.

87. Mogens Müller, 'The Reception of the Old Testament in Matthew and Luke-Acts: From Interpretation to Proof from Scripture', *NovT* 43 (2001), pp. 315–30 (318). See Maarten J.J. Menken, 'Old Testament Quotations Inserted in Markan Contexts', in Maarten J.J. Menken (ed.), *Matthew's Bible: The Old Testament Text of the Evangelist* (BETL, 173; Leuven: University Press, 2004), pp. 227–38.

88. Senior notes that, 'the very word "fulfil" (the verb *plēroō* in Greek) expresses the fundamental meaning of these quotations for Matthew. The evangelist views the total reality of Jesus as the "fulfilment" of his history of Israel and its Scriptures.' See Senior, *Gospel of Matthew*, p. 36.

89. Morgens notes that Matthew's use of Zech. 9.9 has the effect 'by and large [of] replacing the story told in Mark 11.4-5'. See Müller, 'Reception', pp. 318–19. Davies and Allison provide a very helpful table entitled, 'Quotations Common to Matthew and Mark'. See Davies and Allison, *Matthew*, I, pp. 34–35.

90. Hans Hübner, 'OT Quotations in the New Testament', *ABD*, IV.1096–1104 (1099).

91. For more on the issue of Non-LXX forms, see Davies and Allison, *Matthew*, I, pp. 32–58; Boring, 'Matthew', p. 152. See also Maarten J.J. Menken, 'Old Testament Quotations Derived from Mark', in Menken (ed.), *Matthew's Bible*, pp. 205–25.

92. George Kennedy notes that, 'when Matthew cites passages of the Old Testament that are also cited by Mark or Luke, these citations are close to the Septuagint and highly consistent in language, whereas when Matthew cites passages of the Old Testament not found in other gospels, his version is characteristically not that of the Septuagint ...' See George Kennedy, 'Classical and Christian Source Criticism', in W.O. Walker (ed.), *The Relationships among the Gospels* (San Antonio: Trinity University Press, 1978), pp. 125–55 (146, and n. 11).

new situation it became necessary to legitimise Scripture by reference to the Christ faith in order to establish its specific Christian significance.'[93]

Matthew continues the exercise of legitimizing Jesus as the Christ by reference to Scripture – an exercise begun by Mark (Mk 1.2-3; 8.18; 7.6-12, 37; 11.9-10, 17; 12.11, 35-37; ch. 13; 14.49; ch. 15).[94] However, as Müller observes, Matthew takes it to a new level, that is, he legitimizes Old Testament Scripture with reference to Jesus Christ and demonstrates how Jesus Christ surpasses it.[95]

Our contention is that Matthew *emulates* Mark's portrait of Jesus. Mark presents Jesus as greater than Moses, Elijah and, most especially, Elisha. Matthew presents Jesus as greater than the greatest of these three Old Testament figures, Moses:[96] 'In other words, when the First Gospel casts Jesus as a new Moses legitimated like the lawgiver of old, Mark's competing cast of Jesus as a greater Elisha recedes and is, in this instance, overlaid by another image.'[97]

By focusing on the superiority of Jesus relative to Moses, Matthew does not diminish Moses. Rather, he uses the figure of Moses to amplify certain aspects of Jewish theology. He does so, ultimately, in order to amplify aspects of his Christology.[98]

---

93.    Müller, 'Reception', p. 315. Allison writes: 'When Jews looked to the future they saw the past. For them, the distant time of Moses and longed-for latter days mirrored one another.' See Allison, *New Moses*, p. 197. See also Harrington, *Matthew*, p. 17; Hagner, *Matthew 1–13*, pp. xlv, lvi.

94.    Matthew uses the same method as Paul. See ch. 3, section 2. b. above. Donahue and Harrington note that, 'from the very beginning (Mark 1.2-3) the evangelist tells us that the Old Testament is an authoritative text and is being fulfilled in the story of Jesus'. See Donahue and Harrington, *Mark*, p. 1. For a summary of Mark's use of OT Scripture, see also Donahue and Harrington, *Mark*, pp. 34–35.

95.    Donald A. Hagner, 'Balancing the Old and New', *Inter* 51 (1997), pp. 20–30 (21). Hagner notes that Augustine recognized this dynamic: 'The new lies latent in the old and the old is made latent in the new. *In vetere novum lateat, et in novo vetus pateat.* Migne, *Patrologia Latina*, 34.725.' See Hagner, 'Balancing', pp. 20, and 29, n. 1. See also Senior, *Matthew*, p. 26.

96.    Cf. Mt. 11.14; 17.9-13. For a good bibliography on the role of Elijah and Elisha in the New Testament, see Brodie, *Crucial Bridge*, p. 81, n. 5. Matthew presents Jesus as greater than John the Baptist (3.1-17; 11.2-15), Jonah (12.38-41), Solomon (12.42), and the prophets (16.13-14). Allison observes that, 'the explicit comparison of, and especially the implicit drawing of parallels between, Jesus and others, must be reckoned as a compositional habit of Matthew'. See Allison, *New Moses*, p. 137. The literary technique of fashioning deliberate comparisons between characters within a text, or between a text and its source text, was common also in Greco-Roman literature, especially *bioi*. See Ch. 2, sections 1 and 3 above.

97.    Wolfgang Roth, 'Moses and Matthew', *Bib T* 30 (1992), pp. 362–66 (363).

98.    Despite noting the extensive use Matthew makes of mountain symbolism, Kingsbury concludes that Matthew intends to portray Jesus not 'as the new Moses, but as the Son of God'. This is a poor reading of the evidence. These portrayals are not mutually exclusive. In fact, the reality of Jesus as 'Son of God' is precisely what is utterly new about the 'new Moses'. See Kingsbury, 'Form and Message', p. 21.

Such a thesis involving comparison of two great figures, and the emulation of one in relation to the other is in accord with the literary techniques employed in ancient *bioi*. P.L. Shuler's research found that the two main techniques employed in this genre were *amplification* and *comparison*. It may be helpful to note here his description of these techniques:

> Amplification is the process by which the author 'amplifies' those points he is trying to make either by a process of selection, an emphasis upon a few aspects of the character at the expense of a complete account, and/ or the omission of material that does not fit with the author's literary purposes. Comparison demonstrates how the chosen subject excels over (*sic*) those with whom he comes into contact or with whom he may be compared.[99]

Matthew uses these techniques in the service of his literary and theological agenda. He elaborates upon his Markan source, literally, by embedding Old Testament citations, references and allusions into his rewritten material. By the incorporation of the embedded material, he 'expands' it as he 'puts its perceivers in two stories at once'.[100]

We will now examine how Matthew judaizes Mark by his use of Old Testament Scripture. First, we examine briefly how he torahizes the beginning and end ('frames') of his Gospel, under the heading: a. Matthew's Torahized Frame (Mt. 1.1–2.23; 28.16-20). Secondly, we will examine how the Markan material used within this torahized frame is rewritten with an eye to Old Testament Scripture in general, and Moses in particular, under the heading: b. Matthew's Rewriting of Mark within the Torahized Frame (Mt. 3.1–28.15).

### a. *Matthew's Torahized Frame* (Mt. 1.1–2.23; 28.16-20)

Matthew *adds* material to Mark's basic narrative at the beginning and end of his Gospel, namely, the Genealogy and Infancy Narratives in chs 1–2, and the Great Commission in 28.16-20. When we examine these Matthean additions closely we notice that they are embedded with references to the Torah. In particular, the opening chapters contain clear references and allusions to the books of Genesis and Exodus,[101] and the closing verses of

---

99. Shuler, 'Genre(s)', p. 466. In 'Genre(s)', as in his earlier work, *Genre for the Gospels* (1982), Shuler regards the Gospels as belonging to the sub-genre of encomium biography.

100. Allison, *New Moses*, p. 277.

101. H. Frankemölle, *Jahwebund und Kirche Christi: Studien zur Form- und Traditionsgeschichte des 'Evangeliumns' nach Matthäus* (NTAbh, 10; Münster: Aschendorff, 1974), p. 364; Benedict T. Viviano, 'The Genres of Matthew 1–2: Light from 1 Timothy 1.4', *RB* 97 (1990), pp. 31–53 (51); J. Nolland, 'What Kind of Genesis Do We Have in Matt 1.1?', *NTS* 42 (1996), pp. 463–71 (463); Bauer, *Structure*, p. 74, n. 4; J.D. Kingsbury, 'The Birth Narrative of Matthew', in David E. Aune (ed.), *The Gospel of Matthew in Current Study* (Grand Rapids: William B. Eerdmans, 2001), pp. 154–65.

the last chapter incorporate elements of Deuteronomy. Thus Matthew sets his rewriting of Mark *within* a torahized narrative frame. This factor has to be part of any hermeneutical reading of the narrative 'in between the frame', that is, Mt. 3.1–26.15.

We will present just one example from Matthew 1–2 to demonstrate that Matthew has torahized his opening narrative. We will examine his use of Exodus in Matthew 2.

Following Matthew's second fulfilment citation (Mt. 2.15; cp. Hos. 11.1b, 'out of Egypt I called my son'), his narrative presents parallel circumstances to that found in Exodus 1. At the time of Jesus' birth, King Herod orders all the male infants of the Jews in Bethlehem to be killed (Mt. 2.16-18). The third fulfilment citation from Jer. 31.15 in Mt. 2.18 points to a very brutal stage in the exodus. At the time of the birth of Moses, Pharaoh, the king of Egypt, orders all the male children of the Hebrews to be killed (Exod. 1.22).[102]

There is further parallelism between Matthew's Infancy Narrative and the book of Exodus (see Table 5.3 below). Scholars recognize parallels between Matthew's account of the return from Egypt, Mt. 2.19-21 and Exod. 4.19-20:

Table 5.3: *Flight Into/Out of Egypt*[103]

| Exod. 4.19-20 | Mt. 2.19-20 |
|---|---|
|  | 2.19a When Herod died, |
| 4.19a The Lord said | 2.19b an angel of the Lord suddenly appeared in a dream |
| 4.19a to Moses in Midian, | 2.19b to Joseph in Egypt and said, |
|  | 2.20a 'Get up, take the child and his mother and |
| 4.19b 'Go back to Egypt; for all those who were seeking your life are dead.' | 2.20a go to the land of Israel, |
|  | 2.20b for those who were seeking the child's life are dead.' |
| τεθνήκασιν γὰρ πάντες οἱ ζητοῦντές σου τὴν ψυχήν | τεθνήκασιν γὰρ οἱ ζητοῦντες τὴν ψυχὴν τοῦ παιδίου |
| 4.20 So Moses took his wife and his sons, put them on a donkey, and went back to the land of Egypt; ... | 2.21a Then Joseph got up, took the child and his mother, 2.21b and went to the land of Israel. |

---

102. Allison, *New Moses*, p. 145.
103. This table is modelled on that of Allison's. See Allison, *New Moses*, pp. 142–43.

A literary seam created by a narrative incongruity is evident at Mt. 2.20: 'for *those* who were seeking the child's life are dead'. King Herod is the only immediate antecedent; therefore, the plural is grammatically unsuitable here. Allison notes this and concludes that, 'the language of Exod. 4.19 was retained without perfect grammatical adjustment, in order to make the parallel with the sentence from Exodus unmistakable'.[104]

One other significant detail links the narratives, namely, the flight by night. According to Mt. 2.14, Joseph took the child and his mother and left for Egypt 'by night' (νυκτός). The combination of the element 'night' with 'flight' and 'Egypt' also points toward the book of Exodus, specifically 12.30-41:

Pharaoh arose in the *night* (νυκτός) ... Then he summoned Moses and Aaron in the night (νυκτός), and said, 'Rise up, go away from my people' ... The Egyptians urged the people to hasten their departure from the land, for they said, 'We shall all be dead.' ... on that very day, all the companies of the Lord went out from the land of Egypt.

Matthew draws upon the book of Exodus for Matthew 2 to portray Jesus Christ as the 'new Israel' in whom 'the exodus from Egypt is repeated and completed'.[105]

Let us now examine Matthew's torahization of the other side of the narrative frame that encloses the material he draws from his Markan source, that is, the great universal Commission of the Disciples (Mt. 20.16-20).

The final scene of Matthew 28 incorporates elements parallel to the final scene of Deuteronomy 34. Both scenes occur on mountains, and both scenes relate to the matter of succession/transference from the leader to the disciple(s). Just as Moses, who worked signs and wonders, missions Joshua, so Jesus, who worked signs and wonders, missions the disciples. Just as Joshua's concern is for the on-going formation of a nation under God through obedience (Deut. 38.9), so Jesus' concern is for the creation of a new community *in* God through baptism ('Father, Son and Spirit', Mt. 28.19).

Jesus' disciples are commissioned to teach and baptize. In fact, only at this late point do they receive the commission to teach as he himself did (cf. Mt. 7.28; 11.1; 13.53; 19.1; 26.1). Among all the books of the Torah, the portrait of Moses as *teacher* is unique to the book of Deuteronomy (Deut. 4.5, 10; 6.1; 31.12).[106] Matthew sets up the similarities between the narratives, only to also set up the differences. The difference between the

104. Allison, *New Moses*, p. 143.

105. Luz, *Matthew 8–20*, p. 146. See Gundry, *Matthew*, pp. 33–41. For 'new Exodus' motifs in Paul, see 1 Cor. 10.1-4; 11.25; 2 Cor. 3–4.

106. Joseph A. Grassi, 'Matthew as a Second Testament Deuteronomy', *BTB* 19 (1989), pp. 23–29 (26).

two accounts here is not only the difference between the nature of the leaders – Moses, 'Israel's greatest prophet' (Deut. 34.10); Jesus Christ, possessor of 'all authority' (πᾶσα ἐξουσία, Mt. 20.18) – but in the nature and scope of the mission they entrust. Moses entrusts his mission to one, Joshua, for 'all the sons of Israel' to make new descendants upon 'the whole land' (Deut. 34.1, 9). In Matthew, Jesus Christ entrusts his mission to the 'eleven disciples' to make disciples of 'all nations' (πάντα τὰ ἔθνη; 28.19). Jesus Christ's mission is universal, and is therefore greater than Moses' mission to the people of Israel (cf. Mt. 10.37-42).

The influence of Deuteronomy upon the latter stage of Matthew's Gospel is confirmed by some distinctive details. For example, scholars have noted the similarity between the expression – '*this* gospel' (τὸ εὐαγγέλιον τοῦτο) – which Matthew uses at 26.13 (also Mt. 24.14), and the expression '*this* law which is written in *this book*' in Deut. 28.58.[107] The expression in Matthew, placed only on the lips of Jesus, is found nowhere else *in the whole of the New Testament*.[108] (Mark speaks of 'the gospel' in Mk 13.10; 14.9).

The phrase in Deut. 28.58 occurs in the immediate context of people being commanded to 'observe all the words of this law that are written in *this book*, fearing this glorious and awesome name, the Lord your God'; and of people who will be scattered by the Lord 'among all peoples, from one end of the earth to the other' (Deut. 28.58, 64). The thought and vocabulary is similar to Mt. 26.13: 'wherever in all the world *this gospel* is proclaimed' (cf. 26.13).

The next time the phrase 'all the world' occurs in Matthew is at the final commissioning scene, 28.16-20, a context where Jesus also commands his disciples. Here, the thought and vocabulary is even more similar to that of Deut. 28.58 than Mt. 26.13. However, the terms of the vocabulary-cluster based on the words – 'observe', 'name' and 'all the earth' – occur in Mt. 28.19-20 in *reverse order*: 'Go, therefore, make disciples of all nations ... in the name[109] of the Father ... teach them to observe all the commands I gave you'. In Deuteronomy, it is the words in '*this* book' that are to be observed; in Matthew, it is the words of *this* man,[110] Jesus Christ, which

---

107. The phrase 'this day' occurs in Deuteronomy 66 times in all. See Grassi, 'Matthew', p. 24.

108. Grassi, 'Matthew', p. 23.

109. See Gundry, *Matthew*, p. 596.

110. References to Jesus as 'this man' occur three times in Mark – Mk 6.2; 14.71; 15.39, and four times in Matthew – Mt. 9.3; 13.54, 56; 27.47. The last two occurrences in Matthew are telling. At the scene of the crucifixion, Mark has the bystanders, upon hearing Jesus cry, say, 'Listen, he is calling for Elijah' (15.35). In the parallel context, Matthew rewrites the bystanders' comment as, 'This man is calling for Elijah' (27.47). The final occurrence of the expression in Mark is the centurion's great confession, 'Truly this man was God's Son'

are to be observed (Mt. 28.20). Thus Matthew portrays Jesus as replacing 'this law which is written in this book' (Deut. 28.58).

Jesus is the superlative 'new Torah'.[111] This conclusion can be confirmed by another parallel between the reference to '*this* book' in Deuteronomy and to Jesus in Matthew. Moses had ordered '*this* book' to be placed beside the Ark of the Covenant in the Temple (God's dwelling; Deut. 31.26). It was to be read in order to ensure that the community of every generation would contemporize the experience of God's presence at Sinai.[112] The reading was to be done in the Temple by the religious leaders every *seven* years, a symbolic figure emphasizing the complete and perpetual nature of the exercise (Deut. 31.10). In Matthew, after his resurrection, Jesus, the '*I am*' (ἰδοὺ ἐγὼ . . . εἰμι, Mt. 28.20; cf. Exod. 3.14), promises his disciples on the mountain to dwell *with* them to protect them (cf. Gen. 26.24; 28.15; Josh. 1.5, 9; Isa. 41.10; 43.5). Robert H. Gundry rightly notes that, 'thus Matthew closes his gospel – characteristically and appropriately – with an assimilation of Jesus' words to God's word in the Old Testament'.[113]

Therefore, just as Matthew uses Exodus in Matthew 2 to portray Jesus as the 'new Israel' and the 'new Exodus', so he uses Deuteronomy in Matthew 28 to portray Jesus as the 'new Torah' and the 'new Temple'.

Having indicated the torahized nature of Matthew's frame, we now turn to the material within the frame.

### b. *Matthew's Rewriting of Mark within the Torahized Frame* (Mt. 3.1– 28.15)

Our examination of Matthew's judaization of Mark by means of embedding Old Testament citations, references and allusions, *within* the

---

(15.39). Matthew rewrites this confession as, 'Truly, this was God's son' (27.54). By the omission of 'man' (ὁ ἄνθρωπος) in Mt. 27.54, Matthew is emphasising the divine origin of Jesus and concomitantly de-emphasizing his earthly origin.

111.   Keener notes that as early as the sixteenth century Sebastian Münster described Matthew as a 'new Torah' (Pinchas E. Lapide, *Hebrew in the Church: The Foundations of Jewish–Christian Dialogue*, trans. Erroll F. Rhodes, Grand Rapids: Eerdmans, 1986; see Keener, *Matthew*, p. 50. About the debate on the Jewishness of Matthew, Douglas R.A. Hare concludes that, 'those on both sides of this debate can agree that for Matthean Christians Jesus has replaced the Torah as the key to a right relationship with the God of Israel'. See Douglas R.A. Hare, 'How Jewish Is the Gospel of Matthew?', *CBQ* 62 (2000), pp. 264–77 (277).

112.   B.W. Anderson, *Understanding the Old Testament* (Englewood Cliffs, NJ: Prentice-Hall, rev. edn, 1986), p. 380.

113.   Gundry, *Matthew*, p. 597. Beaton comments: 'In many ways, the OT is the sub-text of the gospel itself: the events of Jesus' life represent the fulfillment of the purposes of God in history.' See Beaton, 'How Matthew Writes', p. 122.

torahized frame (Mt. 3.1–28.15), will be given in sample form because a more comprehensive analysis is beyond the scope of this book. While it is in the Sermon on the Mount that, 'the portrayal of Jesus as the greater Moses attains its greatest clarity',[114] there is evidence of it throughout the Gospel. We will examine four pericopae spread across Matthew in order to demonstrate that Matthew uses Mark as a source to this same end. The pericopae are as follows:

1. Fasting in the Wilderness (Mt. 4.1-11 // Mk 1.12-13)
2. Second Feeding Account (Mt. 15.32-39 // Mk. 8.1-10)
3. Transfiguration (Mt. 17.1-8 // Mk 9.2-11)
4. Entry into Jerusalem (Mt. 21.1-11 // Mk 11.1-10)

1. *Fasting in the Wilderness* (Mt. 4.1-11 // Mk 1.12-13)
Matthew's account of Jesus' Fasting in the Wilderness (4.1-11) provides an example of his more precise use of the Torah. For this pericope, Matthew draws upon Mark's already scripture-loaded temptation account (Mk 1.12-13 // Lk. 4.1-13).[115] His modification of the 'forty days' of Mark (so Luke/Q) to 'forty days and forty nights' is significant (Mt. 4.1). While 'forty days' appears frequently in Old Testament Scripture, 'forty days and forty nights' does not.[116] Twice, it is associated with the fasting of the greatest Jewish figure, Moses (Deut. 24.18; 34.28), and once, with Elijah in imitation of Moses (1 Kgs 19.8). The great prophet, Elijah, and the greater prophet, Moses, fast on mountains – Horeb and Sinai respectively.

That Matthew is deliberately linking his text with these figures, particularly Moses, is confirmed by his addition to his account of something not found in Mark (or Luke/Q), that is, that the devil took Jesus 'to a very high mountain' (Mt. 4.8). This *added* phrase demonstrates verbal parallels with Deut. 34.1-4 (see Table 5.4 below).[117]

114. Gundry, *Matthew*, p. 78.

115. Cp. Mt. 4.4 // Lk. 4.3 // Deut. 8.3; cp. Mt. 4.7 // Lk. 4.12 // Deut. 6.16; cp. Mt. 4.10 // Lk. 4.7 // Deut. 6.13.

116. The phrase appears in association with Noah in Gen. 7.4, Moses on Sinai in Exod. 24.18; 34.28, and four times in Deuteronomy in Deut. 9.9, 11, 25; 10.10.

117. In his comment on Mt. 4.1, Gundry writes: 'Matthew wants to display Jesus as the new and greater Moses who goes up into the mountainous part of the wilderness just as Moses went up Mount Sinai in the wilderness (See Deut. 9.9, a passage located in the very section about to supply Jesus' replies to Satan; cf. also Exod 34.1ff. LXX).' See Gundry, *Matthew*, p. 54.

Table 5.4: *The Issue of Food and Fasting in the Wilderness*[118]

| Deut. 34.1-4 | Mt. 4.8-9 |
| --- | --- |
| 34.1: and the Lord showed him the whole land: Gilead as far as Dan | 4.8: Again, the devil took him to a very high mountain and showed him all the kingdoms of the world |
| καὶ ἔδειξεν αὐτῷ κύριος πᾶσαν τὴν γῆν | καὶ δείκνυσιν αὐτῷ πάσας τὰς βασιλείας τοῦ κόσμου |
| 34.4: The Lord said to him [Moses], 'This is the land ... "I will give it to your descendants"' καὶ εἶπεν κύριος πρὸς Μωυσῆν | 4.9: and he said to him [Jesus], 'All these I will give you' καὶ εἶπεν αὐτῷ· |
| αὕτη ἡ γῆ ἣν ὤμοσα ... δώσω αὐτήν | ταῦτά σοι πάντα δώσω |

In Deuteronomy 34, the Lord shows Moses 'the whole land' which he shall not cross into; in Matthew, ironically, the devil, who is not Lord, shows Jesus, the true Lord, the kingdoms of the world. Just as Jesus refuses to bow down before the devil because he knows the falseness of his lordship, the disciples at the final mountain scene fall down before Jesus, because they know the truth of his universal Lordship. Jesus could not accept the pseudo-offer from the devil of what he already had in reality from his Father (Mt. 4.8-10).[119] Further, unlike Moses, Jesus will be with his people as they cross over into all the nations (cp. Mt. 28.20 // Deut. 34.4).

### 2. Second Feeding Account (Mt. 15.32-39 // Mk. 8.1-10)

Links between Mark's two feeding stories (Mk 6.30-44; 8.1-10) and the two Old Testament accounts of the miracle of the manna found in Exodus 16 and Numbers 11 have often been made. At Mk 6.35, for example, Jesus' feeding of the crowd when the hour grows late echoes Num. 11.9 which records that the manna fell in the evening (cf. Exod. 16.6-36). However, 'their single closest Old Testament precedent consists of the multiplying of loaves by Elisha (2 Kgs 4.38-44)'.[120] Elisha commands his servant to feed the one hundred men, and there is still some bread left over.

Matthew wishes to keep the comparison between Jesus and Moses to the fore. In the second feeding story in Matthew, Matthew has Jesus

---

118. The creation of this table was inspired by the comparison made by Allison between Deuteronomy 34 and Matthew 4. See Allison, *New Moses*, p. 170.

119. Allison, *New Moses*, p. 171.

120. Brodie, *Crucial Bridge*, p. 92. See France, *Mark*, p. 262. Cf. 1 Kgs 17.8-16.

ascend the mountain (Mt. 15.29, the third such of *five* ascents in Matthew).[121] This ascending has no parallel in Mark's second account. The opening of Matthew's second feeding account demonstrates clear thematic and verbal parallels, some of which occur in the same order as the opening of the Sermon on the Mount (Mt. 4.18–5.1). The Sermon on the Mount exhibits strong literary references to Moses (see Table 5.5 below).[122]

Table 5.5: *Jesus as the 'New Moses' in Matthew's Second Feeding Account*

| Mt. 4.18–5.1 (SM) | Mt. 15.29-32 |
|---|---|
| 4.18 As he walked by the Sea of Galilee | 15.29 he passed along the Sea of Galilee |
| Περιπατῶν δὲ παρὰ τὴν θάλασσαν τῆς Γαλιλαίας | ἦλθεν παρὰ τὴν θάλασσαν τῆς Γαλιλαίας |
| 5.1 he went up the mountain | 15.29 and he went up the mountain |
| ἀνέβη εἰς τὸ ὄρος | ἀναβὰς εἰς τὸ ὄρος |
| 5.1 he sat down | 15.29 he sat down |
| καθίσαντος αὐτου | ἐκάθητο ἐκεῖ |
| 4.25 great crowds | 15.30 great crowds |
| ὄχλοι πολλοί | ὄχλοι πολλοί |
| 4.24 and he cured them | 15.30 and he cured them |
| καὶ ἐθεράπευσεν αὐτούς | καὶ ἐθεράπευσεν αὐτούς |
| 5.1 his disciples [came to him] | 15.32 [he called] his disciples to him |
| [προσῆλθαν αὐτῷ] οἱ μαθηταὶ αὐτοῦ | [προσκαλεσάμενος] τοὺς μαθητὰς αὐτοῦ |

Matthew sets up similarities between people and events in order to accentuate the similarities, but, most especially, the dissimilarities between them. Matthew's fashioning of the second feeding account in a Moses-type setting serves to recall the story of Moses and the feeding of the

121. Hanson distinguishes five literary units based on mountain locations: the mountain of initiation-ordeal, 4.1-12; the mount of instruction, 4.25–8.1; the mount of healing, 15.29-31; the mount of epiphany, 17.1-8; and, finally, the mount of commissioning, 28.16-20. See K.C. Hanson, 'Transformed on the Mountain: Ritual Analysis and the Gospel of Matthew', *Sem* 67 (1994), pp. 147–70 (157).

122. See Allison, *New Moses*, p. 179; Brown, *John*, I, p. 232. Roth points out that the definite article in the phrase, '*the* mountain', points to a symbolic use. See also Roth, 'Moses and Matthew', p. 365. The 1960s and 1970s saw some scholars reject outright the occurrence of any intended parallelism to Moses in Matthew, for example, Floyd V. Filson, *A Commentary on the Gospel according to St. Matthew* (New York: Harper & Row, 1960), p. 29; William Foxwell Albright and C.S. Mann, *Matthew* (AB; Garden City, NY: Doubleday, 1971). For a more recent positive analysis of same, see Allison, *New Moses*, pp. 173–94; Gundry, *Matthew*, pp. 78–100.

multitude 'in the wilderness' (cf. Exod. 16.32; Mt. 15.33 // Mk 8.4), rather than the feeding at Gilgal by Elisha (so Mark).

What is striking is that while Moses orders that no bread be kept for the following day, Matthew, following Mark, tells us that the disciples took up '*seven* baskets full' (Mt. 15.37 // Mk 8.8; for '*twelve* baskets', cp. Mt. 14.20 // Mk 6.44; cf. 2 Kgs 4.43-44). Secondly, while in Matthew, 'all ate and were satisfied' at this eucharistic scene (Mt. 15.37; cf. 6.11; 26.26;),[123] in Exodus 'all complained against Moses and Aaron in the wilderness' (Exod. 16.2; cf. 16.28).

Matthew's literary links with the feeding account in Exodus 16, in which Moses is portrayed as a less than adept leader whose disciples complained and broke the Sabbath in the hopes of being fed, serves to accentuate his own portrait of Jesus as an adept leader (he questions, commands, and the crowd obeys), who completely satisfied 'all'.

### 3. *Transfiguration* (Mt. 17.1-8 // Mk 9.2-11)

Scholars discern a parallelism between Mark's account of the Transfiguration scene and both the account of the ratification of the Covenant scene in Exodus 24 and the Renewal of the Covenant scene in Exodus 34.[124] Matthew's *addition* of the majestic imperative, 'Look!' (ἰδού, Mt. 17.3) and his *added* detail that the cloud was 'bright' (φωτεινή, Mt. 17.5) increases the solemnity of his account. Matthew, following his Markan source, has a voice from the cloud declare: 'This is my Son, the Beloved' (Mt. 17.5 // Mk 9.7). In both Gospels, 'Jesus is the prophet God has promised to raise up and Jesus surpasses Moses because he is called Son.'[125] Matthew qualifies the heavenly declaration describing Jesus with a quotation from Isa. 42.1: 'in whom I [God] am well pleased' (Mt. 17.5). In this way he recalls the earlier context of Jesus' baptism (Mt. 3.17 // Mk 1.11)[126] and, in so doing, strengthens Matthew's portrait of Jesus as the fulfilment of the Scriptures.

Matthew introduces Moses before Elijah, *reversing* the introductory

---

123. A eucharistic tenor may be attributed to this feeding story in the light of the dense volume of parallel vocabulary between the first feeding story, Mt. 14.13-21, and the account of the Last Supper, Mt. 26.20-29. For a list of these parallels, see Allison, *New Moses*, pp. 259–60.

124. The parallels include (1) a high mountain setting (cp. Mk 9.2 // Exod. 24.12, 15-18; 34.3); (2) the radiance of the central figure (cp. Mk 9.2-3 // Exod. 34.29-30, 35); (3) the presence of a special group of three people (cp. Mk 9.2 // Exod. 24.1); (4) its occurrence after six days (cp. Mk 9.2 // Exod. 24.16); (5) a fearful response from those who saw the radiance (cp. Mk 9.6 // Exod. 34.29-30); (6) a cloud which descends and overshadows this mountain (cp. Mk 9.7 // Exod. 24.15-18 // 34.5); and, finally, (7) a voice coming from the cloud (cp. Mk 9.7 // Exod. 24.16). See Allison, *New Moses*, pp. 243–44.

125. Stan Harstine, *Moses as a Character in the Fourth Gospel* (JSNTSup, 229; Sheffield: Sheffield University Press, 2002), p. 88.

126. Allison, *New Moses*, p. 244.

order of Mark. In this way, he elevates Moses over Elijah (Mt. 17.3 // Mk 9.4).[127]

Matthew *adds* to his Markan source the comment that Jesus' 'face shone like the sun' (Mt. 17.2). Here, Matthew transfers to Jesus what was said of Moses' face on Sinai when he was speaking to God (Mt. 17.2; Exod. 34.29-30, 35). It indicates that Matthew, in his rewriting of Mark's Transfiguration account, is working from the principle that 'the more one exalted Moses, the more one exalted Jesus'.[128] In this way, Matthew elevates the Christology of his Markan source: 'Moses meets "God-with-us" on a new cloud-covered mountain just as he met God on the old cloud-covered Sinai (Exod. 24.15-18; cf. Exod. 40.34-38; Num. 9.15-22; 1 Kgs 8.10-11; 2 Macc. 2.8).'[129]

Matthew further exalts Jesus over Moses by *positivizing* the disciples' response to Jesus' radiance: 'they fell to the ground and were overcome by fear [ἐφοβήθησαν]' (Mt. 17.6). He also *omits* the remark in Mark concerning Peter's ignorance (Mk 9.6a).[130] He replaces the negative response of the disciples in Mark's account: 'for they were terrified [ἔκφοβοι]' (Mk 9.6b) which mirrors Exod. 34.30 where we are told that the Israelites 'were afraid to come near him [Moses]' after he descends from the theophany on the mountain (Exod. 34.29-35). The response of the disciples at the Transfiguration in both Gospels is later mirrored in the respective responses of the disciples after the resurrection (Mt. 28.17; Mk 16.8). Matthew's positivization of Mark's portrait of the disciples continues to the end of the Gospel.

### 4. *Entry into Jerusalem* (Mt. 21.1-11 // Mk. 11.1-10)

The portrait of Jesus as king in Mark's account of Jesus' entry into Jerusalem reflects the influence of Zech. 9.9 (cf. Mk 11.2). This portrait is amplified in Matthew's parallel account by his explicit citation of Zech. 9.9: 'Look, your king is coming to you' (Mt. 21.5), and by his rewriting of Mark's 'blessed is the kingdom of David our father' (*NJB*, Mk 9.10) as, 'hosanna to the Son of David' (Mt. 21.9).

Scholars have long puzzled over Matthew's doubling of Mark's single animal in the account of his entry into Jerusalem (Mt. 21.9 // Mk 9.2). How could Jesus ride two animals at once? Most scholars allude to this. Some see it only as an example of Matthew's habit of doubling elements

127. Gundry, *Matthew*, p. 343.
128. Allison, *New Moses*, p. 275.
129. Gundry, *Matthew*, p. 344.
130. Gundry, *Matthew*, p. 344.

found in Mark, while others note that Matthew, following Zechariah maintains the incongruity that a person would ride two animals at once.[131]

As noted above, the fulfilment citations of the prophets in Matthew usually point to narratives found in the Torah.[132] Narrative incongruities in Matthew, as with other authors in antiquity, very often point to two (literary) directions at once. These two techniques provide the solution to this literary anomaly here.

Let us look at the first of these techniques – Matthew's citation of a prophetic text in order to point to a text of the Torah. Matthew's citation reads: 'Tell the daughter of Zion, "Look, your king is coming to you, humble,[133] and mounted on a donkey, and on a colt, the foal of a donkey"' (ἐπὶ ὄνον καὶ ἐπὶ πῶλον, Mt. 21.5). Immediately after the citation from Zechariah, Matthew rewrites Mark's, 'and they [disciples] went away and found a colt ...' (Mk 11.4), as, 'the disciples went and did as Jesus directed them' (Mt. 21.6; cf. Mt. 15.24-29). Matthew is here orientating his vocabulary towards that of Exod. 12.28, 'The Israelites went (ἀπελθόντες) and did (ἐποίησαν) just as the Lord had commanded (ἐνετείλατο) Moses and Aaron to do (ἐποίησαν)'.[134]

We can be sure that Matthew's vocabulary comes from Exodus here because Matthew provides another close verbal parallel to this phrase in Exod. 12.28 in Mt. 26.19: 'So the disciples did (ἐποίησαν) as Jesus had directed (συνέταξεν) them, and they prepared the Passover meal.' The Israelites did what had been directed by God to them *through* Moses and Aaron. The disciples do what Jesus himself directs. Thus even here Matthew presents Jesus as greater than Moses (cf. Mt. 1.24; 22.24-33).

Link this with the narrative incongruity of Matthew's two donkeys. The similarity of thought and vocabulary between Matthew's citation of Zech. 9.9 in Mt. 21.5 and Exod. 4.20, a context involving Moses, has often been noted by scholars: 'So Moses took his wife and his sons, put them on a donkey ('donkeys', τὰ ὑποζύγια), and went back to the land of Egypt; and Moses carried the staff of God in his hand' (Exod. 4.20; see Table 5.3 above).

We already noted that scholars frequently refer to the parallels between this narrative in Exodus and Mt. 2.12-23. Allison notices that Matthew's

---

131. See ch. 2, section 1. b. above, for an example of how scholars until recently thought that Virgil had cited Homer incorrectly. Current research indicates that he conflated two models, Apollonius and Homer.

132. For examples of Paul's uses of this method, see ch. 3, section 2. above.

133. Matthew's portrayal of Jesus as humble or meek (πραΰς) corresponds to a characteristic of Moses (Mt. 5.5; 11.29; 12.19; cf. Num. 12.3). See Gundry, *Matthew*, p. 69.

134. Senior notes that, 'scholars generally agree that some of the distinctive features found in Matthew's fulfilment quotations are the result of adapting the quotation to the gospel context in which they are used'. See Senior, *Gospel of Matthew*, p. 36.

rewriting of Mark's single donkey as two donkeys serves as a distinctive detail or literary flag linking Matthew's rewriting of Zech. 9.9 to this 'flight' narrative in which two (or more) donkeys are sat upon.[135] The effect of being sent back to this context in Exodus is that it serves to amplify Jesus' courageous response on entering Jerusalem in this fashion. Moses is promised a situation of relative safety. 'Go back to Egypt; for all those who were seeking your life are dead' (Exod. 4.19). Jesus chooses to face the turmoil in the city, even though he is aware that he will be handed over and condemned to death by those who seek his life (Mt. 21.10; cf. Mt. 20.17-19; 2.3).

Thus Matthew's rewriting of Mark recalls Moses. A narrative incongruity serves to betray how his explicit use of an Old Testament citation which was alluded to in Mark could for the ancients serve as a pointer to the prophet Moses.[136] Moreover, to Mark's portrait of Jesus as king, he adds that of prophet: 'This is *the* prophet Jesus ...' (Mt. 21.17). Note his use of the article. Jesus is not another in a line of Jewish prophets; he, not Moses, is *the* prophet. In this subtle way, Matthew's rewriting of Mark presents Jesus as 'greater than' the prophet Moses.

## 3. *Conclusion*

The aim of this chapter has been, first, to present a more in-depth analysis of Matthew's overall literary and theological agenda of judaization which is reflected in his rewriting of Mark; and, secondly, to provide further evidence that the methods and techniques used by Graeco-Roman authors to incorporate earlier sources into their works is also found reflected in his use of Mark as a source.

In the first part, Matthew's strategy in relation to his use of Mark is

---

135.  Allison, *New Moses*, pp. 251–52. Maarten J.J. Menken sees in the reference to the two donkeys a link with the account in 2 Samuel where Ziba offered a pair of donkeys to King David to leave Jerusalem (2 Sam. 16.1-4). Because of the scant evidence of Matthew's use of 2 Samuel, we prefer the above solution. See Maarten J.J. Menken, 'Context and Textual Form of the Quotation from Zechariah 9,9 in Matthew 21,5', in Menken (ed.), *Matthew's Bible*, pp. 105–16; *idem*, 'The Quotation from Zech 9,9 in Mt 21,5 and in Jn 12,15', in Adelbert Denaux (ed.), *John and the Synoptics* (BETL, 101; Leuven: Leuven University Press, 1992), pp. 571–78 (574). Surprisingly, Sabbe, usually an acute discerner of literary contacts, appears to miss the point here. Comparing John's citation of Ps. 22.19 in John 19.24 with Matthew's citation of the same Old Testament text in Mt. 21.5, he concludes that, 'the author [John] has nothing special in mind with the two separate actions just as Matthew's literal interpretation of the now quoted Zechariah 9,9, "the ass and the colt", (Mt 21: 2–7) added no special meaning to the Markan Story'. See Maurits Sabbe, 'The Johannine Account of the Death of Jesus and Its Synoptic Parallels (Jn 19,16b-42)', *ETL* 70 (1994), pp. 34–63 (59).

136.  Goulder recognizes this aspect of Matthew: 'Matthew ... writes his interpretation into scripture'. See Goulder, *Midrash*, p. 36.

outlined: Matthew judaizes Mark. An overview of Matthew's restructuring of Mark as based on key numerals of Judaism is given. Matthew reorganizes Mark's narrative of Jesus into a well-balanced *poly-structure*, a structure based on the numerals two, three, five, seven and twelve. Matthew's dense use of these numerals is one of the two key ways in which he judaizes Mark. Matthew organizes his Markan (and other) material thus in order to steep the narrative of Jesus Christ in Jewish theological overtones.

In the second part, the other key way in which Matthew judaizes his Markan source is presented, namely, his method of embedding Old Testament Scripture, in particular, the Torah, in his reworking of it. He legitimizes Jesus as the Christ by reference to Scripture, as did Mark.

It is demonstrated that Matthew sets his Markan source material within a torahized narrative frame: Matthew 1–2 reflects the influence of Genesis and Exodus; Mt. 28.16-20, the influence of Deuteronomy. This is followed by an examination of Matthew's rewriting of *four* Markan pericopae within this torahized frame, namely, Fasting in the Wilderness (Mt. 4.1-11 // Mk 1.12-13), the Second Feeding Account (Mt. 15.32-39 // Mk. 8.1-10), the Transfiguration (Mt. 17.1-8 // Mk 9.2-11), and the Entry into Jerusalem (Mt. 21.1-11 // Mk 11.1-10). The cumulative evidence confirms not only that Matthew judaizes Mark by means of his extensive use of Old Testament Scripture but also that he uses the figure of Moses to amplify certain aspects of Jewish theology, in order, ultimately, to amplify his Christology.

## Chapter 6

## MATTHEW'S TORAHIZING OF MARK IN TWO KEY TEXTS: MATTHEW 10 AND 18

An analysis of Matthew's use of Old Testament Scripture and Mark as a source in Matthew 10 and 18, the Mission and Community Discourses respectively, provides further evidence of Matthew's judaization of his Markan source. In Matthew 10, he does so by embedding Old Testament citations, references and allusions into his reworking of Mark. In Matthew 18, he does so by placing his rewritten Markan material (Mt. 18.1-15) in between materials that are highly deuteronomized (Mt. 17.22-27; and 18.15-35). In this way, he 'surrounds the material on fraternal correction with material promoting the spirit of generosity, humility, and forgiveness'.[1] In these two discourses we find further evidence of his emulation of his Markan source in terms of structure, and his amplification of Mark's Christology.

We noted above that Matthew 10 and 18 are linked. They share several parallels in terms of vocabulary, themes and length. We observe the following:

1. the phrase 'little ones' (Mt. 10.42 // Mt. 18.6, 10, 14)
2. the theme and vocabulary about the one who 'welcomes you/little child welcomes me [Jesus]' (Mt. 10.40 // Mt. 18.5)
3. the detail of the disciples' experience of 'the name' of Jesus (Mt. 10.22 // Mt. 18.5, 20)
4. the detail of the disciples coming before one or more Gentile 'king(s)' (Mt. 10.17-20 // Mt. 18.23-35; cf. Mt. 17.25)
5. the references to brothers and servants (Mt. 10.21, 24-25 // Mt. 18.15, 24-35)
6. Matthew's use of the verb 'to be moved with compassion' (σπλαγχνίζομαι) in Mt. 9.36, the introduction, to Matthew 10, forms an *inclusio* with the parable with which Matthew 18 ends, as it is also used at Mt. 18.27

---

1. Davies and Allison, *Matthew*, II, p. 751. See Table 5.1 above. See Boring, 'Convergence', p. 593.

Matthew uses the latter part of Mark 9 as a source for both the end of the Mission discourse (Mt. 10.40, 41 // Mk 9.37b, 41) and the beginning of the Community Discourse (Mt. 18.1-2, 5 // Mk 9.34, 36a, 37a).

The distribution of Mark by Matthew in Matthew 10 and 18 may be presented as follows:

Table 6.1: *The Distribution of Mark in Matthew 10 and 18*[2]

| Mark 3, 6, 9, 10, 13 | Matthew 10 |
|---|---|
| 6.34 | 9.36 |
| – – | 9.37-38 Q *logion* |
| 3.13-14, 16-19a; 6.7-8 | 10.1-5a |
| 3.15; 6.8-11 | 10.5b-15 |
| 13.9-13; 10.43-44 | 10.16-25 |
| 4.22 [cf. 8.34-35, 38] | 10.26-39 |
| 9.37b, 41 [cf. 9.35] | 10.40-42 |
| *Mark 9, 10, 14* | *Matthew 18* |
| 9.34, 36, 37a; 10.15 | 18.1-5 |
| 9.42a, 43, 45, 47; 14.21 | 18.6-10 |
| – – | 18.12-35 |

In Matthew 10, Matthew expands Mark's four-verse pericope on mission (Mk 6.7-11) into a ten-verse pericope on mission (Mt. 10.5-15). This ten-verse passage forms the first major part of his mission discourse (Mt. 10.1-38). In Matthew 18, Matthew *conflates* Mark's five-verse pericope on the issue of who is the greatest (Mk 9.33-37) with Mark's *logion* about Entering the Kingdom (Mk 10.15). He reworks it into a five-verse pericope on the issue of True Greatness (Mt. 18.1-5). He then *abbreviates* Mark's nine-verse pericope On Leading Others Astray (9.42-50) into a four-verse pericope on a similar theme (Mt. 18.6-10). For the remainder of the discourse on community, Matthew does not use Mark at all. Rather, he uses the so-called Q source and his own special material (M; Mt. 18.12-35).[3]

---

2. An aspect of Matthew's methodology toward the creation of the macro-structure of his Gospel is reflected in his micro-structural arrangement of these discourses. This is evident from the order in which he uses the pericopae of his Markan source. You will recall how we observed that Matthew distributes elements of Mark creatively before Mt. 12.12, but after that follows the Markan order exactly. The same pattern is discernable with these two discourses. In Matthew 10, Matthew distributes elements from Mark 3, 6, 9, 10 and 13 in mixed order. In Matthew 18, Matthew follows exactly Mark's order, drawing from Mark 9 and 10, except for just one displaced verse from Mark 10 – the *logion* on Entering the Kingdom (Mt. 18.3 // Mk 10.15).

3. Mt. 18.10-14 // Lk. 15.3-7; Mt. 18.15-18 // Lk. 17.3; Mt. 18.19-20 (M); Mt. 18.21-22 // Lk. 17.4; Mt. 18.23-35 (M).

The aim of this chapter is, first, to examine Matthew's judaization of the Markan source material by incorporating Old Testament elements in these two discourses; and, secondly, to demonstrate that the methods and techniques used by Graeco-Roman authors to incorporate earlier sources into their works are also found reflected in his use of Mark as a source in Matthew 10 and 18.

Matthew's judaization of Mark in these discourses will be examined under the following headings:

1.  A Ready Harvest (Mt. 9.35–10.5a // Mk 3.13-14, 16-19a; 6.7-8, 34)
2.  Becoming 'As the Least' Materially (Mt. 10.5-14 // Mk 6.7-8)
3.  Becoming 'As the Least' Socially (Mt. 10.17-25 // Mk 13.9-13; and 10.43-44)
4.  Becoming 'As the Least' Spiritually (Mt. 10.40-42 // Mk 9.37b, 41)
5.  The Temple Tithe Issue Deuteronomized (Mt. 17.22-27)
6.  Becoming as a Little Child (Mt. 18.1-10 // Mk 9.34, 36, 37a; 10.15; 9.42a, 43, 45, 47; 14.21, in that order)
7.  Brotherly Correction Deuteronomized (Mt. 18.15-35)

## 1. *A Ready Harvest* (Mt. 9.35–10.5a // Mk 3.13-14, 16-19a; 6.7-8, 34)

In the introductory narrative to the Mission Discourse, Matthew describes the people as 'a sheep without a shepherd' (πρόβατα μὴ ἔχοντα ποιμένα, 9.36), a phrase taken from Mk 6.34. In the Old Testament, God and the prophets were often imaged as shepherd(s), and the people of Israel as 'lost sheep' (cf. Isa. 53.6; Jer. 50.6; Ezek. 4.5-6).[4] Matthew incorporates this in Mt. 10.6. In Mark, the image of the shepherd-less sheep is found in the context of his first Feeding Story (Mk 6.32-44) where it echoes Exodus 16, as noted above.

In terms of vocabulary, however, the parallel expression in Matthew has its closest verbal parallel in Num. 27.17 (πρόβατα οἷς οὐκ ἔστιν ποιμήν),[5] a context also with clear parallels to Matthew's. In both Old Testament

---

4. Gundry observes that, 'Gentile territories bounded Galilee on all sides except the southern. There, Samaria hemmed it in. Consequently the prohibitions against departure to Gentiles and entry into any city of Samaritans initially limits the disciples to Galilee. In this way Matthew indicates that their ministry must follow the pattern of Jesus' ministry, which he has already taken pains to show, began in Galilee (4.14-16). The limitation of the ministry to Galilean Jews, despised as being among "the people of the land", who failed to observe the rabbinic tradition closely, suggests that "the lost sheep of the house of Israel" are that despised class within the nation.' See Gundry, *Matthew*, p. 185. Also, Matthew, by Mt. 8.28-34, begins to have Jesus move outside Galilee and go to 'the other side' briefly, but return again by Mt. 9.1. This move provides an initial indication of the universal nature of Jesus' mission. Its location may have been dictated by Matthew's structural agenda in chs 8–9.

5. Bauer, *Structure*, p. 214; Davies and Allison, *Matthew*, I, p. 127; Luz, *Matthew 8–20*, p. 64; Gundry, *Matthew*, pp. 181, 308.

contexts – Exodus 16 and Num. 27.16 – the shepherds of Israel appoint a successor or successors (Num. 27.12-23; cp. Mt. 9.36–10.42). Just as Joshua is appointed by the Lord through Moses, so the disciples are appointed by Jesus (Num. 27.18; Mt. 10.5; cf. Mt. 2.6d; Exod. 1.1). Just as Moses, 'a man in whom is the spirit' (Num. 28.18), gives authority to Joshua, so Jesus gives his authority to the disciples to speak 'in the Spirit of your Father' (Mt. 10.20). Finally, just as Moses was called to lay his 'hand upon him [Joshua]' (Num. 28.18), so Jesus summons his disciples to 'cure all kinds of diseases' as he has done when he 'stretched out his hand' (Mt. 8.3, 15; 9.26, 29).[6]

We can be sure that Matthew intends to evoke a comparison between Jesus and Moses in the introduction to the Mission Discourse by the presence of further shared parallel vocabulary and themes between Matthew and the book of Numbers.[7] Matthew's introductory narrative includes the phrase: '*These are the names* [of the twelve disciples]' (τὰ ὀνόματά ἐστιν ταῦτα, Mt. 10.2; cf. Mt. 10.1, 5; 11.1).[8] The introductory narrative of the book of Numbers includes the exact same phrase in a parallel context: Moses missions a group of twelve helpers from the twelve tribes and then lists their names (ταῦτα τὰ ὀνόματα, Num. 1.5). This phrase is only found in Matthew *in the whole of the New Testament*.

What is intriguing, however, is that this same phrase occurs in the opening verse of Exodus: '*These are the names* of the sons of Israel who came to Egypt with Jacob, each with his household'[9] (ταῦτα τὰ ὀνόματα, Exod. 1.1), after which the twelve names are listed.[10] From the combination of this latter data with the earlier detail that Matthew's use of Mk 6.34 at Mt. 9.36b reflects Exodus 16, one can only conclude that this is an example of a double-reference. While Matthew's vocabulary is closer to that of Numbers in terms of theme, his matter is reflected in both Old Testament texts. This is an example of where 'Matthew's text is often polysemous and ... [can] send vectors in several directions at once'.[11]

What of Matthew's use of Old Testament Scripture and Mark in the discourse proper, Mt. 10.5-42? An analysis of a synopsis between Matthew 10 and Mark demonstrates that Matthew uses Mark as a source for three sections of the discourse (see Table 6.1 above): at the

---

6. Bauer, *Structure*, p. 148.

7. Gundry notes that, in Mt. 10.1, Matthew omits the reference to Jesus' going up the mountain in the parallel Markan verse, 3.13, because 'he has already used that piece of information in Matt 5.1'. See Gundry, *Matthew*, p. 182.

8. See Hagner, *Matthew 1–13*, p. 265.

9. Note Matthew's use of 'household' in Mt. 10.25, 36.

10. While many scholars note Matthew's reference to Num. 27.17 in Mt. 9.36b, Bauer is the only scholar, we found, who notes the link between Num. 1.5 and Mt. 10.1, 2. See Bauer, *Structure*, p. 214.

11. Allison, *New Moses*, p. 242.

beginning, Mt. 10.5b-14, he uses elements of Mark 3 and 6; in the middle, Mt. 10.17-25, he uses much of Mark 13 and some of Mark 10; and, for the last literary unit, Mt. 10.40-42, he uses some of Mark 9.

When we examine the three sections in Matthew 10, in which he makes use of Mark in turn, we discover that the disciples are instructed to become *'as the least'* in three ways in imitation of Jesus – materially (Mt. 10.9-13 // Mk 6.8-11), socially (Mt. 10.17-25 // Mk 13.9-13 and 10.43-44) and spiritually (Mt. 10.37-42 // Mk 8.34-35, and 9.37, 41; cf. Mt. 25.31-46). Concomitantly, they are also to become as *'as the greatest'* in three ways in imitation of Jesus, that is, they are 'to do' (Mt. 10.1, 8), 'to speak' (Mt. 10.19, 20) and 'to give and receive hospitality' (Mt. 10.40, 42; cf. 'Words', Matthew 5–7; 'Deeds', Matthew 8–9; 'Giving/Receiving hospitality', Mt. 22.1-11).[12]

## 2. *Becoming 'As the Least' Materially* (Mt. 10.5-14 // Mk 6.7-8)

Matthew's judaizing of Mk 6.7-8 by means of his use of Old Testament Scripture serves to convey two things. First, the disciples are to receive power and authority 'as the greatest', that is, Jesus. They will do as he does (Mt. 10.6-8; cf. Mt. 10.1). Secondly, they are to become 'as the least' materially, that is, to take absolutely nothing material with them on mission, in imitation of him (Mt. 10.9).

Matthew sets out very specific material requirements for mission, making them even more radical than those found in Mark: 'Take no gold, or silver, or copper in your belts, no bag for your journey, or two tunics, or sandals, or a staff' (Mt. 10.8-9 // Mk 6.8-9).[13] While Mark allows staff and sandals, Matthew allows for neither. In fact, in a sequence of *seven* items reflecting a definite graduation from the greater to the lesser, he eliminates completely the possession of anything material (cf. Mt. 5.3;

---

12.    Davies and Allison observe that, 'only after reciting Jesus' words and deeds (chapters 5–9) do the disciples really come into the picture. This is because Jesus and the disciples are two different subjects, and Matthew, with his proclivity for thematic as opposed to historical and chronological thinking, wants to handle one theme at a time. So Jesus, the model, comes first. The disciples, the followers, come second.' See Davies and Allison, *Matthew*, II, pp. 151 and 197. This is in keeping with the Seutonian-type topical biography genre outlined above. See Ch. 4, section 1, and Ch. 4, n. 55.

13.    Hagner clearly misses the point of Matthew's agenda in rewriting Mark here. He writes that, 'the differences between the four lists of what to take on the missionary journey are not significant since essentially the same point is being made by all: one is not to be encumbered by the usual equipment taken on journeys'. So Hagner, *Matthew 1–13*, p. 269. See also Davies and Allison, *Matthew*, II, p. 171. Compare this to, for example, Beare's observation that the rearrangement reflects Matthew's 'desire to add emphasis to the prohibition of gain'. See F.W. Beare, 'The Mission of the Disciples and the Mission Charge: Matthew 10 and Parallels', *JBL* 89 (1970), pp. 1–13 (10).

6.19-34).[14] The inference is that what is essential for the work of mission is spiritual, rather than material, namely, the power and the authority of Jesus, and the gift of the Spirit of the Father (Mt. 10.1, 20).

Matthew's list of the three precious coins in the order of 'gold, silver and copper', reflects an ordering of his vocabulary toward Old Testament usage. It is most especially evocative of Exod. 25.1-3: 'The Lord said to Moses: Tell the Israelites to take for me an offering ... you shall receive the offering for me. This is the offering that you shall receive from them: *gold, silver, and bronze* ...'. Note also the similar vocabulary-cluster based on the words between this text and Matthew 10 – 'take', Mt. 10.8; 'Lord', Mt. 10.24-25; and 'receive', Mt. 10.40-42. The very things that Moses had told the Israelites are required for the building of God's sanctuary – gold, silver and bronze[15] – are the very things that Jesus tells 'the twelve' are *not* required (Mt. 10.2) for the building of 'the kingdom of heaven' (Mt. 10.7), or God's new sanctuary, Jesus (Mt. 10.40).

Matthew presents Jesus as greater than Moses. Recognition of this helps to make sense of the shocking charge made by the Jewish leaders against Jesus and his disciples. They claim that the 'master' [Jesus] and, by association, his 'household' must be working under the power of Beelzebul (a name which means 'lord of the house/dwelling'[16] (Mt. 10.25; cf. Mt. 9.32-34).[17]

## 3. Becoming 'As the Least' Socially (Mt. 10.17-25 // Mk 13.9-13; and 10.43-44)

In Mt. 10.17-25, Matthew draws upon two sections of Mark, namely, Mk 13.9-13; and 10.43-44. His judaization of this section of Mark by means of his use of Old Testament Scripture serves to convey two things. First, the disciples are commissioned to speak (Mt. 10.19-20) as 'the greatest', that is, as Jesus spoke in 'the Spirit of your Father' (Mt. 10.20; cf. Matthew 5–7, 'Words'). Secondly, they are to become 'as the least' socially. They will be hated and treated as criminals. Mark's mission discourse has no

---

14. Luz, *Matthew 8–20*, p. 76.

15. Among the Synoptists, only Matthew refers to 'gold'. He does so four times. His first usage occurs after the Magi do homage to Jesus. By the end of the Gospel, the significance of the gesture is evident. Jesus Christ is himself the locus of true worship (Mt. 2.11; cf. Mt. 28.17). The other three occurrences are found in Matthew's second rewriting of Mark 13 in Matthew 23 (23.16, 17 *bis*).

16. Hagner, *Matthew*, p. 282; Davies and Allison, *Matthew*, II, p. 195.

17. Harrington writes: 'In reading Matt 10.17-18 and 10.21-22 one must be sensitive to both literary convention and actual experience.' See Harrington, *Matthew*, p. 147. Note also the significance of the Beelzebul pericope structurally, as outlined above. See Ch. 5, section 1, a. above.

account of such a persecution.[18] In this way, Matthew prefigures Jesus' own fate. Proleptically, the fate of the disciples is to mirror that of Jesus (Mt. 10.17-25 // Mk 13.9-3; cp. Mt. 27.27-56).[19]

Matthew 10.16 flags the utterly radical nature of the disciples' mission outlined in Mt. 10.17-25. There (Mt. 10.16), Matthew tells us that Jesus sends the disciples among wolves *without even so much as a staff*. This is the utter reversal of human logic. In the next verse, Mt. 10.17, Matthew rewrites Mk 13.9a: Mark's, 'as for yourselves, beware' (Mk 13.9a) becomes in Matthew, 'beware of men' (Mt. 10.17). Thus Matthew sends us back to the warning given in his first discourse: 'Beware of false prophets, who come to you in sheep's clothing but inwardly are ravenous wolves' (Mt. 7.15; cf. Isa. 53.4). He has already shown how Jesus exposes false prophets for what they are, 'wolves'. Ironically, they too are included among 'the lost sheep of the House of Israel', though, as yet, they do not perceive it (Mt. 10.6).

Let us examine, first, the issue of the radical nature of Jesus, and then the issue of the social demands upon those whom he sends on mission.

Who is Jesus that he has the authority to mission people in the manner in which the God of the Old Testament missioned the prophets (Mt. 10.1, 5, 16)?[20] Who is he that people are willing to be dragged and abused before the highest authorities 'for my sake' (Mt. 10.18)? Who is he that his 'name' (Mt. 10.22) should cause such division and hatred among the families of those who use it?

According to Matthew, Jesus is someone with God-like authority – 'behold, I send' (Mt. 10.16).[21] He is 'the Son of Man' who is come (Mt. 10.23). It is the proclamation of such Christological claims that is the ultimate source of the persecution of Jesus and the disciples.

In terms of social cost, Matthew rewrites Mark's 'beating' (δαρήσεσθε, Mk 13.9) as 'flogging' (μαστιγώσουσιν, Mt. 10.17). He draws upon the verb μαστιγόω. The use of it here is evocative of Deuteronomy 25. There, it is used *three* times in relation to flogging a person found in the wrong in

---

18.   H.J.B. Combrink, 'Structural Analysis of Mt 9.35–11.1', *Neot* (1977), pp. 98–114 (100).

19.   Luz, *Matthew 8–20*, p. 89. See Davies and Allison, *Matthew*, II, p. 182, 197; Barbara E. Reid, 'Violent Endings in Matthew's Parables and Christian Nonviolence', *CBQ* 66 (2004), pp. 237–55 (241).

20.   Keener writes: 'Matthew repeatedly emphasizes that the disciples as Jesus' agents are his prophets, even greater than the prophets of old (5:11-12; 11:9; 13:17).' See Keener, *Matthew*, p. 330 and also pp. 314–15.

21.   Gundry notes that, 'the command to "Go" drops out as part of Matthew's deleting the fulfilment of the disciples' mission in Galilee. The omission allows "behold, I send" to come first. The characteristic insertion of ἐγώ (12–13,3) focuses attention on Jesus and his authority (cf. 23.24 with Lk. 11.49)'. See Gundry, *Matthew*, p. 191.

court (Deut. 25.1-3).[22] Matthew further judaizes Mark in his rewriting of Jesus' assurance to the disciples about witnessing in public. Matthew rewrites Mk 13.11, 'do not be troubled ... for it is not you who speak, but the Holy Spirit', as, 'for it is not you who speak, but the Spirit of *your Father* speaking through you' (Mt. 10.20). Matthew reorders his Markan source to the Old Testament vocabulary of God as 'Father'.[23]

Scholars often note contextual parallels between the material on persecution in Mt. 10.19-20 and Exod. 4.10-17.[24] In Exod. 4.10-17, God gives his instructions for the people to Moses, who in turn passes them on to Aaron. Aaron becomes Moses' mouthpiece for the people. Moses is afraid to speak to the people because he is a poor speaker and Aaron is a better one. In Matthew, Jesus instructs his disciples not to fear because the Father will speak *directly* 'through' them (Mt. 10.19). This literary link has the effect of presenting the disciples as even greater than Moses.

It is not surprising then that Jesus warns them that his name is enough to cause division in households (Mt. 10.21-22). Only in Matthew's Gospel is there mention of 'brother against brother'.[25] The persecutions will include 'betrayal,' 'death', 'rising up' and 'hatred' (Mt. 10.21-22). Here again, the choice of vocabulary prefigures aspects of the passion and resurrection of Jesus while, from a proleptic perspective, the lot of the disciples can be seen to mirror that of their master.

In Mt. 10.21, Matthew rewrites Mk 13.12, a verse which implicitly reflects the words of the prophet Micah (Micah 7.6).[26] Mark's prophetic reference is found in a literary context about familial divisions that are the result of depraved actions. Micah 7.6 reads: 'for the son treats the father with contempt, the daughter rises up against her mother, the daughter-in-law against her mother-in-law; your enemies are members of your own household'. Matthew's recognition of Mark's model here is confirmed by the fact that he uses the same Old Testament verse later in the discourse, in Mt. 10.35, where his citation of it is even more exact.[27]

Scholars recognize a connection between Mic. 7.6 and Exodus 5–6 (cf. Isa. 19.2).[28] In this Exodus narrative, we are told that the slave-drivers harassed the Israelites (Exod. 5.13; cf. Mt. 9.35), flogged their foremen

---

22.   A criminal could receive up to forty belts according to the law of Moses. See Davies and Allison, *Matthew*, II, p. 191; Gundry, *Matthew*, p. 193. Deuteronomy is a book that Matthew uses in Matthew 18, as we shall see below (sections 5. and 7.).

23.   See Hagner, *Matthew*, p. 277; Gundry, *Matthew*, p. 193.

24.   Harrington, *Matthew*, p. 142; Davies and Allison, *Matthew*, II, p. 193; Keener, *Matthew*, p. 324.

25.   Hagner, *Matthew*, I, p. 278.

26.   Luz, *Matthew 8–20*, pp. 85, 107–108; Harrington, *Matthew*, p. 150; Davies and Allison, *Matthew*, II, pp. 219–20; Gundry, *Matthew*, p. 193; Keener, *Matthew*, p. 328.

27.   Davies and Allison, *Matthew*, II, pp. 186–87.

28.   Gundry, *Matthew*, p. 9.

(Exod. 5.14, 16; cp. Mt. 10.17), ill-treated the nation and tried to kill the people (Exod. 5.21; cp. Mt. 10.21) because Moses spoke *in the Lord's name* (Exod. 5.22; cp. Mt. 10.22). God proceeded to comfort Moses and, through Moses, the people, by repeating the promise of his covenant to them (Exod. 6.2-13). Moses tells the 'sons of Israel' about God's reassurance. As they do not believe him, he refuses to give further witness before Pharaoh, though he was instructed to do so by God (Exod. 6.6).

This narrative helps to makes sense of Matthew's addition of the *logion*, Mt. 10.22, immediately after his citation of Mic. 7.6 in Mt. 10.21: 'But the one (ὁ δέ) who endures to the end will be saved' (Mt. 10.22; note the use of the singular here).[29] In Matthew, Jesus proceeds to give words of comfort to the disciples and instructs them to stand firm in the face of opposition (Mt. 10.26-33). Sent back to Exodus 5–6 via Mic. 7.6 (two-tier allusion), Matthew indicates that the disciples are to stand more firmly in witnessing to Jesus than Moses did in witnessing to God. They are not to give in before kings or courts, even if it causes severe familial divisions (cf. Mt. 10.28, 32-33). His request of them prefigures his own stance at his passion. Proleptically, we may say that it mirrors it (cf. Mt. 27.11-14).

In Mt. 10.24-25, Matthew shifts to another part of his Markan source, namely, Mk 10.43-44. His use of Mark here is primarily for Christological purposes. It serves to qualify the degree of imitation that is there between the disciples and Jesus: 'A disciple is not above the teacher, nor a slave above the master; it is enough for the disciple to be like the teacher' (Mt. 10.24-25a). In other words, though the disciples may heal with the authority of Jesus and be the channels of the Father's words, they are not equal to either Jesus or the Father.[30] Ironically, the opposing 'wolves', while not recognizing the correct nature of Jesus' lordship, recognize a differentiation between him and his disciples – Jesus is 'master' of the household (harvest/mission); the disciples are the members (labourers/missioners) (Mt. 10.25c-d; cf. Mt. 9.36-38).

### 4. *Becoming 'As the Least' Spiritually* (Mt. 10.40-42 // Mk 9.37b, 41)

We will now examine the third and last section at the end of the second discourse in which Matthew uses Mark. In Mt. 10.40-42, Matthew draws upon Mk 9.37b and 9.41. Matthew's use of Mark here serves to convey Jesus' final instruction to his missioners: the disciples are instructed not only to give and receive hospitality 'as the greatest', that is, in imitation of

---

29. Davies and Allison, *Matthew*, II, p. 187.
30. Gundry, *Matthew*, p. 195.

Jesus (cf. Mt. 22.1-11; 25.31-46);[31] they are also to become 'as the least' spiritually in imitation of him.

We are not unprepared for this conclusion. When the disciples receive his authority, they let go of material security (Mt. 10.5-15); when they receive the power to speak in his name, they let go of their own social security (Mt. 10.17-25); and now, as we shall see, when they receive God in another disciple, they let go personal security, that is, they become as 'little ones' interiorly (Mt. 10.40-42).

The three verses of Mt. 10.40-42 begin with the phrase, '(if) anyone receives' (ὁ δεχόμενος, cf. Mt. 10.37-39). Matthew has composed this final triadic unit in such a way that, first, the disciples are instructed to imitate both the host ('anyone') and the one hosted. Part of their mission is to give practical hospitality to one another. Part of their mission is to receive practical hospitality from one another. Secondly, the disciples are instructed about the universality of the mission. There is no longer any qualification for the recipients of the mission, in terms of race or religious tradition (Mt. 10.6). The only requirement is the act of receiving Jesus.

We notice that as the description of the nature of a disciple expands and becomes more explicit, the description of the nature of his reward or wages contracts and becomes more implicit. The kind of disciple to be welcomed is described first as 'you' (Mt. 10.40, so Mk 9.37b); secondly, as 'a prophet' and 'righteous person' (Mt. 10.41); and, thirdly, as 'one of these little ones ... [who] is a disciple' (Mt. 10.42; Matthew *adds* the adjective 'cold' to Mk 9.41).[32] The kind of reward or wages for the host-disciple is first described as 'me [Jesus] and the one who sent me [God]' (Mt. 10.40); then as the reward of 'a prophet'/'righteous person' (Mt. 10.41);[33] and thirdly, an unnamed reward or wage (Mt. 10.42).

What is the implication of this arrangement? Luz notes that nowhere else does Matthew 'like to use the idea of a graduated reward'.[34] However, it is not the reward that is graduated. That remains the same – Jesus and the one who sent him, God. Rather, it is the degree of spiritual 'littleness' of a disciple that is graduated. The more one becomes 'little' spiritually, the less one has need for the naming of the reward. Here, Matthew is at his most contemplative.

---

31.  Keener, *Matthew*, p. 314. Keener notes that, 'diaspora Judaism was especially scrupulous about hospitality, as ancient texts regularly attest ...' See Keener, *John*, I.146. For a list of such texts, see Keener, *John*, I, p. 146, n. 48. He also notes that, 'after this time [70 CE] the custom of hospitality to travellers would have required definitions of which sort of Jews were acceptable and which were not (those linked with Palestinian revolutionaries presumably would not have been). The same kinds of connections existed among Christians scattered throughout the empire.' See Keener, *John*, I, p. 148.

32.  Davies and Allison, *Matthew*, II, p. 228.

33.  H. Preisker, 'μισθός', *TDNT*, IV, pp. 695–728.

34.  Luz, *Matthew 8–20*, p. 121.

In terms of a disciple's reward or wages, the first element in the triad is explicit: the host-disciple in welcoming a disciple receives Jesus, and not only Jesus but God himself. What then is a prophet or holy man's reward or wage? The diction of 'prophet' and 'holy man', in that order, in a context of instruction on the hospitality God offers to those in need, has directed many scholars to see behind this Matthaean composition references to Elijah, called 'prophet', and Elisha, his disciple, and 'man of God' (1 Kgs 17.1-16; 2 Kgs 4).[35]

It has already been demonstrated that Matthew draws upon both these narrative contexts. What is their significance here? In the Elijah narrative, God rewards a widow with a store of food that will never be emptied through the intercession of the prophet (1 Kgs 17.16); in the Elisha text, God rewards a widow with enough food for herself and her children through the work of this 'man of God' (τὸν ἄνθρωπον τοῦ θεοῦ, 2 Kgs 4.42); and, on a second occasion, God rewards a hundred men with enough food such that they have 'some left over' through the intercession of Elisha (2 Kgs 4.44). When compared, Elisha's reward is less than Elijah's: for the former, some food is left over, for the latter there remains food that will *never* be spent (cf. Mt. 15.32-39). Matthew recognizes the message common to these two narratives, that the practical hospitality of God to the needy knows no bounds. However, he goes even further. He also makes explicit that the source of the food, God, is received as a guest in the act of hospitality (cf. Mt. 5.46).[36]

This is confirmed by the mention of 'prophets and holy men' by Matthew in Mt. 13.16. Many of these men longed to see 'the secrets of the kingdom of heaven' revealed. The disciples now receive the reward of their longing. They see and hear the mysteries of the kingdom of heaven revealed in the giving and receiving of hospitality in a spirit of lowliness (cf. Mt. 13.11).

This helps us to interpret Mt. 10.40-42. The practical hospitality of a disciple too must know no bounds (cf. 10.10): 'As one treats God's prophet, so one treats the God who sent the prophet (Exod. 16.8; 1 Sam. 8.7).'[37] However, there is more. There is no longer need for prophetic intermediaries like Elijah and Elisha to facilitate an exchange between

---

35.   Hagner writes: 'Possibly behind this idea of reward to those who show hospitality to prophets are the stories of those who did so to Elijah (1 Kgs 17.9-24) and Elisha (2 Kgs 4.9-37).' See Hagner, *Matthew*, I, p. 296. Also, Luz notes that, 'while the combination of prophets and righteous person occurs only in Matthew, in the two other texts (13.17 and 23.29) it is related to the Old Testament period'. See also Luz, *Matthew 8–20*, p. 119, n. 3

36.   Reid, 'Violent Endings', p. 247; Hermann W. Beyer, 'διακονέω', *TDNT*, II, p. 88.

37.   Keener, *Matthew*, p. 330.

God and his people.[38] God the Father, in Jesus, dwells *within* his disciples.[39] This internalization is radical theology to Jewish ears.[40] Thus ironically, the leaders who earlier claim that Jesus is spiritual 'Lord of the house' (οἰκοδεσπότην, Mt. 10.25) are yet again proved correct.[41]

In Mt. 10.41, Matthew's use of the conditional – 'if anyone ... because he believes' – is instructive. The explicit use of 'if' evokes the implicit use of 'if not'. On the one hand, the implication is that if, as host-disciple, one does not give the least hospitality ('a cup of *cold* water') to the least person 'because he believes', one will not receive Jesus, nor the one who sent him, God (cf. Mt. 25.27-46). On the other hand, if the receiving-disciple cannot receive the lowliest hospitality as 'one of these little ones', he cannot receive Jesus, nor the one who sent him, God (cf. Mt. 1.23).

Matthew's concluding reference to 'the twelve' (Mt. 11.1) forms an *inclusio* with the opening (Mt. 10.1, 2).

10.1   Then Jesus summoned his *twelve* (δώδεκα) disciples
10.2   These are the names of the *twelve* (δώδεκα) apostles
11.1   Now when Jesus had finished instructing his *twelve* (δώδεκα) disciples

The repetition of this theologically symbolic number, *twelve*, in a context of the theme of littleness and greatness suggests that for Mt. 10.40–11.1, Matthew draws upon the *logion* found in Mark's pericope concerning the exorcist:[42] Mark writes that Jesus 'sat down, called the *twelve* (δώδεκα), and said to them, "Whoever wants to be first must be last of all and servant of all"' (Mk 9.35).

Through his use of the Old Testament Scripture and Mark, Matthew gradually accentuates the spiritual nature of mission as the discourse unfolds. In his rewriting of Mk 9.37b; and 9.41 in Mt. 10.40-42, he creates a unit rich in Christology. The disciples are instructed to become 'as the

---

38.   Luz notes that, 'with the addition of v. 42, which puts the "little ones" on the level of the prophets and righteous, the latter are stripped of their special status'. See Luz, *Matthew 8–20*, p. 121.

39.   Davies and Allison, *Matthew*, II, p. 225.

40.   Keener, *Matthew*, p. 320. Hagner rightly notes that Matthew's use of '"receive", in 10.40 means not merely to welcome, e.g., into one's home, but to receive in a deeper sense (cf. 10.13-14). It is to accept the message of the disciples and thus the message of Jesus and his person, which is inseparable from the disciples' message (cf. 1.5; John 12.44; 13.20; for a negative statement of the same point, see Luke 10.16)'. See Hagner, *Matthew 1–13*, p. 295. See also, Luz, *Matthew 8–20*, p. 65.

41.   Luz observes that, 'while "teacher" and "servant" emphasise primarily the subordination under Jesus, "member of the household" suggests the relationship with him ...'. See Luz, *Matthew 8–20*, p. 96 and n. 21. See also Otto Michel, 'οἶκος', *TDNT*, V, p. 135.

42.   Luz notes that, 'for formal reasons the Markan pericope of the strange exorcist (Mark 9.38-40) did not fit his [Matthew's] discourse'. See Luz, *Matthew 8–20*, p. 119.

greatest' in terms of the unlimited extent of their hospitality on mission, in imitation of Jesus-God. Paradoxically, in the giving of this unlimited hospitality, they receive 'the greatest' hospitality themselves. The divine host becomes their guest. Concomitantly, the disciples are instructed to become 'as the least' spiritually, which is manifest externally in terms of the lowliness of the hospitality that they are willing to give to anyone who is a disciple, or receive from anyone, in imitation of Jesus.

## 5. *The Temple Tithe Issue Deuteronomized* (Mt. 17.22-27)

Matthew's use of Mark as a source in Mt. 18.1-10 is set between two deuteronomized narratives – Mt. 17.22-27; and 18.15-35.[43] The strong influence of Deuteronomy upon Matthew at the end of the First Gospel has already been noted above where it was demonstrated how Matthew uses Deuteronomy in 28.16-20 to portray Jesus as the 'new Torah' and 'new Temple'.[44]

The pericope concerning the Temple Tax, 17.22-27 (M), serves as the narrative introduction to the Community Discourse in a way that the pericope on the crowd's distress, 9.35-10.4, does to the Mission Discourse. In terms of Matthew's use of Deuteronomy, Mt. 17.22-27 reflects a similar theme as well as parallel vocabulary in parallel order, with the discourse material concerning the Clean and Unclean Animals and the Annual Tithe requirement in that order in Deut. 14.1-27.

Jesus not only does what the Jewish law requires, he exceeds it by generously and gratuitously paying the debt of another – his disciple, Peter. Jesus exceeds the law by extending the principle of paying one's tax debt not only to God's 'very own people out of all the peoples of the earth' (Deut. 14.2) but to all the 'kings of the earth', whether Gentile or Jew (Mt. 17.27). Thus he universalizes the issue. More importantly, theologically, is that, in Matthew, Jesus spiritualizes the issue of indebtedness: the ultimate debt is to God (Mt. 17.25).

The detail of Matthew's duplication of the tax, τέλη ἢ κῆνσον, provides a literary indication that there are two debts to be paid, the earthly and the spiritual. That the real debt is spiritual, rather than material and is owed to the king of heaven, and not to kings of the earth (cf. Mt. 2.2; 21.5; 27.11, 29, 37, 42), is confirmed by the detail of Peter's going 'into the

43. For a detailed analysis of Matthew's use of Deuteronomy in Mt. 17.22-27 and 18.15-34, see Thomas Brodie, 'Fish, Temple Tithe, and Remission: The God-Based Generosity of Deuteronomy 14–15 as One Component of Matt 17.22–18.35', *RB* 4 (1992), pp. 697–718.

44. See ch. 5, section 2. a. above. The strong influence of Deuteronomy upon Matthew is also evident because 'it is from Deuteronomy, rather than from Isaiah or the Psalms, that Matthew takes the greatest number of explicit quotations (13, as against 10 from Isaiah and 9 from the Psalms)'. See Brodie, 'Fish, Temple Tithe', p. 699.

house' with Jesus and coming before him (καὶ ἐλθόντα εἰς τὴν οἰκίαν προέφθασεν, Mt. 17.25a). The wise men also, having gone into the house (καὶ ἐλθόντες εἰς τὴν οἰκίαν), fell down and paid the little child, Jesus, homage (προσεκύνησαν, Mt. 2.11; cf. Mt. 10.25).

The effect of Matthew's deuteronomizing of his source here has been to emulate and internalize the requirements of the Law of Moses. In terms of function, it serves to encapsulate a profound Christological fact: Jesus is one with God, the source of everything. Thus he is the one to whom all on earth, whether Gentiles or Jews, are spiritually indebted (cf. Mt. 10.42). Moreover, this is the disposition with which disciples must approach their relationships with one another in community and the world. The matter of spiritual debt introduced here is further expanded upon in the second part of the Mission Discourse, Mt. 18.15-35, as we shall see below (section 7).

### 6. *Becoming as a Little Child* (Mt. 18.1-10 // Mk 9.34, 36, 37a; 10.15; 9.42a, 43, 45, 47; 14.21, *in that order*)

We saw how in Mt. 10.40-42 the disciples are instructed to become 'as the least' spiritually. This is manifest externally in terms of the least degree of hospitality that they are willing to give to and receive from one another in imitation of Jesus. In Mt. 18.1-14, Matthew rewrites parts of Mark 9 and 10 in order to internalize further the demand for the disciples to become 'as the least' spiritually.

Matthew 18.1-14 divides into three units, each of which is structured triadically: the first, Mt. 18.1-5, concerns the issue of Who is the Greatest?, and is a rewriting of Mk 9.34, 36a; 10.15; and 9.37a in that order; the second, Mt. 18.6-10, concerns the issue of Leading Others Astray, and is a rewriting of Mk 9.42a, 43, 45, 47; the third, Mt. 18.12-14, a parable concerning the Lost Sheep, is not a rewriting of Mark, but is added to create a complementary third triad because of its thematic or topological suitability (par. Lk./Q 15.3-7; cf. Mt. 9.36; 10.16).[45]

What was in Mark a heated dispute among the disciples about the issue as to which of them was the greatest (Mk 9.33-37) is rewritten in Matthew as a calm conversation between the disciples and Jesus about the more spiritual issue of the greatest in the kingdom of heaven (Mt. 18.1; cf. Mt. 18.4).[46] Matthew's addition of the double-reference to the 'kingdom of heaven' (18.3, 4) links this pericope to the preceding passage where he portrays the disciples as 'sons of a king' (Mt. 17.24-27).[47]

---

45. This is in keeping with the Suetonian-type topical biography genre outlined above. See Ch. 4, section 1, and Ch. 4, n. 55.

46. Harrington, *Matthew*, p. 264; Davies and Allison, *Matthew*, II, p. 755; Gundry, *Matthew*, p. 359.

47. Gundry, *Matthew*, p. 359.

Jesus places a child in front of the disciples (Mt. 18.2). By his action ['deed'], Jesus answers the disciples' dispute. The greatest in the kingdom of heaven is like a child. He qualifies his action with a 'word'. For Jesus' word here, Matthew has transposed up the *logion* from Mk 10.15 which is found in a pericope where Jesus also 'enacts his own words'[48] (Mk 10.13-16 // Mt. 19.13-15, where Mk 10.15 is omitted). Matthew's rewriting serves to stress the point that it is those who become as 'little children' (τὰ παιδία, Mt. 18.4; cp. παιδίον, Mt. 18.3, 5)[49] who receive Jesus himself.

In Mt. 18.5, Matthew uses the first half of another Markan *logion*, Mk 9.37a, the second half of which he has already used at the end of the Mission Discourse, Mt. 10.40 (so Mk 9.37b): 'Whoever receives (δέξηται) one such child in my name receives me'. Thus Matthew creates a literary and theological link between the Mission and Community Discourses. In both, the host-disciple, in receiving the hosted-person – 'you' (Mt. 10.40)/ 'one such child' (Mt. 18.5), receives Jesus. An equation becomes clear: 'child' and 'disciple' are interchangeable. Thus in Mt. 18.1-5, Matthew confirms and further deepens two aspects of what is already indicated in the discourse for Mission: the requirement to become 'little' in one's inner self, and the indwelling of Jesus in each disciple who becomes 'little' in this way.

Matthew 18.6-10 is punctuated by an *inclusio* and a continuity based on the phrase 'one of these little ones' (Mt. 18.6, 10, 14), which is found in Mk 9.42; and 10.42.

18.6 If any of you put a stumbling block before *one of these little ones* (τῶν μικρῶν τούτων) who believe in me

18.10 Take care that you do not despise *one of these little ones* (τῶν μικρῶν τούτων)

18.14 So it is not the will of your Father in heaven that *one of these little ones* (τῶν μικρῶν τούτων) should be lost

Matthew uses the phrase *three* times. It mirrors his use of 'little child/ren' thrice in the first pericope (Mt. 18.3, 4, 5). The phrase 'one of these little ones' creates a further literary link with the final instruction to the disciples sent on Mission in Mt. 10.42: 'and whoever gives even a cup of cold water to *one of these little ones* ...'. Matthew's 'little ones' and 'little child/children' in close contextual proximity play off one another in terms of levels of understanding. By means of this literary link and interplay, Matthew 'refers both to the external conditions and to the internal attitude'[50] necessary for life in community.

---

48. Davies and Allison, *Matthew*, II, p. 760.

49. See Davies and Allison, *Matthew*, II, p. 759.

50. Luz, *Matthew 8–20*, p. 429. Luz also notes the fact that, 'the words παῖς and παιδίον can also mean "slave", says a great deal about the legal standing of children ... the root word [humble] means the entire condition of lowliness, not merely the inner attitude of humility'. See Luz, *Matthew 8–20*, pp. 428–29. See Albrecht Oepke, 'παῖς', *TDNT*, V, p. 649.

In its original setting in Mt. 10.42, the phrase 'one of these little ones' is set in a negative conditional clause: '*If* anyone gives to one of these little ones he will certainly *not* lose ...'. In Mt. 18.6-10, Matthew uses three of four positive conditional clauses found in his Markan source: 'Whoever/If anyone ... it would be better' (Mt. 18.6, 8, 9 // Mk 9.42, 43, 47). In the first pericope (Mt. 18.1-5), Jesus indicates clearly that, 'one must work at the practice of lowliness',[51] and that, if one does, one will gain the reward of the kingdom of heaven/receiving Jesus.

So too, in the second pericope (Mt. 18.6-10), Jesus indicates forcibly that one must not hinder such work. If one does, the great punishment of 'eternal fire' is promised (Mt. 18.8 // Mk 9.43). In this way, both the preciousness of each 'one of these little ones' and the conditional nature of entering the kingdom of heaven (Mt. 18.3-4)/receiving Jesus (Mt. 18.5) is emphasised. Further, the emphasis on the inner littleness of the disciples in 18.1-5, and again in 18.6-10, makes the issue of anyone placing obstacles to bring down little ones all the more scandalous. This prefigures the fate of Jesus and of the disciples on mission (cf. 'obstacle', Mt. 26.69-75; 'littleness', Mt. 27.46-50).

## 7. *Brotherly Correction Deuteronomized* (Mt. 18.15-35)

We now turn to the deuteronomized material of Mt. 18.15-35 (cp. Lk. 17.3-4). In this section, Matthew draws upon Deuteronomy's account of Remission in the Sabbatical Year (Deut. 15.1-15).

In Deut. 15.1-15, the neglect to release debtors in the seventh year is considered to be a sin ('remission', ἄφεσις, Deut. 15.1, 2, 3, 9; 'sin', ἁμαρτία, Deut. 15.9). This is reflected in Mt. 18.15-18 in terms of the forgiveness of sin being compared to the release of debts ('forgiveness', ἀφίημι, Mt. 18.21, 27, 32, 35; 'sin', ἁμαρτάνω, Mt. 18.15, 21).[52]

In both Matthew 18 and Deuteronomy 15, initially, an erring brother is to be approached privately by a fellow-brother (cp. Mt. 18.15a // Deut. 15.1-4).[53] If the erring brother 'hears' his fellow-brother, there will be gain – money and power in Deuteronomy (ἐὰν δὲ ἀκοῇ εἰσακούσητε, Deut. 15. 5-6), 'your brother' in Matthew (Mt. 18.15b; cf. Lev. 19.17).[54] If this approach fails, there is need then for witnesses in the assembly/community – ἐκκλησία (Mt. 18.16-17 // Deut. 18.16; cp. Deut. 17.6; 19.15; 23.1-3; Lev.

---

51. Luz, *Matthew 8–20*, p. 429.

52. Brodie, 'Fish, Temple Tithe', pp. 708–709

53. Harrington notes that, 'the keyword that holds the material together is "brother"'. See Harrington, *Matthew*, p. 270.

54. Davies and Allison note that the verb 'to point out' a fault (ἐλέγχω), found in Lev. 19.17, is a *hapax* in Matthew. See Davies and Allison, *Matthew*, II, p. 783. See also, Luz, *Matthew 8–20*, p. 450; and Gundry, *Matthew*, p. 367.

19.15-18).[55] Here a distinctive detail links the two texts. Nowhere else does the term ἐκκλησία occur outside Mt. 18.17 (*bis*; and 16.18) *in the whole of the Gospels*, and outside Deuteronomy *in the whole of the Torah* (Deut. 4.10; 9.10; 18.16; 23.2, 3, 4 *bis*, 9; 31.30; for the verb form, see Deut. 4.10; 31.22, 28; cf. Lev. 8.3; Num. 20.8).

Matthew, however, *adds* something not found in Deuteronomy: Jesus who has the power to forgive sins, something which only God has (cf. Mt. 9.1-8), gives it to *all* of the disciples (18.18-19; cf. Mt. 16.19).

Matthew then returns to another issue found in Deuteronomy 15: a brother must let the remission/forgiveness be complete. In Matthew, the requirements of Jesus 'the Lord' exceed that of the Law of Moses. Literally every *seven* years, of Deuteronomy (Deut. 15.1, 9-10), becomes symbolically '*seventy* times *seven*' in Matthew (Mt. 18.21-24).[56] A brother must not only be generous in terms of his brother who owes a debt (δάνειον) as the Law of Moses required (Deut. 15.8), he must practise 'unbounded generosity in imitation of the Father in heaven (cf. Mt. 5.48)'[57] to his brother who incurs a debt (δάνειον, Mt. 18.27).[58]

Thus Matthew's Jesus demands that the power to forgive, that is, to give spiritual hospitality, must also be unbounded within the community.[59] All share it. In so doing, Matthew's Jesus places the disciples ahead of Moses and the prophets.

What becomes clear is that just as the experience of God in the exchange of external hospitality in Mt. 10.42 is conditional upon giving even the least material hospitality to the least, here too the experience of God in the parabolic account of the forgiveness of debts in Mt. 18.33-35 is conditional

55. Harrington, *Matthew*, p. 269; Davies and Allison, *Matthew*, II, pp. 784–85; Luz, *Matthew 8–20*, p. 452; Keener, *Matthew*, pp. 454–55; Gundry, *Matthew*, p. 368.

56. 'Seventy times seven' is a NT *hapax* which connects Mt. 18.21 to Gen. 4.24, a context that also deals with forgiveness. See Harrington, *Matthew*, p. 269; Davies and Allison, *Matthew*, II, p. 793; and Keener, *Matthew*, p. 457. Brodie points out the presence of a parallel vocabulary-cluster unique to Deut. 15.12 and Mt. 18.23-35: the 'to sell into service' (δουλεύσει) of Deut. 15.12 is reflected in the vocabulary of 'servants' (δούλων) in Mt. 18.23, and 'to sell' (ῥαθῆναι) in Mt. 18.25; the 'seventh/seventy' (τῷ ἑβδόμῳ) of Deut. 15.12 is reflected in the 'seven ... seventy times seven' (ἑπτάκις ἀλλὰ ἕως ἑβδομηκοντάκις) of Mt. 18.22; 'his brother' (ὁ ἀδελφός σου) of Deut. 15.12 is reflected in 'your brother' (τῷ ἀδελφῷ αὐτοῦ) in Mt. 18.35. Brodie notes that, 'this combination ... is otherwise virtually unkown in the Bible'. See Brodie, 'Fish, Temple Tithe', p. 713. See also Harrington, *Matthew*, p. 271; Keener, *Matthew*, p. 458. Cf. Lev. 25.

57. Davies and Allison, *Matthew*, II, p. 804.

58. The term used here for 'debt', δάνειον, also constitutes a *hapax* in Matthew. It occurs only here in Matthew *in the whole of the NT*, and in Deut. 15.5, 8; 24.11, *in the whole of the Old Testament*. See Brodie, 'Fish, Temple Tithe', p. 711; Harrington, *Matthew*, p. 270; Davies and Allison, *Matthew*, II, p. 800.

59. Harrington, *Matthew*, p. 269; Gundry, *Matthew*, p. 369. Reid writes: 'Real power ... depends on a transformation of heart (18.35) that impels the disciples to imitate the One who has first shown unearned graciousness and love'. See Reid, 'Violent Endings', p. 254.

upon extending even the least spiritual hospitality to the least brother.[60] The effect is that, 'the essential generosity of the Old Testament text has been maintained, but it has been cast into a form which both fits the flow of the parable story and which lays emphasis on interior dispositions (the obeisance of the servant, and the idea of large-mindedness)'.[61]

The effect of Matthew's deuteronomizing of his Markan source here has been to emulate and internalize the requirements of the Law of Moses. In terms of function, it serves to encapsulate a profound Christological fact: Jesus is one with God, the source of all forgiveness. Therefore, just as the final unit of the discourse on Mission ended with the instruction that the disciples must become 'as the greatest' in receiving Jesus Christ by extending even the least material hospitality to the 'littlest one', so in Mt. 18.15-35, they must become 'as the greatest', by practicing unbounded spiritual hospitality to the least in the community, that is, an erring brother.

## 8. *Matthew's Judaization: A Comment on the Sitz im Leben*

As with Mark, Matthew was intended to circulate to wide and far-flung audiences. What would it communicate to Jews or Jewish-Christians, all of whom would be familiar with Old Testament Scripture, and some among the latter who would have been familiar with the Gospel of Mark? What would it communicate to Gentiles or Gentile-Christians, almost all of whom would have been unfamiliar with Old Testament Scripture, and some of whom would have been familiar with the Gospel of Mark?[62]

The Jews and Jewish-Christians would have registered clearly Matthew's message as one that emphasises the continuity between Judaism and Jesus.[63] Matthew's dense structural use of Jewish numerals rivals any found in the Mishna texts of the Rabbinic movement, itself bent on claiming authentic continuity with Judaism.[64] Jewish-Christians

---

60. Brodie, 'Fish, Temple Tithe', pp. 709–16, 718.

61. Brodie, 'Fish, Temple Tithe', p. 711.

62. Keener notes that, 'we must take into account the historical context not only *in which* but also *to which* they communicated their message. Such a context naturally shaped the form of their message ...'. See Keener, *Matthew*, p. 2.

63. Harrington, *Matthew*, p. 21.

64. Davies and Allison note that, 'Rabbinic texts are full of numbers and numerical schemes. The Mishnah in particular is memorable in this regard. *m.' Abot* 1, for instance, contains many triads, while in *m.' Abot* 5, the numbers ten, seven and four are named again and again. And *m. Kelim* 24 contains triad after triad – seventeen triads in all. Matthew's penchant for numbers would thus appear to place him squarely in the Jewish world, and perhaps specifically in the world of the rabbis.' See Davies and Allison, *Matthew*, I, p. 86. Beaton, citing U. Luz (1922 [sic], 50), 'notes that Matthew's Greek occasionally betrays a "clear relationship to the linguistic development in the rabbinic Judaism of the time"'. See Beaton, 'How Matthew Writes', p. 122.

familiar with the Gospel of Mark would recognize from Matthew's judaization of Mark's account of Jesus, the message that Jesus is the fulfilment of the messianic hopes found in Old Testament Scripture.

Hearers/readers familiar with Mark would know that he presents Jesus as greater than Elijah and Elisha. These same hearers/readers would also recognize how, in Matthew's account, Jesus is presented as greater even than Moses. Matthew does not diminish Moses in order to raise Jesus up.[65] Rather, he uses the high status of Moses to tell of the superlative status of Jesus. Among the many Jews 'divided by a sort of paternity dispute',[66] Matthew presents Jesus as one with God. This form of emulation counters any who would claim a superlative role for Moses.

To Gentile-Christians and would-be Gentile-Christians, Matthew's Gospel assures them of a spiritual heritage and identity in common with the Jews: 'Matthew's Jesus, the son of David and the son of Abraham (1.1), by fulfilling the prophecies of the Jewish Bible and by being like Moses, became the heir of Jewish history and tradition (cf. Mt. 21.43), which in turn made his followers joint heirs of the same'.[67] Moreover, by means of stressing that the disciples model themselves wholly on Jesus, as he does in Matthew 10 and 18, Matthew counters all who continued to claim Moses and the prophets as their primary models.

The above evidence demonstrates the 'inseparability of the message and the story form in which it is embodied ...'.[68]

## 9. Conclusion

The aim of this chapter has been, first, to examine Matthew's judaization of the Markan source material by incorporating Old Testament elements in two key texts, namely, the discourses on Mission (ch. 10) and Community (ch. 18); and, secondly, to continue to demonstrate that the methods and techniques used by Graeco-Roman authors to incorporate earlier sources into their works are also found reflected in his use of Mark as a source in these discourses.

Matthew's judaizes Mark in Matthew 10, the Mission Discourse, by embedding Old Testament citations, references and allusions into his reworking of his Markan source such that each (would-be) disciple is called to become 'as the least' – materially (Mt. 10.5-14 // Mk 6.7-8), socially (Mt. 10.17-25 // Mk 13.9-13; and 10.43-44) and spiritually (Mt. 10.40-42 // Mk 9.37b, 41) – in imitation of Jesus. Concomitantly, they are also to become 'as the greatest' in three ways in imitation of Jesus, that is,

---

65. Bauer, *Structure*, pp. 275–76.
66. Bauer, *Structure*, p. 281.
67. Bauer, *Structure*, p. 278.
68. Boring, 'Matthew', p. 108.

they are 'to do' (Mt. 10.1, 8), 'to speak' (Mt. 10.19, 20), and 'to give and receive hospitality' (Mt. 10.40, 42; cf. 'Words', Matthew 5–7; 'Deeds', Matthew 8–9; 'Giving/Receiving hospitality', Mt. 22.1-11).

He does so in Matthew 18, the Community Discourse, by placing his rewritten Markan material (Mt. 18.1-10 // Mk 9.34, 36, 37a; 10.15; 9.42a, 43, 45, 47; 14.21, in that order) in between materials that are highly deuteronomized ('sandwich' technique; Mt. 17.22-27; and 18.15-35). The effect is to instruct each (would-be) disciple that he or she must become 'as the least' like 'a little child' (Mt. 18.5 // Mk 10.15) in order to gain the reward of the kingdom of heaven/receiving Jesus; and 'as the greatest' by practising unbounded spiritual hospitality to the least in the community, that is, an erring brother [/sister], in order to gain the very same reward.

CONCLUSION

The aim of this book is to demonstrate the thesis that Matthew used Mark as a literary source, and that the way in which he did so was in accord with the literary conventions of Graeco-Roman antiquity. This has been achieved. The aim of the Conclusion is to provide a summary of the whole. Here there is, as it were, a 'pulling through of the thread' of the material of this book, from beginning to end. This involves a brief résumé of the chapters and their conclusions, after which the key recommendations that emerge as a result of this study are presented.

This study is presented in two parts. In Part 1 the background for the examination of Matthew's rewriting of Mark is set out in three chapters, chs 1–3. It is entitled, the 'Use of Sources in Graeco-Roman Antiquity: Towards a Context and Criteria for Examining Matthew's Use Of Mark as a Source'.

Chapter 1 examines the 'Use of Sources in Graeco-Roman Antiquity'. From the evidence analysed, we draw the following three conclusions: (1) the most common method of literary composition in the Graeco-Roman world from the fourth century BCE onwards was the rewriting of earlier texts by means of creative imitation (Gk, *mimēsis*; Lt., *imitatio*); (2) while the relatively small volume of theoretical handbooks on imitation are instructive, most of our information on the use of sources in antiquity comes from the analysis of authors whose texts reveal evidence of the practice of rewriting; and (3) the use of criteria for identifying source texts was not required in antiquity as the convention of rewriting was so pervasive; and, while the application of criteria came later, the formulation of the same into an explicit methodology at the present time may be viewed as a new departure.

Chapter 2, entitled 'Rewriting: Evidence from Graeco-Roman Texts', examines several examples of the practice of rewriting in Graeco-Roman antiquity. Evidence from the works of four Graeco-Roman authors is presented, namely, Virgil's *Aeneid*, Seneca's *Phaedra*, Livy's *History of Rome* and Plutarch's Greek and Roman *Lives*.

Chapter 3, entitled, 'Rewriting: Evidence from Jewish Texts', examines several examples from Jewish antiquity. Judaea was part of the great Graeco-Roman empire before and up to the first century CE. Evidence from the works of two sacred Jewish texts, namely, Tobit's book of that name and Paul's First Letter to the Corinthians is examined.

In Chs 2 and 3, the primary external criteria outlined in Ch. 1 are applied and satisfied. Then the internal criteria for establishing literary dependence also outlined in Ch. 1 are applied to the selected texts. From the examination of the internal evidence of the above texts, we conclude that the methods and techniques used by Graeco-Roman authors to incorporate earlier sources into their works are also found reflected in Jewish sacred works. The techniques which all of the above authors used to achieve their literary and ideological or theological purposes include: parallels in vocabulary, themes and events, in parallel order; and shared distinctive details in the form of particular words. Most of the authors also used the techniques of abbreviation, addition, conflation, elaboration, emulation, negativization, omission, positivization, reordering and variation.

Evidence of systematic rewriting is found in both the secular and sacred texts examined, namely, Virgil's *Aeneid*, Livy's *History of Rome*, the book of Tobit, and 1 Corinthians. Of the Graeco-Roman works examined, one of the key effects of the rewriting was positivization. Of the two Jewish works examined, the shared key effect of the rewriting was the Torahization of the text, albeit for different purposes. In Tobit, Torahization was used to boost a community in exile; in 1 Corinthians, it was used to correct the theology and practice of a community in relation to eating idol food.

Part 2 focuses solely on 'Matthew's Use of Mark as a Source'. In three chapters, chs 4–6, we demonstrate not only *that* Matthew uses Mark but *how* and *why* he does so. An in-depth examination of the 'how' and the 'why' of his use of Mark has been a major dimension missing in research on Matthew to date.

Chapter 4 examines 'Matthew's Use of Mark as a Source'. It provides evidence that Matthew and the Gospels belong within the genre of ancient historical βίοι, and to the sub-genre of βίοι Ἰησοῦ, because of their portrayal of Jesus as the Christ and Son of God. The central purpose of this genre is the establishment of the essence of the subject. This is reflected in terms of Christology throughout Matthew, as it is in each of the Gospels.

The external criteria for establishing literary dependency outlined above are applied and satisfied. The case for the chronological priority of Mark is made. Evidence for the dating of the Gospel of Mark to c. 68 CE and Matthew to c. 80 CE is presented. A case is made for the plausiblity of the thesis that Matthew could have had access to a copy of Mark, given the level of book production in Rome, the movement of texts throughout the Graeco-Roman empire, and the established network of Christian communities at the time he was writing. Mark's association with Peter would have made the circulation of his Gospel all the more likely.

The internal criteria for establishing literary dependence outlined and applied in chs 1–3 are applied to Matthew. Some initial evidence of Matthew's rewriting of Mark is presented. In terms of parallel vocabulary, themes and events, 90 + per cent of Mark appears in Matthew, 51 per cent of which reflects Mark's exact words. In the first half of his Gospel, Matthew creatively re-orders the pericopae taken from his Markan source. In the second half, he follows the Markan order exactly.

Some of the more simple techniques by which Matthew rewrites Mark are then examined. Matthew uses the techniques of omission and variation for the purpose of positivizing his portrait of Jesus and the disciples, and the techniques of addition and conflation for the purpose of amplifying his Christology, relative to his Markan source.

Chapter 5 is entitled 'Matthew's Judaization of Mark'. Matthew legitimizes Jesus as the Christ by reference to Scripture, as did Mark. However, the way in which he does so reflects a particular strategy in relation to his use of this source, namely, that of judaization. Matthew judaizes Mark.

This strategy is seen, first, in Matthew's restructuring of Mark by means of the use of the key numerals of Judaism. Matthew re-organizes Mark's narrative of Jesus into a well-balanced *poly-structure*, a structure based on the numerals – two, three, five, seven and twelve. Matthew's dense use of these numerals is one of the two key ways in which he judaizes Mark. Matthew organizes his Markan (and other) material thus in order to steep the narrative of Jesus Christ in Jewish theological overtones.

The other key way in which Matthew judaizes his Markan source is then examined, namely, his method of embedding Old Testament Scripture, in particular, the Torah, in his reworking of Mark. It is demonstrated that Matthew sets his Markan source material within a torahized narrative frame: Matthew 1–2 reflects the influence of Genesis and Exodus; Mt. 28.16-20 reflects the influence of Deuteronomy. This is followed by an examination of Matthew's rewriting of *four* Markan pericopae within this torahized frame, namely, Fasting in the Wilderness (Mt. 4.1-11 // Mk 1.12-13), the Second Feeding Account (Mt. 15.32-39 // Mk: 8.1-10), the Transfiguration (Mt. 17.1-8 // Mk 9.2-11) and the Entry into Jerusalem (Mt. 21.1–11 // Mk. 11.1-10). In all four cases, we find evidence that Matthew's agenda in conflating Mark and the Old Testament involved emulation: the demonstration of Jesus as greater than Moses.

The title of Ch. 6 reflects its purpose: 'Matthew's Torahization of Mark in Two Key Texts: Matthew 10 and 18'. Matthew torahizes Mark in Matthew 10, the Mission Discourse, by embedding Old Testament citations, references and allusions into his reworking of Mark. He torahizes Mark in Matthew 18, the Community Discourse, by placing his rewritten Markan material (Mt. 18.1-15) between materials that are highly deuteronomized (Mt. 17.22-27; and 18.15–35).

The net effect of the analysis of all of the above in chs 4–6 augurs for a thesis of Matthew's literary dependency upon Mark. The analysis of the methods and techniques used by Matthew in his rewriting of Mark enhances our interpretation of the Gospel of Matthew. From the cumulative internal evidence presented, we conclude, first, that Matthew's strategy in his use of Mark as a source was toward christianizing Judaism; and secondly, that the way in which he does so reflects the methods and techniques used by Graeco-Roman authors to incorporate earlier sources into their works.

In establishing Matthew's use of Mark as a source, this research provides a new model for examining the relationship. It does this by broadening the context for the discussion, that is, by setting the issue in the context of the use of sources in Graeco-Roman antiquity, and by outlining suitable criteria for discerning literary dependency. It is recommended that Scripture scholarship use and hone the inter-critical approach used here, that is, the use of both biblical and classical methodologies (particularly ancient literary criticism), in further exercises in relation to the issue of Matthew's use of Mark. This methodology may also be fruitfully applied to the so-called 'Synoptic problem' and the 'John-Synoptic problem', or, indeed, any intertextual study of the Scriptures. Such studies would in turn contribute, as this one does, to the research upon how authors used sources in antiquity.

Despite detailed research on the matter of the similarities and differences between Matthew and Mark as found in commentaries, it was discovered that there has been little in-depth analysis of Matthew's overall literary and theological agenda reflected in his rewriting of Mark. It is recommended that this continue to be addressed in future research.

Finally, in each text examined above, we demonstrated briefly how instructive the literary evidence is toward the understanding of its *Sitz im Leben* or context of origin. It is recommended that this approach be used on a larger scale upon the historical milieu of each of the Gospels, or any other part of the Old or New Testament, in future research. As noted above, 'the results of literary analysis may well supply useful information for historical reconstructions of the milieu of the Gospel' [so any Scripture text].[1]

This list of recommendations, like the study itself, is not exhaustive. There are more. However, it is hoped that what is presented above bears something of the fruitfulness for the reader that it did for the writer:

---

1. See Ch. 1, n. 96.

A positive global criterion is the fruitfulness of the interpretation . . . if an interpretation renders the text meaningless or banal, especially if the text has a history of significance, one suspects the validity of the interpretation. On the other hand, an interpretation, even if new or startling, that 'makes the text speak', that, for example, exploits the potentiality of the text to illuminate the faith of the community without violating the canons of good exegetical and critical method, should be taken seriously.[2]

2.   Sandra M. Schneiders, *The Revelatory Text: Interpreting the New Testament as Sacred Scripture* (San Fransisco: Harper, 1991), p. 165.

BIBLIOGRAPHY

Achtemeier, Paul J. '*Omne Verbum Sonat*: The New Testament and the Oral Environment of Late Western Antiquity'. *JBL* 109 (1990), pp. 3–27.

Achtemeier, Paul J., Roger S. Boraas, Michael Fishbane, Pheme Perkins and William O. Walker, Jr., (eds). *The HarperCollins Bible Dictionary*. San Francisco: HarperSanFrancisco, 1996.

Aland, Kurt. *Synopsis of the Four Gospels*. English edn. United Bible Societies, 1982.

Aland, Kurt, and Barbara Aland, *The Text of the New Testament*. Grand Rapids: William B. Eerdmans, 1989.

Aland, Kurt and Barbara Aland (eds). *Greek-English New Testament*. Stuttgart: Deutsche Bibelgesellschaft, 27th edn, 1998.

Albright, William Foxwell, and C.S. Mann. *Matthew*. AB. Garden City, NY: Doubleday 1971.

Alexander, Loveday. 'Ancient Book Production and the Circulation of the Gospels', in Bauckham (ed.), *The Gospel for All Christians*, pp. 71–105.

Allison, Dale C. *The Intertextual Jesus: Scripture in Q*. Harrisburg, PA: Trinity Press International, 2000.

—*The New Moses: A Matthean Typology*. Edinburgh: T & T Clark, 1993.

Alter, Robert. *The Art of Biblical Narrative*. New York: Basic Books, 1981.

Anderson, B.W. *Understanding the Old Testament*. Englewood Cliffs, NJ: Prentice-Hall, rev. edn, 1986.

Apollonius Rhodius. *The Argonautica*. Trans. R.C. Seaton. Loeb Classical Library. London: William Heinemann, 1967.

Aristotle. *Physics*. Trans. P.H. Wicksteed and F.M. Cornford. Loeb Classical Library. 2 vols. Cambridge, MA: Harvard University Press, 1996 and 2000.

Aristotle, Longinus, Demetrius. *Poetics, On the Sublime, On Style*. Trans. Stephen Hallibwell, W. Hamilton Fyfe and Doreen C. Innes. Loeb Classical Library. Cambridge, MA: Harvard University Press, 1995.

Aulus Gellius. *Attic Nights*. Trans. John C. Rolfe. Loeb Classical Library. 3 vols. Cambridge, MA: Harvard University Press, 1998–2002.

Aune, David E. 'Greco-Roman Biography', in Aune (ed.), *Greco-Roman Literature and the New Testament*, pp. 107–26.

—*The New Testament in Its Literary Environment*. Philadelphia: Westminster, 1987.

Aune, David E. (ed.). *The Gospel of Matthew in Current Study: Studies in Memory of William G. Thompson*. Grand Rapids: William B. Eerdmans, 2001.

—*Greco-Roman Literature and the New Testament: Selected Forms and Genres*. SBLSBS, 21. Atlanta: Scholars, 1988.

Baar, Allan. *A Diagram of Synoptic Relationships*. Edinburgh: T & T Clark, 1976.

Baar, D.L. 'The Drama of Matthew's Gospel: A Reconsideration of Its Structure and Purpose'. *TD* 24 (1976), pp. 349–59.

Bacon, B.W. *Studies in Matthew*. New York: Henry Holt, 1930.

—'The "Five Books" of Matthew against the Jews'. *ExpTim* 15 (1918), pp. 56–66.

Baldwin, Charles Sears. *Ancient Rhetoric and Poetic: Interpreted from Representative Works*. New York: Macmillan Company, 1924.

Barrett, C.K. 'The Place of John and the Synoptics within the Early History of Christian Thought', in Denaux (ed.), *John and the Synoptics*, pp. 63–79.

Bauckham, Richard, 'For Whom Were the Gospels Written?', in Bauckham (ed.), *The Gospel for All Christians*, pp. 9–48.

Bauckham, Richard (ed.). *The Gospel for All Christians: Rethinking the Gospel Audiences*. Grand Rapids: William B. Eerdmans, 1998.

Bauer, David R. *The Structure of Matthew's Gospel: A Study in Literary Design*. JSNTSup, 31. 3rd repr. Sheffield: Sheffield Academic Press, 1996.

Beare, F.W., 'The Mission of the Disciples and the Mission Charge: Matthew 10 and Parallels'. *JBL* 89 (1970), pp. 1–13.

Beaton, Richard C. 'How Matthew Writes', in Bockmuehl and Hagner (eds), *The Written Gospel*, pp. 116–34.

Ben-Porat, Ziva. 'The Poetics of Literary Allusion'. *JDPTL* (1976), pp. 105–28.

Berkley, Timothy W. *From a Broken Covenant to a Circumcision of the Heart: Pauline Intertextual Exegesis in Romans 2.17-29*. Atlanta: SBL, 2000.

Bieringer, R. (ed.). *The Corinthian Correspondence*. BETL, 125. Leuven: Leuven University Press, 1996.

Bockmuehl, Markus. 'The Making of Gospel Commentaries,' in Bockmuehl and Hagner (eds), *The Written Gospel*, pp. 274–95.

Bockmuehl, Markus, and Donald A. Hagner (eds). *The Written Gospel*. Cambridge: Cambridge University Press, 2005.

Borgen, Peder. *Philo of Alexandria: An Exegete for His Time.* NovTSup, 86. Leiden: Brill, 1997.

Boring, M. Eugene, 'The Convergence of Source Analysis, Social History and Literary Structures in the Gospel of Matthew', in E.H. Lovering (ed.), *Society of Biblical Literature Seminar Papers.* Atlanta: Scholars, 1994, pp. 587–611.

—'Matthew', in E. Keck Leander *et al.* (eds), *The New Interpreters Bible.* Nashville: Abingdon, 1995, VIII, pp. 87–505.

Boyd, Barbara Weiden (ed.). *Brill's Companion to Ovid.* Leiden: Brill, 2002.

Breisach, Ernst. *Historiography: Ancient, Medieval and Modern.* London: University of Chicago Press, 2nd edn, 1994.

Brenk, F.E. *In Mist Apparelled: Religious Themes in Plutarch's Moralia and Lives, Mnemosyne.* Sup, 48. Leiden: Brill, 1977.

Briscoe, John. *A Commentary on Livy: Books 31–33.* Oxford: Clarendon Press, 1973.

Brodie, Thomas. 'Fish, Temple Tithe, and Remission: The God-Based Generosity of Deuteronomy 14–15 as One Component of Matt 17.22–18.35'. *RB* 4 (1992), pp. 697–718.

Brodie, Thomas L. *The Crucial Bridge: The Elijah-Elisha Narrative as an Interpretative Synthesis of Genesis-Kings and a Literary Model for the Gospels.* Collegeville: Liturgical Press, 1999.

—*Genesis as Dialogue: A Literary, Historical, and Theological Commentary.* Oxford: Oxford University Press, 2001.

—'Greco-Roman Imitation of Texts as a Partial Guide to Luke's Use of Sources', in Charles H. Talbert (ed.), *Luke-Acts: New Perspectives from the Society of Biblical Literature Seminar.* New York: Crossroad, 1984, pp. 17–46

—'Luke-Acts as a Systematic Rewriting and Updating of the Elijah-Elisha Narrative in 1 and 2 Kings'. Unpublished doctoral dissertation. Rome: St. Thomas Aquinas University, 1984.

—'The Systematic Use of the Pentateuch in 1 Corinthians: An Exploratory Survey', in Bieringer (ed.), *The Corinthian Correspondence.* pp. 441–57.

—'Towards Tracing the Gospels' Literary Indebtedness to the Epistles', in MacDonald (ed.), *Mimesis and Intertextuality in Antiquity and Christianity,* pp. 104–116.

Brown, Raymond E. *The Birth of the Messiah: A Commentary on the Infancy Narratives in Matthew and Luke.* Garden City: Doubleday, 1977.

– *An Introduction to the New Testament.* ABRL. New York: Doubleday, 1997.

Brown, Raymond E., Joseph A. Fitzmyer and Roland E. Murphy (eds). *The Jerome Biblical Commentary.* London: Geoffrey Chapman, 1968.

—*The New Jerome Biblical Commentary*. London: Geoffrey Chapman, 1990.

Buckley, T.W. 'The Christology of Matthew'. *ChicStud* 40 (2001), pp. 251–60.

Bultmann, R. *The History of the Synoptic Tradition*. Trans. John Marsh. Oxford: Blackwell, 1963.

Burridge, Richard A. 'About People, by People, for People: Gospel Genre and Audiences', in Bauckham (ed.), *The Gospel for All Christians*, pp. 113–45.

—*What Are the Gospels?: A Comparison with Graeco-Roman Biography*. Cambridge: Cambridge University Press, 1992.

—'Who Writes, Why, and for Whom?', in Bockmuehl and Hagner (eds), *The Written Gospel*, pp. 99–115.

Cairns, Francis. *Generic Composition in Greek and Roman Poetry*. Edinburgh: Edinburgh University Press, 1972.

—*Virgil's Augustan Epic*. Cambridge: Cambridge University Press, 1989.

Carmichael, Calum M. *The Laws of Deuteronomy*. London: Cornell University Press, 1974.

Casson, Lionel. *Travel in the Ancient World*. London: George Allen & Unwin, 1974.

Castle, E.B. *Ancient Education and Today*. Harmondsworth: Penguin, 1961.

Cheung, Alex T. *Idol Food in Corinth: Jewish Background and Pauline Legacy*. JSNTSup, 176. Sheffield: Sheffield Academic Press, 1999.

Ciampa, Roy E. *The Presence and Function of Scripture in Galatians 1 and 2*. WUNT, 2. Series, 102. Tübingen: Mohr Siebeck, 1998.

Cicero. *De Oratore*. Trans. E.W. Sutton and H. Rackham. Loeb Classical Library. 2 vols. Cambridge, MA: Harvard University Press, 1969.

—*Letters to Atticus*. Ed. and trans. D.R. Shackleton Bailey. Loeb Classical Library. 3 vols. Cambridge, MA: Harvard University Press, 1999.

—*Philippics*. Trans. Walter C.A. Ker. Loeb Classical Library. London: William Heinemann, 1926.

—*Pro Caelio*. Trans. R. Gardner. Loeb Classical Library. Cambridge, MA: Harvard University Press, 1969.

Clark, Donald Lemen. 'Imitation: Theory and Practice in Roman Rhetoric'. *QJS* 37 (1951), pp. 11–22.

Coffey, Michael, and Roland Mayer (eds). *Seneca Phaedra*. Cambridge: Cambridge University Press, 1990.

Collins, Adela Yarbro. *Is Mark's Gospel a Life of Jesus?: The Question of Genre*. The Père Marquette Lecture in Theology 1990. Milwaukee: Marquette University Press, 1990.

Collins, Raymond F. 'Reflections on 1 Corinthians as a Hellenistic Letter', in Bieringer (ed.), *The Corinthian Correspondence*, pp. 39–61.

Combrink, H.J.B., 'Structural Analysis of Mt 9.35–11.1'. *Neot* 11 (1977), pp. 98–114.

Conte, Gian Biagio. *Genres and Readers: Lucretius, Love Elegy, Pliny's Encyclopedia*. Trans. Glenn W. Most. London: The Johns Hopkins University Press, 1994.

—*The Rhetoric of Imitation: Genre and Poetic Memory in Virgil and Other Latin Poets*. Ed. Charles Segal. Trans. from Italian. Ithaca, New York: Cornell University Press, 1996.

Court, John M (ed.). *New Testament Writers and the Old Testament: An Introduction*. London: SPCK, 2002.

Cousland, J.R.C. 'Tobit: A Comedy in Error?' *CBQ* 65 (2003), pp. 535–53.

Cox, Patricia. *Biography in Late Antiquity: A Quest for the Holy Man*. Berkley: University of California Press, 1983.

Davies, Philip R. *Scribes and Schools: The Canonization of the Hebrew Scriptures*. London: SPCK, 1998.

Davies, W.D., and Dale C. Allison, Jr. *A Critical and Exegetical Commentary on the Gospel according to Saint Matthew*. ICC. 3 vols. Edinburgh: T & T Clark, 1988–2000.

Davis, Stephan K. *The Antithesis of the Ages: Paul's Reconfiguration of Torah*. CBQMS, 33. Washington DC: The Catholic Biblical Association of America, 2002.

Dawes, Gregory W. 'The Danger of Idolatry: First Corinthians 8.7–13'. *CBQ* 58 (1996), pp. 82–109.

De Jonge, H.J., 'Sonship, Wisdom, Infancy: Luke 2.41–51a'. *NTS* 24 (1977–78), pp. 317–54; 337–39.

Delobel, Joël. 'Coherence and Relevance of 1 Cor 8–10', in Bieringer (ed.), *The Corinthian Correspondence*, pp. 177–190.

Denaux, Adelbert, 'The Q-Logion Mt 11.27/Lk 10.22 and the Gospel of John', in Denaux (ed.), *John and the Synoptics*, pp. 163–99.

Denaux, Adelbert (ed.). *John and the Synoptics*. BETL, 101. Leuven: Leuven University Press, 1992.

Dewar, Michael. '*Siquid Habent Ueri Uatum Praesagia*: Ovid in the 1st–5th Centuries A. D.', in Boyd (ed.), *Brill's Companion to Ovid*, pp. 383–412.

Dewey, Joanna. *Markan Public Debate: Literary Technique, Concentric Structure and Theology in Mark 2.1–3.6*. SBLDS, 48. Chico, CA: Scholars Press, 1977.

Di Lella, Alexander A. 'The Book of Tobit and the Book of Judges: An Intertextual Analysis'. *Hen* 22 (2000), pp. 197–205.

—'The Deuteronomic Background of the Farewell Discourse in Tob 14.3–11'. *CBQ* 41 (1979), pp. 380–89.

Dionysius of Halicarnassus. *Critical Essays*. Trans. Stephen Usher. Loeb Classical Library. 2 vols. Cambridge, MA: Harvard University Press, 1985–2000.

Donahue, John R., and Daniel J. Harrington. *The Gospel of Mark*. SPS, 2. Collegeville, MN: Liturgical Press, 2002.

Dorsey, D.A. *The Roads and Highways of Ancient Israel*. ASORLBNEA. Baltimore: Johns Hopkins University Press, 1991.

Downing, F.G. 'Compositional Conventions and the Synoptic Problem'. *JBL* 107 (1988), pp. 69–85.

—'A Paradigm Perplex: Luke, Matthew and Mark'. *NTS* 38 (1992), pp. 1–28.

—'Redaction Criticism: Josephus' *Antiquities* and the Synoptic Problem'. *JSNT* 8 (1980), pp. 46–65.

—'Redaction Criticism: Josephus' *Antiquities* and the Synoptic Problem'. *JSNT* 9 (1980), pp. 28–48.

Drury, J. 'What Are the Gospels?' *ExpTim* 87 (1976), pp. 324–28.

Duckworth, G.E. 'The Architecture of the *Aeneid*', in Hardie (ed.), *Virgil*, IV, pp. 13–25.

Dungan, David L. (ed.). *The Interrelations between the Gospels*. BETL, 95. Leuven: Leuven University Press, 1990.

Ellis, Peter F. *Matthew: His Mind and His Message*. Collegeville: Liturgical Press, 1974.

Enslin, M.S. '"The Five Books of Matthew": Bacon on the Gospel of Matthew'. *HTR* 24 (1931), pp. 67–97.

Euripides. *Hippolytus*. Ed. David Kovacs. Trans. David Kovacs. Loeb Classical Library. Cambridge, MA: Harvard University Press, 1995.

Eusebius. *The Ecclesiastical History*. Trans. Kirsopp Lake. Loeb Classical Library. 2 vols. London: William Heinemann, 1926.

Evans, Craig A. 'How Mark Writes', in Bockmuehl and Hagner (eds), *The Written Gospel*, pp. 135–48.

Evans, Craig A., and James A. Sanders (eds). *Paul and the Scriptures of Israel*. JSNTSup, 83. Studies in Scripture and Early Judaism, 1. Sheffield: JSOT Press, 1993.

Fantham, Elaine. 'Virgil's Dido and Seneca's Tragic Heroines'. *GR* 22–23 (1975–76), pp. 1–10.

Fenton, J.C. 'Inclusio and Chiasmus in Matthew', in *Studia Evangelica*. TU, 73. Berlin: Akademie-Verlag, 1956, I, pp. 174–9.

Filson, Floyd V. *A Commentary on the Gospel according to St. Matthew*. New York: Harper & Row, 1960.

Finkelpearl, Ellen. 'Pagan Traditions of Intertextuality in the Roman World', in MacDonald (ed.), *Mimesis and Intertextuality in Antiquity and Christianity*, pp. 78–90.

Fishbane, Michael. *Biblical Interpretation in Ancient Israel*. Oxford: Clarendon Press, 1988.

Fiske, G.C. *Lucilius and Horace: A Study in the Classical Theory of Imitation*. New York Westport, CT: Greenwood Press, rev. edn, 1971.

Fitzmyer, Joseph A. *The Dead Sea Scrolls and Christian Origins.* Grand Rapids: William B. Eerdmans, 2000.

—*The Genesis Apocryphon of Qumran Cave 1: A Commentary.* Rome: Biblical Institute, 2nd edn, 1971.

France, R.T. *The Gospel of Mark: A Commentary on the Greek Text.* Grand Rapids: William B. Eerdmans, 2002.

Frankemölle, H. *Jahwebund und Kirche Christi: Studien zur Form- und Traditionsgeschichte des 'Evangeliumns' nach Matthäus.* NTAbh, 10. Münster: Aschendorff, 1974.

Freedman, David Noel (ed.). *Anchor Bible Dictionary.* New York: Doubleday, 1992.

Freedman, William. 'The Literary Motif: A Definition and Evaluation'. *Nov* 4 (1971), pp. 123–31.

Gahan, J.J. 'Imitation and Aemulation in Seneca's Phaedra'. *Lat* 46 (1987), pp. 380–87.

Gamble, Harry Y. *Books and Readers in the Early Church: A History of Early Christian Texts.* New Haven: Yale University Press, 1995.

Goulder, Michael D. *Midrash and Lection in Matthew.* Speaker's Lectures in Biblical Studies 1969–71. London: SPCK, 1974.

Grassi, Joseph A. 'Matthew as a Second Testament Deuteronomy'. *BTB* 19 (1989), pp. 23–29.

Guelich, Robert A. *Mark 1–8.26.* WBC, 34A. Dallas: Word Books, 1989.

Gundry, Robert H. *Mark: A Commentary on His Apology for the Cross.* Grand Rapids: William B. Eerdmans, 1993.

—*Matthew: A Commentary on His Handbook for a Mixed Church under Persecution.* Grand Rapids: William B. Eerdmans, 2nd edn, 1994.

—'Matthew: Jewish-Christian or Christian-Jewish? At an Intersection of Sociology and Theology', in Robert H. Gundry (ed.), *The Old Is Better.* NTESTI. WUNT, 178. Tübingen: Mohr Siebeck, 2005, pp. 111–19.

Hadas, Moses, and Morton Smith, *Heroes and Gods: Spiritual Biographies in the Greco-Roman World.* New York: Harper & Row, 1965.

Hagner, Donald A. 'Balancing the Old and New'. *Int* 51 (1997), pp. 20–30.

—*Matthew 1–13.* WBC, 33A. 2 vols. Dallas, TX: Word Books, 1993.

Hammond, N.G.L., and H.H. Scullard (eds). *The Oxford Classical Dictionary.* Oxford: Clarendon Press, 2nd edn, 1970.

Hanson, K.C. 'Transformed on the Mountain: Ritual Analysis and the Gospel of Matthew'. *Sem* 67 (1994), pp. 147–70.

Hardie, Philip (ed.). *Virgil: Critical Assessments of Classical Authors.* 4 vols. London: Routledge, 1999.

Hare, Douglas R.A. 'How Jewish Is the Gospel of Matthew?'. *CBQ* 62 (2000), pp. 264–77.

Harrington, Daniel J. 'The Gospel according to Mark', *NJBC*, pp. 596–629.

—*The Gospel of Matthew*. SPS, 1. Collegeville: Liturgical Press, 1991.

Harstine, Stan. *Moses as a Character in the Fourth Gospel*. JSNTSup, 229. Sheffield: Sheffield University Press, 2002.

Hays, Richard B. *Echoes of Scripture in the Letters of Paul*. London: Yale University Press, 1989.

Heinze, Richard. *Virgil's Epic Technique*. Trans. Hazel Harvey, David Harvey and Fred Robertson. London: Bristol Classical Press, 1993.

Hengel, Martin. 'Eye-Witness Memory and the Writing of the Gospels', in Bockmuehl and Hagner (eds), *The Written Gospel*, pp. 70–96.

—*The Four Gospels and the One Gospel of Jesus Christ: An Investigation of the Collection and Origin of the Canonical Gospels*. London: SCM Press, 2000.

Hickling, C.J.A. 'Paul's Use of Exodus in the Corinthian Correspondence', in Bieringer (ed.), *The Corinthian Correspondence*, pp. 367–376.

Hollander, John. *Figure of Echo: The Mode of Allusion in Milton and After*. Berkley: University of California Press, 1981.

Homer. *Iliad*. Trans. A.T. Murray. Revised by William F. Wyatt. Loeb Classical Library. 2 vols. Cambridge, MA: Harvard University Press, rev. edn, 1969.

—*Odyssey*. Trans. A.T. Murray. Loeb Classical Library. 2 vols. Cambridge, MA: Harvard University Press, 1995.

—*Odyssey*. Trans. A.T. Murray. Revised by George E. Dimock. Loeb Classical Library. Vol. 1. Cambridge, MA: Harvard University Press, rev. edn, 1998.

Horace. *Ars Poetica*. Trans. by H.R. Fairclough. Loeb Classical Library. Cambridge, MA: Harvard University Press, 1999.

Hornblower, Simon, and Anthony Spawforth (eds). *The Oxford Classical Dictionary*. Oxford: Oxford University Press, 3rd edn, 1996.

Horsfall, Nicholas (ed.). *A Companion to the Study of Virgil*. Leiden: Brill, 1995.

Howard, F. 'The Anti-Marcionite Prologue'. *ExpTim* (1936), pp. 534–38.

Isocrates. Trans. George Norlin. Loeb Classical Library. 3 vols. London: William Heinemann, 1961.

Jones, C.P. 'Towards a Chronology of Plutarch's Works'. *JRS* 54 (1966), pp. 61–74.

Josephus. *Jewish Antiquities*. Trans. H. St. J. Thackery. Loeb Classical Library. 9 vols. Cambridge, MA: Harvard University Press, 1996–2001.

—*The Jewish War*. Trans. H. St. J. Thackery. Loeb Classical Library. 3 vols. Cambridge, MA: Harvard University Press, 1997.

Kealy, Seán P. *Mark's Gospel: A History of Its Interpretation: From Beginning until 1979*. New York: Paulist Press, 1982.

Keegan, Terence J. 'Introductory Formulae for the Matthean Discourses'. *CBQ* 44 (1982), pp. 415–30.

Keener, Craig S. *A Commentary on the Gospel of Matthew*. Grand Rapids: William B. Eerdmans, 1999.

—*The Gospel of John: A Commentary*. 2 Vols. Peabody, MA: Hendrickson, 2003.

Kennedy, George. *The Art of Persuasion in Greece*. Princeton, NJ: Princeton University Press, 1963.

—'Classical and Christian Source Criticism', in W.O. Walker (ed.), *The Relationships among the Gospels*. San Antonio: Trinity University Press, 1978, pp. 125–55.

—*Classical Rhetoric and Its Christian and Secular Tradition from Ancient to Modern Times*. Chapel Hill: University of North Carolina Press, 1980.

—*New Testament Interpretation through Rhetorical Criticism*. Chapel Hill: University of North Carolina Press, 1984.

Kenney, E.J. 'Books and Readers in the Roman World', in Kenney and Clausen (eds), *The Cambridge History of Classical Literature II*, pp. 3–32.

Kenney, E.J., and W.V. Clausen (eds). *The Cambridge History of Classical Literature II: Latin Literature*. Cambridge: Cambridge University Press, 1982.

Kidd, D.A. 'Imitation in the Tenth *Ecologue*', in Hardie (ed.), *Virgil*, I, pp. 404–17.

Kingsbury, Jack Dean. 'Form and Message of Matthew'. *Int* 29 (1975), pp. 13–23.

—'The Birth Narrative of Matthew', in E. Aune (ed.), *The Gospel of Matthew in Current Study*, pp. 154–65.

—*Matthew: Structure, Christology and Kingdom*. London: SPCK, 1975.

Kittel, G., G. Friedrich (eds). *Theological Dictionary of the New Testament*. (trans. G.W. Bromily; 10 vols., Grand Rapids: Eerdmans, 1964–76)

Knauer, Georg N. *Die Aeneis und Homer: Studien zur poetischen Technik Vergils mit Listen der Homerzitate in der Aeneis*. Hypomnemanta, 7. Göttingen: Vandenhoeck & Ruprecht, 1964.

—'Vergil's *Aeneid* and Homer', in Hardie (ed.), *Virgil*, III, pp. 93–113.

Koch, Deitrich-Alex. *Die Schrift als Zeuge des Evangeliums: Untersuchungen zur Verwendung und zum Verständnis der Schrift bei Paulus*. Tübingen: J.C.B. Mohr (Paul Siebeck), 1986.

Koester, Craig R. *Symbolism in the Fourth Gospel: Meaning, Mystery, Community*. Minneapolis: Fortress Press, 2nd edn, 2003.

Kraft, Robert A. 'Philo's Treatment of the Number Seven in *On Creation*'. Paper presented for the Society of Biblical Literature Philo Group. New Orleans, 1996.

Kristeva, J. *Desire in Language: A Semiotic Approach to Literature and Art*. Ed. L.S. Roudiez. Trans. T. Gora, A. Jardine and L. Roudiez. New York: Columbia University Press, 1980.

Kümmel, Werner Georg. *Introduction to the New Testament*. London: SCM Press, 1975.

Lapide, Pinchas E. *Hebrew in the Church: The Foundations of Jewish–Christian Dialogue*, trans. Erroll F. Rhodes, Grand Rapids: Eerdmans, 1986; see Keener, *Matthew*, p. 50.

Lee, George. 'Imitation in the Poetry of Virgil', in Ian McAuslan and Peter Walcot (eds), *Virgil*. GRS, 1. New York: Oxford University Press, 1990, pp. 1–14.

Legg, S.C.E. *Novum Testamentum Graece: Evangelicum Secundum Marcum*. Oxford: Clarendon Press, 1935.

Lieu, Judith. 'How John Writes', in Bockmuehl and Hagner (eds), *The Written Gospel*, pp. 171–83.

Livy. *History of Rome*. Trans. B.O. Foster *et al*. Loeb Classical Library. 13 vols. Cambridge, MA: Harvard University Press, 1919–2002.

Lohr, Charles H. 'Oral Techniques in the Gospel of Matthew'. *CBQ* 23 (1961), pp. 403–35.

Luce, T.J. *Livy: The Composition of History*. Princeton, NJ: Princeton University Press, 1977.

Luz, Ulrich. *Matthew 1–7: A Commentary*. Trans. Wilheim C. Linss. CC. Minneapolis Press: Fortress, 1989.

—*Matthew 8–20: A Commentary*. Trans. James E. Crouch. HCHCB. Minneapolis: Fortress Press, 2001.

Lyne, R.O.A.M. 'Vergil's *Aeneid*: Subversion by Intertextuality: Catullus 66.39 and Other Examples'. *GR* 41 (1994), pp. 187–204.

MacDonald, Dennis R. *Christianizing Homer: The Odyssey, Plato and the Acts of Andrew*. Oxford: Oxford University Press, 1994.

—'Tobit and the *Odyssey*', in MacDonald (ed.), *Mimesis and Intertextuality in Antiquity and Christianity*, pp. 11–40.

MacDonald, Dennis R. (ed.). *Mimesis and Intertextuality in Antiquity and Christianity*. Harrisburg, PA: Trinity Press International, 2001.

McKeon, Richard. 'Literary Criticism and the Concept of Imitation in Antiquity'. *ModPhil* 34 (1936), pp. 1–35.

McKenzie, John L. 'The Gospel of Matthew', in Brown, Fitzmyer, and Murphy (eds), *JBC*, pp. 62–114.

Malley, Edward J. 'The Gospel according to Mark', in *JBC*, pp. 21–61.

Meeks, Wayne A. *The First Urban Christians: The Social World of the Apostle Paul*. New Haven: Yale University Press, 1983.

Meier, John P. *Matthew*. NTM, 3. Dublin: Veritas, 1980.

Menken, Maarten J. J. 'Context and Textual Form of the Quotation from Zechariah 9,9 in Matthew 21,5', in Menken (ed.), *Matthew's Bible*, pp. 105–16.

—*Numerical Literary Techniques in John: The Fourth Evangelist's Use of Numbers of Words and Syllables*. NovTSup, 55. Leiden: E.J. Brill, 1985.

—'Old Testament Quotations Derived from Mark', in Menken (ed.), *Matthew's Bible*, pp. 205–25.

—'Old Testament Quotations Inserted in Markan Contexts', in Menken (ed.), *Matthew's Bible*, pp. 227–38.

—'The Quotation from Zech 9,9 in Mt 21,5 and in Jn 12,15', in Deneaux (ed.), *John and the Synoptics*, pp. 571–78.

Menken, Maarten J.J. (ed.). *Matthew's Bible: The Old Testament Text of the Evangelist*. BETL, 173. Leuven: Leuven University Press, 2004.

Metzger, B. *The Text of the New Testament: Its Transmission, Corruption, and Restoration*. New York: Oxford University Press, 1964.

Mitchell, Margaret M. *Paul and the Rhetoric of Reconciliation: An Exegetical Investigation of the Language and Composition of 1 Corinthians*. Louisville, KY: Westminster, 1991.

Mlakuzhyil, George. *The Christocentric Literary Structure of the Fourth Gospel*. AnBib, 117. Rome: Biblical Institute Press, 1987.

Moessner, David P. 'How Luke Writes', in Bockmuehl and Hagner (eds), *The Written Gospel*, pp. 149–70.

Moloney, Francis J. *The Gospel of Mark: A Commentary*. Peabody, MA: Hendrickson, 2002.

Moore, Carey A. *Tobit: A New Translation with Introduction and Commentary*. AB, 40A. London: Doubleday, 1996.

Moyise, Steve. 'Intertextuality and the Study of the Old Testament in the New Testament', in Steve Moyise (ed.), *The Old Testament in the New Testament: Essays in Honour of J.L. North*. JSNTSup, 189. Sheffield: Sheffield Academic Press, 2000, pp. 14–41.

Müller, Mogens. 'The Reception of the Old Testament in Matthew and Luke-Acts: From Interpretation to Proof from Scripture'. *NovT* 43 (2001), pp. 315–30.

Murphy, Frederick J. 'The Jewishness of Matthew: Another Look', in Alan J. Avery-Peck, Daniel Harrington and Jacob Neusner (eds), *When Judaism and Christianity Began: Essays in Memory of Anthony J. Saldarini*. Fest. Anthony J. Saldarini. JCB. SupJSJ, 85. Leiden: Brill, 2004, II, pp. 377–403.

Murphy-O'Connor, Jerome. *Paul the Letter-Writer: His World, His Options, His Skills*. GNS, 41. Collegeville: Liturgical Press, 1995.

Neirynck, Frans. 'The Synoptic Problem', *NJBC*, pp. 587–95.

Nelis, Damien, *Virgil's Aeneid and the Argonautica of Apollonius Rhodius*. ARCA, 39. Leeds: Francis Carins, 2001.

Neville, David J. *Mark's Gospel – Prior or Posterior?: A Reappraisal of the Phenomenon of Order*. JSNTSup, 222. Sheffield: Sheffield Academic Press, 2002.

Nickelsburg, George W.E. 'The Search for Tobit's Mixed Ancestry: A Historical and Hermeneutical Odyssey'. *RevQ* 17 (1996), pp. 339–49.

—'Tobit and Enoch: Distant Cousins with a Recognizable Resemblance', in David J. Lull (ed.), *Society of Biblical Literature Seminar Papers*, pp. 54–68. Atlanta: Scholars Press, 1988.

—'Tobit, Genesis, and the *Odyssey*: A Complex Web of Intertextuality', in MacDonald (ed.), *Mimesis and Intertextuality in Antiquity and Christianity*, pp. 41–55.

Nolland, J. 'What Kind of Genesis Do We Have in Matt 1.1?' *NTS* 42 (1996), pp. 463–71.

Noonan Sabin, Marie. *Reopening the Word: Reading Mark as Theology in the Context of Early Judaism*. Oxford: Oxford University Press, 2002.

Nowell, I. 'The Book of Tobit: Narrative Technique and Teheology'. Ph.D. dissertation, Catholic University of America, Washington DC; Ann Arbor, MI: University Microfilms International, 1985, No. 8314894.

O'Day, Gail R. 'Jeremiah 9.22–23 and 1 Corinthians 1.26–31: A Study in Intertextuality'. *JBL* 109 (1990), pp. 259–67.

O'Leary, Anne M. 'John's Use of Matthew as a Source in the Context of the Use of Sources in Graeco-Roman Antiquity'. Part-published Dissertation. Limerick: Mary Immaculate College, University of Limerick, 2004.

Oakley, S.P. *A Commentary on Livy: Books 6–10: Volume I: Introduction and Book VI*. Oxford: Clarendon Press, 1997.

Ogden White, Harold. *Plagiarism and Imitation during the English Renaissance: A Study in Critical Distinctions*. Cambridge: Harvard University Press, 1935.

Ogilvie, R.M. 'Livy', in Kenny and Clausen (eds), *The Cambridge History of Classical Literature II: Latin Literature*, pp. 458–66.

Ong, W.J. *Rhetoric, Romance and Technology*. Ithaca, NY: Cornell University Press, 1971.

Oropeza, B.J. 'Animadversiones: Laying to Rest the Midrash: Paul's Message on Meat Sacrificed to Idols in Light of the Deuteronomic Tradition'. *Bib* 79 (1998), pp. 57–68.

Otis, Brooks. 'The Originality of the Aeneid', in D.R. Dudley (ed.), *Virgil*. London: Routledge & Kegan Paul, 1969, pp. 27–66.

Ovid. *Heriodes*. Trans. Grant Showerman. Revised by G.P. Goold. Loeb Classical Library. Cambridge, MA: Harvard University Press, rev. edn, 2002.

—*Metamorposhes*. Trans. Frank Justus Miller. Revised by G.P. Goold. Loeb Classical Library. 2 Vols. Cambridge, MA: Harvard University Press, rev. edn, 1999.

Pate, C. Marvin. *The Reverse of the Curse: Paul, Wisdom and the Law*. WUNT, 2. Series, 114. Tübingen: Mohr Siebeck, 2000.

Pelling, C.B.R. 'Plutarch's Adaptation of His Source Material'. *JHS* 100 (1980), pp. 127–40.

—'Plutarch's Method of Work in the Roman Lives'. *JHS* 99 (1979), pp. 74–96.

Pelling, Christopher. *Literary Texts and the Greek Historian*. London: Routledge, 2000.

—'Truth and Fiction in Plutarch's *Lives*', in D.A. Russell (ed.), *Antonine Literature*. Oxford: Clarendon Press, 1990, pp. 19–52.

Philo. *On Moses*. Trans. F.H. Colson. Loeb Classical Library. Cambridge, MA: Harvard University Press, 1969.

Plato. *Ion*. Trans. W.R.M. Lamb. Loeb Classical Library. Cambridge, MA: Harvard University Press, 2001.

—*Republic*. Trans. Paul Shorey. Loeb Classical Library. 2 vols. Cambridge, MA: Harvard University Press, 1999–2000.

Plutarch. *Lives*. Trans. Bernadotte Perrin. Loeb Classical Library. 11 vols. Cambridge, MA: Harvard University Press, 1989–2001.

Pöschl, Viktor. *The Art of Vergil: Image and Symbol in the Aeneid*. Trans. Gerda Seligson. Michigan: University of Michigan Press, 2nd edn, 1966.

Quintilian. *The Institutio Oratoria*. Trans. H.E. Butler. Loeb Classical Library. 4 vols. Cambridge, MA: Harvard University Press, 1953–80.

Reid, Barbara E. 'Violent Endings in Matthew's Parables and Christian Nonviolence'. *CBQ* 66 (2004), pp. 237–55.

Richardson, Neil. *Paul's Language about God*. JSNTSup, 99. Sheffield: Sheffield Academic Press, 1994.

Robbins, Veron. *The Tapestry of Early Christian Discourse: Rhetoric, Society and Ideology*. London: Routledge, 1996.

Roberts, Michael. *Biblical Epic and Rhetorical Paraphrase in Late Antiquity*. ARCA, 16. Liverpool: Francis Carins, 1985.

Rotelle, John E. (ed.). *On Genesis: A Refutation of the Manichees Unfinished Literary Commentary on Genesis: The Literal Meaning of Genesis*. Trans. Edmund Hill. WSA, I. New York: New City Press, 2002.

Roth, Wolfgang. 'Moses and Matthew'. *Bib T* 30 (1992), pp. 362–66.

Russell, D.A. 'De Imitatione', in David West and Tony Woodman (eds), *Creative Imitation and Latin Literature*. Cambridge: Cambridge University Press, 1979, , pp. 1–16.

—'On Reading Plutarch's *Lives*.' *GR* 13 (1966), pp. 139–54.

Russell, D.A., and M. Winterbottom (eds). *Ancient Literary Criticism: The Principle Texts in New Translations*. Oxford: Clarendon Press, 1972.

Sabbe, Maurits. 'The Johannine Account of the Death of Jesus and Its Synoptic Parallels (Jn 19,16b-42)'. *ETL* 70 (1994), pp. 34–63.

Sandmel, S. *The Hebrew Scriptures: An Introduction to Their Literature and Religious Ideas*. New York: Oxford University Press, 1978.

Schnackenburg, Rudolph. *The Gospel of Matthew*. Trans. Robert R. Barr. Grand Rapids: William B. Eerdmans, 2002.

Schneiders, Sandra M. *The Revelatory Text: Interpreting the New Testament as Sacred Scripture*. San Fransisco: Harper, 1991.

Schweizer, Eduard. *The Good News according to Mark*. Trans. Donald H. Madvig. London: SPCK, 1987.

Scott, James M. 'Paul's Use of Deuteronomic Tradition'. *JBL* 112/4 (1993), pp. 645–65.

—' "For as Many are Works of the Law are Under a Curse" (Galatians 3.10)', in Evans and Sanders (eds), *Paul and the Scriptures of Israel*, pp. 187–221.

Segal, C.S. *Language and Desire in Seneca's Phaedra*. Princeton, NY: Princeton University Press, 1986.

Seneca. *Epistles*. Loeb Classical Library. 3 vols. Cambridge, MA: Harvard University Press, 2000–2002.

—*Phaedra*. Ed. John G. Fitch. Trans. John G. Fitch. Loeb Classical Library. Cambridge, MA: Harvard University Press, 2002.

Senior, Donald. 'Directions in Matthean Studies', in Aune (ed.), *The Gospel of Matthew in Current Study*, pp. 5–21.

—*The Gospel of Matthew*. IBT. Nashville: Abingdon, 1997.

—*Matthew*. ANTC. Nashville: Abingdon, 1998.

Shuler, P.L. *A Genre for the Gospels: The Biographical Character of Matthew*. Philadelphia: Fortress Press, 1982.

—'The Genre(s) of the Gospels', in Dungan (ed.), *The Interrelations between the Gospels*, pp. 459–83.

Smart, Ninian, (ed.). *Atlas of the World's Religions*. Oxford: Oxford University Press, 1999.

Smit, Joop F.M. *'About the Idol Offerings': Rhetoric, Social Context and Theology of Paul's Discourse in First Corinthians 8.1–11.1*. Leuven: Peeters, 2000.

Smit Sibinga, Joost. 'The Composition of 1 Cor 9 and Its Context'. *NovT* 40 (1998), pp. 136–163.

—'The Structure of the Apocalyptic Discourse, Matthew 24 and 25'. *ST* 29 (1975), pp. 711–79.

Smit Sibinga, J. 'Matthew 14.22-33 – Text and Composition', in Jay Eldon Epp and Gordon D. Fee (eds), *New Testament Textual Criticism: Its Significance for Exegesis: Essays in Honour of Bruce. M. Metzger*. Oxford: Clarendon Press, 1981, pp. 15–33.

Smith, Christopher R. 'Literary Evidences of a Fivefold Structure in the Gospel of Matthew'. *NTS* 43 (1997), pp. 540–51.

Smith, D. Moody. *Johannine Christianity: Essays on Its Setting, Sources, and Theology*. Edinburgh: T & T Clark, 2nd edn, 1987.

Smith, Kym. *The Amazing Structure of the Gospel of John*. Blackwood, Aus.; Sherwood, 4th edn, 2005.

Smith, Morton. 'Prolegomena to a Discussion of Aretalogies, Divine Men, the Gospels, and Jesus'. *JBL* 90 (1971), pp. 174–99.

Snodgrass, Klyne. 'The Gospel of Jesus', in Bockmuehl and Hagner (eds), *The Written Gospel*, pp. 31–44.

Soll, Will. 'Misfortune and Exile in Tobit: The Juncture of a Fairy Tale Source and Deuteronomic Theology'. *CBQ* 51 (1989), pp. 209–31.

Stanley, Christopher D. *Arguing with Scripture: The Rhetoric of Quotations in the Letters of Paul*. London: T & T Clark, 2004.

—*Paul and the Language of Scripture: Citation Technique in the Pauline Epistles and Contemporary Culture*. New York: Cambridge University Press, 1992.

Stanton, Graham N. *The Gospels and Jesus*. Oxford: Oxford University Press, 2nd edn, 2002.

Stanton, G.N. 'Matthew: ΒΙΒΛΟΕ ΕΥΑΓΓΕΛΙΟΝ ΒΙΟΕ?', in F. Van Segbroeck, C.M. Tuckett, G. Van Belle, and J. Verheyden (eds), *The Four Gospels 1992: Festschrift Frans Neirynck*. 3 vols. Leuven: Leuven University, 1992, pp. 1187–1201.

Stern, David H. *Jewish New Testament Commentary*. Clarksville, MD: Jewish New Testament Publications, 1992.

Stibbe, M.W.G. *John as Storyteller: Narrative Criticism and the Fourth Gospel*. SNTSMS, 73. Cambridge: Cambridge University Press, 1994.

Stock, Augustine. *The Method and Message of Mark*. Wilmington, DE: Michael Glazier, 1989.

Stockhausen, C.K. *Moses' Veil and the Story of the New Covenant: The Exegetical Substructure of 2 Cor. 3.1–4.6*. AnBib, 116. Rome: Pontifical Biblical Institute, 1989.

—'2 Corinthians 3 and the Principles of Pauline Exegesis', in Evans and Sanders (eds), *Paul and the Scriptures of Israel*, pp. 143–64.

Streeter, B.H. *The Four Gospels*. London: Macmillan, 1924.

Stuhlmacher, P. 'The Genre(s) of the Gospels: Response to P.L. Shuler', in Dungan (ed.), *The Interrelations between the Gospels*, pp. 484–94.

Suetonius. *The Lives of the Caesars*. Trans. J.C. Rolfe. Loeb Classical Library. 2 vols. London: William Heinemann, 1959–69.

Swanson, Reuben J. *The Horizontal Line Synopsis of the Gospels*. Dillsboro, NC: Western North Carolina Press, 1975.

Tacitus. *Agricola*. Trans. M. Hutton and W. Peterson. Revised by R.M. Oglive, E.W. Warmington and M. Winterbottom. Loeb Classical Library. Cambridge, MA: Harvard University Press, rev. edn, 2000.

Talbert, Charles H. *What Is a Gospel?: The Genre of the Canonical Gospels*. Macon, GA.: Mercer University Press, 2nd edn, 1985.

Tarrant, R.J. 'Senecan Drama and Its Antecedents'. *HSCP* 82 (1978), pp. 213–63.

Theissen, Gerd. *Introduction to the New Testament*. Minneapolis: Fortress Press, 2003.

—*A Theory of Primitive Christian Religion*. London: SCM Press, 1999.

Thielman, F. 'Unexpected Mercy: Echoes of a Biblical Motif in Romans 9–11'. *SJT* 47 (1994), pp. 169–81.

Thomas, R.F. 'Virgil's *Georgics* and the Art of Reference', in Hardie (ed.), *Virgil*, II, pp. 58–82.

Thompson, Michael B. 'The Holy Internet: Communication between Churches in the First Century Generation', in Bauckham (ed.), *Gospel for All Christians*, pp. 49–70.

Throckmorton, Burton. H. Jr. *Gospel Parallels: A Synopsis of the First Three Gospels*. Nashville: Thomas Nelson, 4th edn, 1979.

Thucydides. *History of the Peloponnesian War*. Trans. C.F. Smith. Loeb Classical Library. 4 vols. Cambridge, MA: Harvard University Press, 1996–99.

Todorov, Tzvetan. 'Primitive Narrative', in *idem, The Poetics of Prose*. Trans. R. Howard. Oxford: Basil Blackwell, 1977, pp. 53–65.

Tolbert, Mary Ann. *Sowing the Gospel: Mark's World in Literary-Historical Perspective*. Minneapolis: Fortress Press, 1989.

Van Erp Taalman Kip, A. Maria. 'Intertextuality and Theocritus 13', in Irene J.F. de Jonge and J.P. Sullivan (eds), *Modern Critical Theory and Classical Literature*. New York: Leiden, 1994, pp. 151–69.

Van Iersel, Bas. M.F. *Mark: A Reader-Response Commentary*. JSNTSup, 164. Sheffield: Sheffield Academic Press, 1998.

—*Reading Mark*. Edinburgh: T & T Clark, 1989.

Van Wolde, Ellen. 'Trendy Intertextuality?', in Spike Darisma (ed.), *Intertextuality in Biblical Writings: Essays in Honour of Bas van Iersel*. Kampen: Uitgeversmaatschappij J.H. Kok–Kampen, 1989, pp. 43–49.

Vines, Michael E. *The Problem of Markan Genre: The Gospel of Mark and the Jewish Novel*. SBLAB, 3. Atlanta: SBL, 2002.

Virgil. *Aeneid*. Trans. H.R. Fairclough. Revised by G.P. Goold. Loeb Classical Library. 2 vols. Cambridge, MA: Harvard University Press, rev. edn, 2002.

Viviano, Benedict T. 'The Genres of Matthew 1–2: Light from 1 Timothy 1.4'. *RB* 97 (1990), pp. 31–53.

—'The Gospel according to Matthew', *NJBC*, pp. 630–74.

Von Rad, G. *Deuteronomy*. Philadelphia: Westminister, 1966.

Votaw, C.W. 'The Gospels and Contemporary Biographies in the Greco-Roman World'. *AJT* 19 (1915), pp. 45–49.

Walker, W.O. (ed.). *The Relationships among the Gospels*. San Antonio: Trinity University Press, 1978.

Walsh, P.G. *Livy: Historical Aims and Methods*. Cambridge: Cambridge University Press, 1976.

Wardman, A.E. 'Plutarch's Methods in the *Lives*'. *CQ* (1971), pp. 254–61.

—*Plutarch's Lives*. London: Paul Elek, 1974.

Weitzman, Steven. 'Allusion, Artifice, and Exile in the Hymn of Tobit'. *JBL* 115 (1996), pp. 49–61.

West, David, and Tony Woodman (eds). *Creative Imitation and Latin Literature*. Cambridge: Cambridge University Press, 1979.

Williams, R. Deryck. 'The *Aeneid*', in Kenny and Clausen (eds), *The Cambridge History of Classical Literature II*, pp. 333–69.

Wills, Jeff. *Repetition in Latin Poetry: Figures of Allusion*. Oxford: Clarendon Press, 1996.

Wiseman, T.P. *Roman Studies: Literary and Historical*. Liverpool: Francis Cairns, 1987.

Witherington III, Ben. *The Gospel of Mark: A Socio-Rhetorical Commentary*. Grand Rapids: William B. Eerdmans, 2001.

—*Jesus the Sage*. Philadelphia: Fortress Press, 1994

Woodman, A.J. *Rhetoric in Classical Historiography*. London: Croom Helm, 1988.

Wrede, William. *Das Messiasgeheimnis in den Evangelien*. Göttingen: Vandenhoeck & Ruprecht, 1901.

Wright, N.T. *The Climax of the Covenant: Christ and the Law in Pauline Theology*. Minneapolis: Fortress Press, 1991.

Wuellner, W. 'Greek Rhetoric and Pauline Argumentation', in W.R. Schoedel (ed.), *Early Christian Literature and the Classical Intellectual Tradition: Festschrift R.M. Grant*. ThH, 53. Paris: Beauchesne, 1979, pp. 177–87.

Xenophon. *Agesilaus*. Trans. E.C. Marchant and G.W. Bowersock. Loeb Classical Library. 2 vols. Cambridge, MA: Harvard University Press, 1969.

Zimmerman, Frank. *The Book of Tobit: An English Translation with Introduction and Commentary*. New York: Harper, 1958.

# Index of Authors

# Index of References